Profitable Small, Cottage, Tiny and Home Industries

(A Complete Hand Book on Home & Small Scale Industries)

Profitable Small, Cottage, Tiny and Home Industries

(A Complete Hand Book on Home & Small Scale Industries)

Written By

EIRI Board of Consultants & Engineers

ENGINEERS INDIA RESEARCH INSTITUTE

4449, Nai Sarak, Main Road. Delhi - 110006 (India)

Ph: +91-11-23918117, 23916431, 45120361, 23947058, 64727385

*** E-Mail: eiribooks@yahoo.com & eiriprojects@gmail.com**

***Website: www.eiriindia.org & www.industrialprojectreports.com**

PRINTED & PUBLISHED BY

ENGINEERS INDIA RESEARCH INSTITUTE

4449, Nai Sarak, Main Road, Delhi - 110006 (India)

Ph: +91-11-23918117, 23916431, 45120361, 23947058, 64727385

* E-Mail: eiribooks@yahoo.com & eiriprojects@gmail.com

*Website: www.eiriindia.org & www.industrialprojectreports.com

Sole Distributor:

EIRI PROJECT CONSULTANTS AND PUBLISHERS

4/54 Roop Nagar, Delhi-110007

and

Industrial Technologies, India

Nai Sarak, Delhi-110006

2nd Revised & Enlarged Edition

ISBN: 9788186732793

Printed in New Delhi (INDIA)

₹ 900/-

Printed & Published by Sudhir Gupta for "Engineers India Research Institute", 4449 Nai Sarak, Main Road, New Delhi -110006

Preface

The role played by the small scale industry in the economic activity of advanced industrialised countries like Japan, Germany, Great Britain and the United States of America is significant. Many Nations, both developed and developing exteriorized that the small industry sector is a useful vehicle for growth, in the later for the creation of new employment opportunities on a wide scale in the shortest possible time. Hundreds of thousands of people start their own businesses every year, and untold more dream about the possibility of becoming their own bosses. While entrepreneurship has its many potential rewards, it also carries unique challenges.

Starting a business involves planning, making key financial decisions and completing a series of legal activities. To run a successful business, you need to learn all about your existing and potential customers, your competitors and the economic conditions of your market place. The Government has announced series of steps to promote industrial development by way of rationalization of the policies to encourage the new entrepreneurs as well as existing units. In both developed and developing countries, the Government is turning to small and medium scale industries and entrepreneurs, as a means of economic development and a veritable means of solving problems.

It is a seedbed of innovations, inventions and employment. You do not need to be a genius to run a successful small business, but you do need some help. And that is exactly what this book is, a guide into the stimulating world of small business ownership and management.

Entrepreneurship helps in the development of nation. A successful entrepreneur not only creates employment for himself but for hundreds. Deciding on a right project can lead you to the road to successproducts, shuttle cocks for badminton, neon sign boards etc.

The book **Profitable Small, Cottage, Tiny & Home Industries** covers almost all the basic and advanced details to setup your own Small/Cottage & Home Industry. The main chapters are *Setting of Home Scale Industries, Steps in Setting up a Small Scale Industry, Aonla Products, Automatic Candle Making Plant, Acid Slurry (L.A.B), Agarbatti Industry, Automatic Book Binding Unit, Adhesive (Polyvinyl Butyral Based), Adhesive Based of Vinyl Acetate (Fevicol), Bakery Unit (Pastries, Bread, Buns, Cake, & Toffee etc), Ball Pen, Bread Manufacturing, Cane and Bamboo Industry, Processing of Cereals and Pulses Industry, Confectionery Industry-Semi Automatic Plant, Corrugated Sheet Board and Boxes, Coolant (Engine), Cleaning Powder (Vim Type), Cosmetics Industry, Dry Cleaning, Distilled Water, Detergent Powder, Dhoop Batti Sticks , Dal Moth, Chanachur & Bhujia Namkeen Industry, Dairy Farm, Food Supply/Catering Business, Gem Clips, Paper Clips & Staples, Herbals Cosmetic, Ice Cream & Ice-Candy, Jam, Jellies, Pickles and Squashes , Tissue Paper/Toilet Roll Paper, Leather Garments, Liquid Toilet Cleaner (Harpic Type), Masala (Spices), Mustard Oil (Edible Oil), Menthol Crystals, Mineral Water, Mini Flour Mill (Atta), Note Book, Register & Files, Paper Carry Bags, Pan Masala, Pappad Plant (Automatic), Pet Bottle from Pre-form (Capsules), Plastic Injection Moulding Products, Polythene Bags, Phenyl (Black & White), P.V.C Granules from P.V.C Scraps, P.V.C Pipe & Fittings, Paint Industry, Potato Chips/Waffers, Paper Envelopes (Including Self Sealing Type), Readymade Garments, Repacking of Medicines, Rice Puff, Shoe Polish, Shampoo Industry, Sock Knitting, Shaving Cream, Softeners (Cationic An-Ionic andNon-Ionic), Silver Extraction from Waste Hypo Solution X-Ray, Colour Paper Bleach and Cinema Film by Chemical Process, Tooth Brush and Suppliers of Machineries and Raw Materials etc.*

The book has been written for the benefit and to prove an asset and a handy reference guide in the hands of new entrepreneurs & well established industrialists.

EIRI Board of Consultants & Engineers

Contents and Subject Index

Chapters	Page No.	Chapters	Page No.

CHAPTER 12

Bread Manufagcturing 66-70

CHAPTER 13

Cane and Bamboo .... 71-79 Industry

CHAPTER 14

Procesing of Cereals and Pulses Industry 80-102

Chapters	Page No.	Chapters	Page No.

Chapters	Page No.	Chapters	Page No.

Chapters	Page No.

Chapters	Page No.	Chapters	Page No.

Chapters	Page No.	Chapters	Page No.

Chapters	Page No.	Chapters	Page No.

Chapter - 1

Setting of Home Scale Industries

Home Scale Industries involve artisans, skilled craftsmen and technician who can work in their own house or some small work areas without engendering any kind oi casualties, eventualities and pollution.

Home Scale Industries are adaptable to semi-urban, and rural environment where infrastructure is underdeveloped.

However, Home Scale Industries provide employment facilities to people mostly in rural areas so as to enable them to earn their livelihood and improve their socio-economic status.

A special feature of home Scale Industries is that very small investment is required.

In Home Scale Industries labour can be well utilised and fairly good amount of capital is saved. Thus they attract small savings and divert them into productive channels.

Another special feature of Home Scale Industries is that no sophisticated machines are used for the manufacture of their products.

Above all, they are instrumental in obliteration of regional disparities and economic backwardness in the rural/less developed segments.

Tiny industries which are establishment covering personal or house hold services located in urban and rural areas with population of 5 lakhs comprise investment for plant & machinery not exceeding 5 lakhs.

Government is taking all possible measures and special legislation for protecting the interest of cottage and house hold industries with a view to ensure that these activities which provide self-employment in large numbers get due recognition in our industrial development the overall development of home scale industries provides a significant contribution to the economic status of a country.

Chapter - 2

Steps in Setting up a Small Scale Industry

In an industry, as in any work, one has to go through various steps before he reaches the goal. These are enunciated below :

STEP-I. DECIDING TO BE AN ENTREPRENEUR

A strong entrepreneurial attitude is the most vital fact behind every successful project. Therefore, the imperative need is to know one's qualities, strenth and weaknesses as an entrepreneur. One's strength could be his qualifications, training, experience, personality traits, knowledge etc.

Every person, irrespective of his financial status posesses sufficient strength to become an entrepreneur. One may even start with a low investment enterprise and gradually build it up.

After one has resolved himself in regard to the above consideration, the next step would be to gear himself for the endeavour.

STEP-II. TRAINING

There are organisations which provide training to potential entrepreneurs which is motivating as well as encouraging.

Training may be technical or managerial. The entrepreneurship development training is conducted by over 700 organisations all over the country such as by SISIs (Small Industries Service Institute), District Industries Centres (DICs), Banks, State Financial Corporations, Institutes or Centres of Entrepreneurship Development, Technical Consultancy Organisations, Small Industries of Entrepreneurs Association, Chamber of Commerce & Industries and others. Such training is usually given freely and in certain cases one may even get a stipend particularly when EDPs (Entrepreneurship Development Programme) are conducted by the SISIs.

STEP-III. PROJECT IDENTIFICATION AND SELECTION

Scrutinization of the selective project of one's choice out of the many existing items, is the discretary prerequisite for starting of any industry. First, short listing of ideas generated, can be done by considering availability of technical know-how, investment, health of industry, raw material availability, market demand and supply position etc.

However, the final selection should be done based on an actual market survey. One's personal assessment with regard to his experience, qualification, aptitude, personality characteristics, family background, financial position and the like, serves as a vital fact for project identification.

Further, the project should be profitable enough to meet his financial requirements at present as well as in the years to come.

STEP-IV. LOCATION OF THE ENTERPRISE

Location is of the paramount importance for ensuring success of any business including an industrial enterprise. An ideal location will be one where all raw materials/inputs/feed stocks are available locally, market is in the vicinity, skilled labour is abundant and infrastructural facilities, particularly power, ensured. The site selected should be suitable for construction of industrial structure to house the plant and machinery etc. Also, the area should have an industrial culture and market to send one's project.

Further, an entrepreneur can arrive at a worthwhile decision after taking into account the following aspects :

1. Nearness to market and raw materials, 2. Availability of adequate transport system for the procurement of raw materials, despatching finished goods to markets, 3. Availability of an industrial area/estate or an industrial zone with essential services viz. power, water supply and facilities for effluent disposal, 4. Availability of required skills at reasonable wage rates, 5. Climatic conditions/environmental factors effecting the industry, 6. Incentives/concessions applicable for industrially backward areas.

STEP-V. ARRANGING TECHNICAL KNOW-HOW

Appropriate technical know-how is the key to entrepreneurial success. Quality products are ensured with right technology. However, care should be taken the technology chosen is commercially acceptable and is similar to or better than that acquired by one's present and potential competitions.

One significant consideration to be kept in view is that for any product there may be more than one way of manufacturing. A close study of the advantages and disadvantages of each of the processes should be made prior tc choosing the best option.

STEP-VI. CONSTITUTION OF THE FIRM

Constitution of a firm can be done in variety of forms; proprietorship, partnership, private limited company, public limited company or a co-operative society. A co-operative society as a form of enterprise is avery convenient form to arrange loans, but extremely difficult to run. A co-operative society is recommended only if the members are confident of ensuring smooth operations under all circumstances and for all times. Also, there is a limit on the distribution of dividends in case of a co-operative society. However, certain advantages are offered like getting exclusive facilities under various government schemes.

Whether the firm is sole proprietorship or partnership, one's liability is unlimited. The firm's creditors can sue one and recover their debts from one's personal assets also. When size of operations are huge, a private limited company may be the answer. This way when the firm faces bankruptcy, one's liability is limited to the extent of his shareholding the personal assets are not at stake.

A public limited company shall come in handy when one expands and graduates into a medium or large scale industry.

STEP-VII. REGISTRATION

After the formation of an enterprise, the entrepreneur while establishing a unit has to get his firm registered with Registrar of Firms, Income Tax Department and DT/DIC.

If the firm is a partnership firm the partners may get their partnership registered with the Registrar of Firms. For corporate entities (Private or Public Limited Companies) registration with Registrar of Company is essential.

Registration with Directorate of Industries DOI or DISTRICT INDUSTRIES CENTRE (DIC) is not compulsory but, helpful in obtaining various facilities. Such registration is done in two stages : (a) Provisional Regisration, (b) Permanent Registration.

STEP-VIII. ARRANGING FINANCE

Finance for the industrial project should be obtained before applying for registration. Finance for business has two components :

(a) Fixed Capital, (b) Working Capital.

Fixed capital comprises the amount required for land, building, plant and machinery, office equipment, furniture, fixtures, fittings, installations and other fixed assets etc.

Working capital is required for day to day operations of the unit for payment of wages, manufacturing/administrative expenses, purchasing, processing and storing raw materials, goods in process, finished goods, consumable stores/spares, etc. provide credit to trade on sales, to meet expenses on workers wages, transport and the like.

Fixed capital can be had in the form of term loan, hire purchase, or different payment facility. Working capital can be arranged from a commercial bank in the form of cash credit, overdraft and bills purchase/ discount facility.

Term loans are provided by State Financial Corporation (SFCs). Almost every State/Union Territory has one SFC. Where there is no SFC, the State Industrial Development Corporation (SIDC) perform the functions. Apart from these corporations, banks (Commercial, Co-operateive and Regional, Rural Banks) also sanction term loans although their main operations are extension of working capital facilities. All SSIs engaged or proposed to be engaged in legally permissible process/service activity are eligible for financial assistance.

Among other sources for raising finance is National Small Industries Corporation Limited (NSIC) which gives machinery, indigenous and imported, on hire-purchase and leasing basis besides extending assistance (including financial) for procurement of raw material, imported and indigenous, and for sale to government agencies.

For margin money which is the amount of money that one has to invest in the project from his own sources, there area number of schemes through which partially or completely margin money required to set up the project is available. These are Special Capital Scheme, Seed Capital Scheme, National Equity Fund and Engineers Equity Fund.

Chapter - 3

Aonla Products

Abstract

Aonla, the Indian gooseberry (Emblica officinalis Gaertn) belongs to the family eurphorbiaceae is one of the important fruits indigenous to India. It is one of the high medicinal value and can be consumed in the various form of processed products like jam, squash, sauce and candy. This enriched food value endorses for future establishment of herbal processing industries.

Introduction

Aonla is known to be commercially grown only in India since ancient times. The fruit occupies a prominent place in ancient Indian Mythological Literature like Ramayana, Kadambari and Charak Samhita as "Amrit Phal'. In India, Aonla is grown in an area of about 20,000 hectares with a production of around 2,00000 MT. Uttar Pradesh accounts for nearly 60 percent of this production. Pratapgarh in U.P. is a major aonla producing area covering 10,000 hectares under this crop. The fruit is acrid cooling, refrigerant, diuretic and laxative, hence, used for treating chronic dysentery, bronchitis, diabetes, fever, diarrhoea, jaundice, dyspepsia, cough etc. It is highly nutritive and is one of the richest natural sources of Vitamin 'C'. It contains 500-1500 mg. of ascorbic acid per 100g for pulp. This is much more than Vitamin 'C' content of guava, citrus and tomato fruits. The fruit juice contains nearly 20 times as much Vitamin 'C' as in orange juice and a single fruit is equal in anti-ascorbic value to two oranges. The gallic acid present in aonla fruit has antioxidant property. The excellent nutritive and therapeutic values of fruit have great potentiality for processing into number of quality produces. Keeping in view of the importance of aonla processed products, present attempt was undertaken with following objective i.e.

1. To examine physico-chemical composition of aonla and its suitability for processed products.

2. To judge organoleptic quality of prepared aonla processed products and workout its economics.

Material and Method

The present investigation incorporates the preparation of aonla pulp based process product (jam, squash, sauce and non-pulp based product candy).

Results and Discussion

Physico-chemical analysis are displayed in Table 1 & 2. The average fruit weight of NA-7 variety of aonla recorded 41.75g.

Table 1. Physical Composition of NA-7 Aonla

Physical Character	Percent Content
Av. Fruit weight	41.75
Pulp	91.85
Fibre	1.34
Seed	5.80

Table 2. Chemical Composition of NA-7 Aonla

Particulars	Percent chemical content
TSS	10.98
Acidity	1.97
Ascorbic acid (mg)	739.52
Phenols (mg)	186.40

pulp 91.85%, fibre 1.34% and seed 5.80%.

Aonla NA-7 showed appreciable percentage of total acidity, ascorbic acid and least presence of total solid and phenol content.

At present, majority of the people diversified into health oriented consumption pattern, thereby aonla is becoming important in dietary intake either wholesome or in processed form. As such processed products can be prepared viz., squash, jam, candy and sauce.

Extraction of pulp from NA-7 Aonla

The technique used for extraction of NA-7 Aonla fruit is used for making squash, jam and sauce (Flow Sheet 1).

Aonla fruit

↓

Washing

↓

Heating in boiling water for 10 minutes

↓

Separation of segments and removal of seed

↓

Addition of water in ratio 1:1

↓

Passing through a pulping machine

↓

Pulp

↓ ↓ ↓

Squash Jam Sauce

Fig.1 Flow Sheet for extraction of Aonla Fruit pulp

Aonla fruit pulp

↓

Mixing with asparagus root extract

↓

Mixing with sugar syrup solution

↓

Addition of sodium metabisulphite

↓

Addition of essence

↓

Bottling

↓

Capping

↓

Labelling

↓

Storage

Fig.2 Flow Sheet for preparation of Aonla Squash

The chief products jam, squash, sauce and candy were prepared for their organoleptic assessment. In this regard NA-7 Aonla variety was used for attaining better qualities.

Squash

By using the variety of NA-7 aonla preparation of squash was followed by earlier technique (Fig. 1). 10 liters of squash of recipe containing 25% pulp, 15g sugar, 1.2% acidity, 5% asparagus root extract and 2.25% ginger juice was prepared. Sodium metabisulphite (350 ppm) was used as preservative and squash was filled in sterilized bottles of 750 ml. capacity and further sealed it.

Jam

By examining various possible preparations of jam, best one recipe containing 50% aonla pulp, 67% sugar, 1.2% acidity, 5% asparagus and 2% aswagandha extracts was prepared and packed in sterilized bottles of 500g, capacity and made it air tight.

Candy

Mature aonla fruits of NA-7 variety was used for the preparaion of candy. It was subjected by using the method of segmented fruit with pectin coating. Candies were prepared with stated technique (Fig. 3). Therefore, ready candies were packed in polythene bags of 500 gram capacity.

Aonla fruit pulp

↓

Addition of sugar & herbal

↓

Cooking

↓

Addition of citric acid

↓

Judging of end point (TSS 68%)

↓

Filling into clean sterilized bottles

↓

Capping

↓

Labelling

↓

Storage

Fig.3 Flow Sheet for preparation of Aonla Jam

Sauce

Five kg of sauce containing 50% aonla pulp, and 50% tomato pulp with 75g.sugar, 10g salt, 60g onion, 6g garlic, 12g ginger, 5g red chillies, 12g hot spices were prepared with using acetic acid sodium benzoate as preservatives at the rate of 1ml. and 0.3g/kg of final product, respectively. Finally sauce was filled up in bottles and crown corked and pasteurized for 30 minutes in boiling water, air cooled.

Mature Aonla fruit
↓
Washing
↓
Picking
↓
Dipping in 2% salt solution (24-hour)
↓
Washing
↓
Dipping in 2% alum solution (24-hour)
↓
Washing in running water
↓
Blanching in boiling water
↓
Separation of segment and seed removal
↓
Steeping in 50% syrup solution (24-hour)
↓
Steeping 60% syrup solution (24-hour)
↓
Steeping in 70% syrup solution (3-days)
↓
Draining of excess sugar
↓
Coating with pectin solution
↓
Shade drying up to 15% moisture
↓
Packaging in polythene pouches (400-gauge)
↓
Storage

Fig.4 Flow Sheet for preparation of Aonla Candy

Organoleptic Quality of Aonla Processed Products

Further final products were evaluated for organoleptic quality rating by using the nine point Hedonic Rating Test and respective results pertaining to aonla processed products are given in Table 3.

Table 3. Evaluation of NA-7 Aonla Processed Products and Respective Organoleptic Rating

S. No.	Recipes	Aonla pulp (%)	Asparagas Juice (%)	Ginger Juice (%)	TSS (%)	Acidity (%)	Organoleptic Quality	
							Score (%) *	Rating ***
1.	Squash	25	5	2.25	52	1.22	8.0	LVM
2.	Jam	50	10	2.25	69	1.22	8.2	LVM
3.	Candy							
i.	Whole fruit (Pectin Coated)	–	–	–	–	–	8.5	LVM
ii.	Segmented fruit (Pectin Coated)	–	–	–	–	–	9.0	LE
4.	Sauce**	–	–	–	–	–	8.8	LVM

*Above 7 are acceptable

**Combinations of composition (0.5 kg Aonla pulp + 0.5kg Tomato pulp + Sugar 75 gm + 10g Salt + Onion 50g + Garlic 5g + Ginger 10g + Chillies 5g + Hot spice 10g)

***LVM -linked very much, LE liked extremely.

Table 4. Economics of NA-7 Aonla Processed Products (per kg/litre basis)

S.No.	Particulars	Squash	Jam	Candy	Sauce
1.	Aonla	0.45	3.50	6.50	4.50
2.	Transportation Cha.	0.5	0.5	0.5	0.5
3.	Fuel	2.5	2.75	-	2.25
4.	Sugar	2.0	5.50	2.25	1.20
5.	Asparagus	0.5	-	-	0.75
6.	Ginger	0.10	-	-	0.05
7.	Tomato	-	-	-	2.50
8.	Salt	-	-	-	0.05
9.	Onion	-	-	-	0.20
10.	Garlic	-	-	-	0.05

11.	Chillies	-	-	-	0.02
12.	Hot spices	-	-	-	0.50
13.	Labour expenses	3.75	4.75	3.50	5.25
14.	Packing/Bottling	2.50	3.50	0.75	3.50
15.	Interest on working Capital	0.80	1.33	1.07	1.45
	Total	**13.90**	**21.83**	**17.57**	**22.77**

1. **Cost of one litre squash = Rs.14.00**
2. **Cost of jam 1 kg = Rs.22.00**
3. **Cost of candy 1 kg = Rs.17.00**
4. **Cost of sauce 1 litre = Rs.22.75**

Aonla candy (segmented fruit with pectin coated) have secured maximum rating followed by sauce, candy (whole fruit with pectin coated), jam and squash.

Table 4 reveals that, the per litre processing cost of squash came to Rs.14.00 whereas, per kg processing cost of jam, candy and sauce exhibited Rs.22.00, 17.00, and Rs.22.75 respectively.

Therefore, it may be concluded that NA-7 aonla processed products opened new dimensions for establishing commercial processing industries as in the form of value added products by utilizing raw aonla as available in abundance during glut in the market when the prices rule at lower level. As such this may enhance profitability of aonla products manifold this new and effective results would certainly be helpful to industrial sector.

Chapter - 4

Automatic Candle Making Plant

Automatic Candle making unit is a profitable unit now-a-days as designed and perfumed candles are being exported to various other countries.

Since long, people used to burn cotton in mud cups filled with oil. In European countries previously people used to burn wooden sticks by dipping. These in facts due to the shortage of vegetable oils. About 25% of total population of India is living in villages where electricity was not available. But electricity is no problem these days, so kerosene oil lamps or wax candles are generally used for lighting purpose on special occasions. In the night or dark room, whenever electricity fails these candles play a big role in illuminating small and big cities, candles importance is also given in the encyclopedia of Britanica. In catholic church, candle was much preferred. The demand and consumption of candle is increasing day by day. In every village and town big & small grocer, general merchant, panwari, and perry shopkeepers sell candles. Paraffin wax was first time used in 1854. These days also candles are made of paraffin wax.

Previously candles made by Burmah Oil Co. Ltd. and Indo Burma Petroleum Industries were imported and in India candles were made out of stearin.

RAW MATERIALS

Imported plant is quite suitable to produce Perfumed and Designed Candles because Small/Cottage scale producers will not be the competitors as they shall not be in a position to invest this much amount.

Most modern candles are made from a mixture of several ingredients. They are paraffin wax, stearic acid, small quantities of other waxes being added usually for the sake of appearance. Probably this mixture which can be used in all method of making candles will prove most suitable for nearly all projects. However details of other materials which can be used are given below :

Paraffin wax is distilled from coal and oil shales and semi refined grades are used by most candle makers. It is usually supplied in the form of large blocks by petrol reining companies. For the several grades available the melting point is between 50° and 70°. For temperature climates 58°C melting point climate a higher melting point is necessary. Stearic Acid is a component of animal an vegetable fats and is supplied in flakes by oil and chemicals companies. It is added to wax to improve burning qualities and in removing the finished candle from the mould easily. It also reduce the amount of smoke produced white burning. Between 5% and 50% of stearic acid can be used depending upon the quality of candle required on an average 10% is added. The more percentage of stearic acid the better the candle but the cost of the material should also be taken into account.

FORMULATION FOR CANDLES MAKING

1.	Paraffin Wax	60%
	Stearic Acid	35%
	Bees Wax	5%
2.	Paraffin Wax	70 Parts
	Stearic Acid	15 Parts
	Petroleum (Or β-Napthal)	15 Parts
3.	Paraffin Wax	90 Parts
	Stearic Acid	5 Parts
	Petroleum	5 Parts

PARAFORM CANDLES

1.	Paraffin Wax	40
	Stearic Acid	20
	Paraformaldehyde	20
2.	Paraffin Wax	16
	Stearic Acid	16
	Paraformaldehyde	8
	Formaldehyde	5.5

CANDLES

Colouring Creasine Candles for the Christmas Tree. For coloring these candles only dye stuff, soluble in oil can be employed. Blue : 23-24 lavender blue, pale or dark, 100-120 parts per 5,000 parts of ceresine. Violet 26 fast violet R, 150 parts per 5,000 parts of ceresine. Silver gray: 29 silver gray, 150 parts per 5000 parts of ceresine. Yellow and orange : 30 wax yellow, medium, 200 parts per 5000 parts of ceresene; 61 old gold, 200 parts per 5000 ceresene. Pink and red : 27 peach-pink, or 29 chamois, about 100 parts per 5000 parts of ceresine. Green, 16-17, brilliant green, 33 may gre, 41 may green, 200-250 parts per 5000 parts of ceresene. The above-named colors should be ground in oil and the ceresene tinted with them afterwards.

MANUFACTURE OF COMPOSITE PARAFFIN CANDLES

Three parts of hydroxy stearic acid are dissolved in I part of a suitable solvent (e.g. stearic acid), and solution is mixed with paraffin wax to form a stock for the manufacture of composite candles.

TRANSPARENT CANDLES

The following are two recipe given in a German patent specification. The figures denote parts by weight:

1. Paraffin wax, 70; stearine, 15; petroleum 15.
2. Paraffin wax 90; stearine, 5; petroleum 5.

Recipe I of course gives candles more transparent than does recipe II. The 15 percent may be regarded as the extreme limit consistent with proper solidity of the candles.

MANUFACTURING PROCESS

Four different method of manufacture are described briefly.

THE DIPPING PROCESS

The technique consists of immersing the candle wick in molten wax then withdrawing it so that it pick up wax as it emerges. The wax is allowed to cool and the process is repeated until the required thickness has been built up. The equipment is very simple.

THE POURING PROCESS

This technique consist of suspending a wick over a container of melted wax and pouring hot wax from a small ladle so that it runs down the wick cooling as it goes. Any surplus wax dips back into the main container and can be used again. In terms of equipment, this is the simplest method. To produce good candles in this way a fair degree of skill must be acquired.

THE MOULDING OR CASTING PROCESS

The moulding process consists of filling a mould, in which a wick has been positioned, with melted wax to cool and then removing the completed candle from the mould. Except for very small outputs per day a certain degree of sophistication in mould design and fairly large number of moulds are needed. Machines for casting candles in large numbers are available and they do not require power for operation.

THE DRAWING PROCESS

A long length of wick is passed back and forth horizontly through a bath of wax forming a candle rope which is accommodated large diameter drums with a manually operated. The rope is then cut into candle lengths. A mechanized version of this machine does give much higher output but at greatly increased capital cost.

The process mentioned below is regarding the moulding or casting process.

Casting is most suitable for the following conditions. An automatic plant making candles only for its own use so that the number required is very large. For candles which are decorative rather than strictly utilitarian in which many technique of colouring, texturing and the production of special shades are used and for candles over 4 cm in diameter.

The technique of moulding the candle involves melting the wax, fixing the wide inside the mould and pouring the wax inside the die and cooling. After cooling the candle is drawn out. If the candle sticks inside the mould even after cooling the composition has to be changed.

Comparatively a hard wax is required for casting as it is less likely to stick to the mould. Hardness can be gauged by high melting point wax which melts in the region of 60° to 69°C is required for casting. The temperature for filling a mould should not be lower than 80°C and not higher than 88°C.

A good paraffin wax should be selected for casting. It should be hard and be of the required melting point. A relatively high percentage of stearic acid between 10 to 30% should be added and to obtain a good surface finish resistant to abrasion and dust penetration 3% of Microcrystalline wax is necessary. This will also ensure an easy release from the mould. This blend will produce a high quality long burning candle. A perfectly adequate simple candle can be made using nothing other than paraffin wax which should be sufficient depending on the market demand. As the wax in the mould cools each candle should be probed with a laythin rod and opened. If a hole is seen this should be filled with fresh wax. The process may have to be repeated until all the wax has solidified. During solidification wax contracts by 20% so that this procedure is not followed.

There are likely to be holes in the candles particularly in the region of the wick. Once the wax is solid but not get cool the mould can be immersed in water. If in running water cooling is much quicker. When the wax is cool the wick can be taken off the top metal bars and the candle can be pushed out of the moulds by pressing the bottom plug or bungs through. In case of problem for the release the following can be tried increase th appropriation of stearic acid. Tin plate the mould surface spray silicon inside the mould.

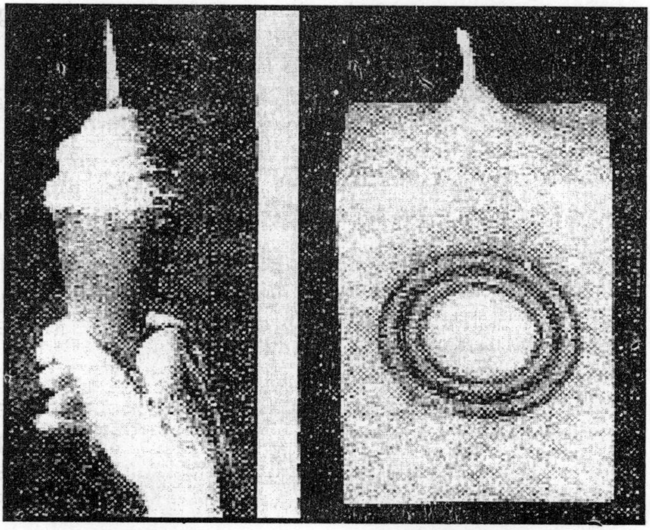

ICE-CREAM CANDLE

BULL'S-EYE CANDLE

PLANT ECONOMICS OF COLOUR FLAME PERFUME CANDLE

Rated Plant Capacity	=	3000.00 Pkt./Day
LAND & BUILDING (Total Land 800 sq.mt)	=	Rented

PLANT & MACHINERY

1. Wax melting pan made of iron and jacket for steam heating
2. Baby boiler
3. Semi automatic candle making machine
4. Colour making vessel made of mild steel
5. Other accessories

FIXED CAPITAL

1. Plant & Machinery	Rs.	3,00,000.00
2. Other Fixed Assets	Rs.	93,000.00
TOTAL	Rs.	3,93,000.00

RAW MATERIALS

1. Paraffin wax
2. Cotton wick
3. Colour compound
4. Other perfumed materials like, musk ambrette, musk zylon, ciret, yara powder, red rose, bragomot oil etc.
5. Packing material

TOTAL WORKING CAPITAL/ANNUM

1. Raw Material	Rs.	1,46,10,000.00
2. Salary & Wages	Rs.	5,50,620.00
3. Utilities & Overheads	Rs.	3,94,300.00
TOTAL	Rs.	1,55,54,920.00

TOTAL CAPITAL INVESTMENT

Total Fixed Capital	Rs.	3,93,000.00
Total Working Capital for 1 Month	Rs.	12,96,243.00
TOTAL	Rs.	16,89,243.00

TURN OVER/ANNUM

Receipt through sale of 9,00,000 Packets (each contain 12 candles)	Rs.	1,98,00,000.00

PROFIT SALES RATIO = Profit / Sales x 100 = 20.00 %

RATE OF RETURN = Operating profit / T.C.I x 100 = 234.39 %

BREAK EVEN POINT (B.E.P) = 14.36 %

Chapter - 5

Acid Slurry (L.A.B.)

Acid slurry is also known as linear alkyl benzene sulphuric acid, which is manufactured with alum or stabilized free SO_3 or mixture of alum linear alkyl benzene is the basic raw material for manufacturing slurry. It is an important raw material for the production of synthetic detergent, tablets and liquid detergents.

Linear alkyl benzene is a colourless liquid with a characteristic odour. It is the most widely used basic raw material for the manufacture of synthetic detergents.

Manufacture of linear alkyl benzene is based on the latest technology developed by universal oil production (U.O.P), U.S.A. It is characteristics by the latest techniques such as separation of the normal paraffins from superior kerosene using molecular sienes, dehydrogenatation of the normal paraffin to normal olefins and coupling of tube olefins with benzene is the presence of an acid catalyst.

Typical Quality of LAB

Distillation 95%	320°C Max
Normal Alkyl Benzene wt.%	92 Min
Bromine Index	30 Max
Doctor Test	-ve
Molecular Wt.	238 to 292 or 283 to 257 (As required)
Appearance	Clear and water white

MANUFACTURING PROCESS OF ACID SLURRY

Acid slurry is the economical name of linear alkyl benzene sulphonic acid, which is produced by the sulphonations of linear alkyl benzene with oleum or free sodium trioxide or concentrated sulphuric acid, solvent features are as given below:

a) Oleum
b) Free liquid sodium trioxide
c) Mixture of oleum and sulphuric acid.
d) 20% Oleum

Acid slurry is produced by due sulphonations of linear alkyl benzene with 20% oleum.

Reaction carried out as given below:

1. Sulphonations Stage:

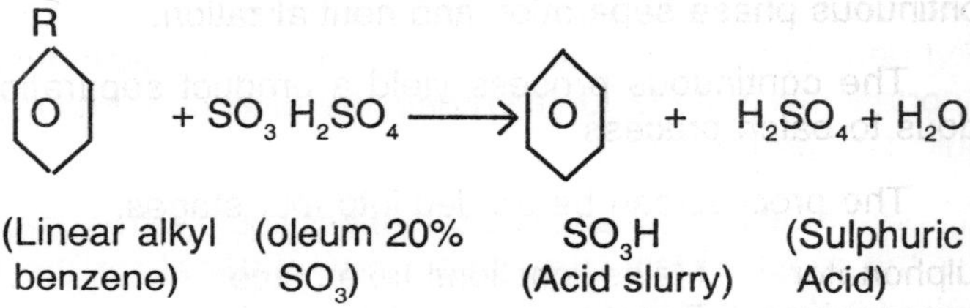

2. Dilution Stage & Separation Stage

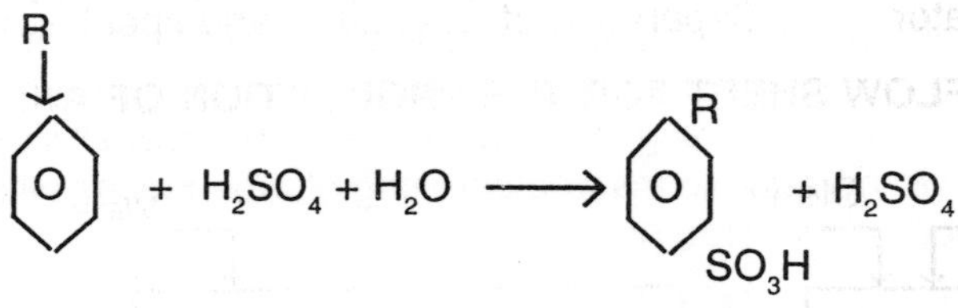

88% Sulphonic Acid
12% Sulphuric Acid

Batch Sulphonations Process

Reaction vessel is charged with 300 kgs of linear alkyl benzenone. The stirrer is turned on & cooling coates is circulated through the jacket 20% oleum is metered slowly to maintain the temperature of the reaction mass between 40°C. and 45°C. Normally the total weight of the oleum to be charged for complete the cooling is regulated in such a way to allow digested at a temperature of 45°C for atleast one hour.

Further for the separations of spent acid 18% of water calculated on the total weight of oleum are added to obtain good spent acid. During this stage of dilutions, the temperature rise gradually and addition of water is carefully controlled. Keeping the temperature at above 60°C. When the addition of water is completed.

The mass in again stirred for another 15 minutes, after which it is allowed to stir for about 10 or 12 hours. The separations of the upper sulphonic phase and the lower sulphuric acid phase can be effective only if the temperature during dilution is kept at 60°C. After 12 hours of billing, the lower acid layer is with down and the sulphuric acid stored in stainless steel barrels.

Continuous Sulphonations Process

The reaction is conducted in a small turbine reaction and operated continuously on overflow acid displacement principles followed by continuous phase separation and neutralization.

The continuous process yield a product separation in colour and odous to batch process.

The process can be divided into four stages.

Sulphonator - Mains reactions take place
Homozenizer - Reaction is completed here.
Dilutor - Dilute with water is affected here.
Separator - Separation of acid slurry and spent acid takes place.

FLOW SHEET FOR THE PRODUCTION OF ACID SLURRY

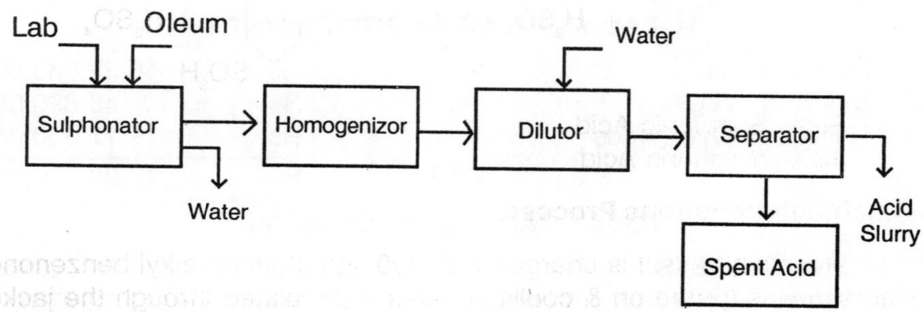

PLANT ECONOMICS OF ACID SLURRY

Rated Plant Capacity	=	2.00 Ton/Day
LAND & BUILDING (Land area 500 sq. mt.)	=	RENTED

PLANT & MACHINERY

1. Sulphonator
2. Homogenizer
3. Dilution vessel
4. Separator
5. Storage Tank
6. Storage vessel
7. Miscellaneous
9. Water, cooler & Control

FIXED CAPITAL

1. Plant & Machinery	Rs.	11,40,000.00
2. Other Fixed Assets	Rs.	2,45,000.00
TOTAL	Rs.	13,85,000.00

RAW MATERIALS

1. Linear Alkyl Benzene
2. Sulphuric Acid

TOTAL WORKING CAPITAL/MONTH

1. Raw Material	Rs.	16,33,080.00
2. Salary & Wages	Rs.	43,890.00
3. Utilities & Overheads	Rs.	1,17,000.00
TOTAL	Rs.	17,93,970.00

TOTAL CAPITAL INVESTMENT

Total Fixed ASSETS	Rs.	13,85,000.00
Total Working Capital for 1 Month	Rs.	17,93,970.00
TOTAL	Rs.	31,78,970.00

TURN OVER/ANNUM

By selling 600 tons of acid slurry	Rs.	2,64,00,000.00

PROFIT SALES RATIO = Profit / Sales x 100 = 15.92 %
RATE OF RETURN = Operating profit / T.C.I x 100 = 132.18 %
BREAK EVEN POINT (B.E.P) = 25.56 %

Chapter - 6

Agarbatti Industry

Agamya shastra and Ayurveda recommended the use of Dhoop Agarbatti which is mixture of natural ingredients having medicinal properties. Dhoop can be made with six to sixteen ingredients. Some combinations are good for subtle fragrance, other combinations have antifungal properties, while yet others are meant to stipulate the mind or elevate a person's mood.

In our ancient literature, there is a formula for making a dhoop called "SHODASHANG DHOOP" which is meant to emit fragrance as well as ward off colds and similar infections. Agarbatti reportedly clears lung congestion and is very popular with consumers.

MAN REQUIRES FRAGRANCE IN LIFE

Agarbatti is a fragrant frame ambassador of India. Agarbatti industry is basically a handifcrafts / cottage industry. In one respect this industry - unlike the traditional conception of a handicraft industry associated with carving etc. and which thus provides employment to very limited persons - is a real employment generator and is capable of providing employment to the weaker sections of both the urban and rural people. Most of the workers are uneducated. No educational/technical qualification or specialised experience is required. The required experience is gathered while rolling. No money is invested in plant or machinery in agarbatti manufacturing sector which bears the dignified title of industry. It is an industry in the sense, it is an organised effort by a group of people to produce a commodity. In fact, if a person can save Rs.10,000 he can start his own manufacturing in a small way.

Agarbatti rolling can be called as the ideal industry which can be spread with missionary zeal in areas where most people are under-employed or unemployed, belong to landless labour or artisans. Agarbatti rolling does not physically tire the rollers unlike in other industries as it is a light work.

Agarbatti is an alternative form of raw products like scented woods and grass found in the forests. The manufacture of Agarbatti is a traditional industry in many parts of the country. As there is an increase in demand for Agarbatti within the country and abroad, there is enormous scope for the development of this industry as a viable cottage industry.

NAMES OF THE RAW MATERIALS AND USES

(i) Jiggat Powder

This powder is made out of the skin/bark of a tree which is having self-adhesive property. Its botanical name is mochilas makrantha. Being in powder form, it encourages burning process. The Jiggat powder is used in Agarbatti mixture powder which helps in keeping intact all the compositions together.

(ii) Nurva Powder

In the pre-bath rolling various fragrant woods and country herbs like - kostom tulsi patra, kachura, kasturi, potohouli leaves, marugh, dhavana etc. are mixed which is known as Nurva powder. The Nurva powder is used in Agarbatti manufacturing as filler which helps in generating mild smoke having good smell and get mixed with fragrance.

These two powders i.e. Jiggat and Nurva are used by all manufacturing agencies throughout the country. So far no better substitute of the two powders have been developed. Entire demand of these two types of powders are mostly met out by the main suppliers of Tamil Nadu and Karnataka States.

(iii) Charcoal Powder

Ordinary charcoal is crushed and made into powder. It is used in Agarbatti manufacturing as a filling compound to encourage burning.

MANUFACTURING PROCESS

The whole production process for manufacture of Agarbatti can be divided into five stages.

(i) Sorting : The bamboo sticks are sorted out and cleaned i.e. fibres of splints are removed and then bottom 5 cm of splints are coloured. On an average, one kg. of bamboo splints contains about 3,000 sticks of 8" variety.

(ii) Mixing : The powders i.e. Jiggat, Nurva, waste sandal wood or charcoal are mixed in definite proportion.

The semi solid paste or watered dough (Atta) from 5 kg. masala powder, 11 kg watered dough may be obtained. Raw battis prepared on Bamboo splints with this Atta, after drying will come to about 7 kg. weight.

(iii) Rolling : Semi-solid paste (Atta) is distributed for rolling of raw battis. First gum is applied on sticks and then it is rolled with Atta. After rolling, battis are kept in sun light for drying.

(iv) Perfuming : Preparation of perfume and dipping is the fourth process. Raw battis are dipped therein with a view to give sweet fragrance while burning. Ready mixed, compounds of different fragrances are also available in market. There are 3 types of perfuming raw batti i.e. dipping, brushing and spraying. Out of these methods, dipping is the best method to maintain quality of the product.

(v) Packing : Wrapping / packing is the fifth process in which butter paper and cartons are used. Agarbatti in bunch of 10 sticks is wrapped in butter paper bags and is put in cartons for disposal.

PROJECT PROFILE FOR MANUFACTURE OF AGARBATTI

1.	Type of unit	:	Agarbatti Manufacturing Unit.
2.	Annual Capacity of production	:	2,500 kg in 3,00,000 packets of finished Agarbatti containing 10 sticks in each packet.
3.	Nature of the activity	:	Manufacture of different varieties of Agarbatti.
4.	Estimated work period	:	250 days in a year with 8 hours work in a day.
5.	Number of persons required for working	:	15 persons including one supervisor (mostly women workers).

6. Cost of the Project

TERM LOAN (CAPITAL EXPENDITURE)

(a)	Workshed and office 800 sq. ft.	Rs.	1,60,000
(b)	Machinery / Equipment		
(a)	Wooden desk for rolling 10 Nos.	Rs.	1,200
(b)	Patla 15 Nos.	Rs.	450

(c)	Kadai 1	Rs.	175
(d)	Spoon (big) 1	Rs.	60
(e)	Spoons (small) 2	Rs.	60
(f)	Measuring glass 1	Rs.	160
(g)	Tin trays and aluminium vessels 1	Rs.	1,500
(h)	Blow lamp stove 1 No.	Rs.	350
(i)	Balance laboratory 2 sets	Rs.	2,600
(j)	Big jars glass 1 No.	Rs.	1,300
(k)	Covered Rack 1 No.	Rs.	1,500
(l)	Furniture and fittings (office tables, chairs; cupboards)	Rs.	20,000
(m)	Other small tools	Rs.	2,000
	Total	**Rs.**	**31,355**
	Capital Expenditure - Term Loan	Rs.	1,91, 355
	or say	Rs.	1,91,400

7. RAW MATERIAL (per annum)

(a)	Raw material - Bamboo sticks	986 kg or 34,00,000 sticks of 20 cm. including 15 per cent defective sticks	Rs.	34,510
(b)	Waste sandal wood powder/ charcoal powder	603.5 kg @ 70 per kg being 34 per cent of total masala powder required (1,775 kg)	Rs.	42,245
(c)	Jiggat powder	426 kg @ Rs.40 per kg being 24 per cent of total masala powder required	Rs.	17,040
(d)	Pure sandal wood powder	142 kg @ Rs.120 per kg. being 8 per cent of total masala powder required (1,775 kg)	Rs.	17,040
(e)	Nurva powder	426 kg @ Rs.35 per kg being 24 per cent of total masala required (1,775 kg)	Rs.	14,910

(f)	Other ingredients of natural herbs in powder form to be suitably used.	177.5 kg @ Rs.35 per kg. being 10 per cent of total masala powder (1,772 kg)	Rs. 22,188
(h)	Pure perfume compound of different varieties on an average	340 kg @ Rs.400 per kg.	Rs. 1,36,000
(i)	DEP (Di-ethyl phthalate) 2 per cent in pure perfume and 5 per cent of DEP has been taken into consideration as wastage.	578 kg @ Rs.65 per kg.	Rs. 37,570
(j)	Packing materials such as butter paper	3,00,000 nos. @ Rs.120 per 1,000 nos.	Rs. 36,000
(k)	Carton	3,00,000 nos. @ Rs.540 per 1,000 nos.	Rs. 1,62,000
(l)	Roll paper	30 rolls @ 300 per roll	Rs. 9,000
(m)	Tapioca powder for pasting	60 kg @ 6 per kg.	Rs. 360
			Rs. 5,28,863

8. SALARY AND WAGES

(i)	Wages for 14 workers	Rs. 17,500
(ii)	Salary for supervisor-cum-chemist	Rs. 54,000
		Rs. 2,29,000

9. OVERHEAD CHARGES

(i)	Interest on capital expenditure @ 16% p.a.	Rs.	30,624
(ii)	Insurance @ 1%		
	(a) Stock in hand of raw materials	Rs.	5,289
	(b) Capital expenditure	Rs.	1,914
		Rs.	7,203
(iii)	Depreciation		
	(a) Building @ 5%	Rs.	8,000
	(b) Machinery and equipment @ 10%	Rs.	3,136
	Total	Rs.	11,136

10. INDIRECT EXPENSES

(a)	Freight and octroi charges	Rs.	15,000
(b)	Packing and forwarding charges	Rs.	10,000
(c)	Office expenses such as postage, printing and stationery	Rs.	6,000
(d)	Promotional expenses for publicity and propaganda.	Rs.	12,000
	Total	Rs.	43,000

11. WORKING CAPITAL REQUIREMENT

A. Fixed Working Capital

(1) Salary	Rs.	54,000
(2) Office expenses	Rs.	6,000
(3) Interest on capital expenditure	Rs.	30,624
(4) Insurance	Rs.	7,203
(5) Publicity and propaganda	Rs.	12,000
	Rs.	1,09,827

Fixed cost for one operating cycle (25% of total) Rs.27,456.75 or say Rs.27,500

B. Variable Working Capital

(1)	Wages	Rs.	1,75,800
(2)	Interest on working capital	Rs.	37,800
(3)	Raw material	Rs.	5,28,863
(4)	Packing material	Rs.	10,000

(5)	Freight and octroi	Rs. 15,000
		Rs. 7,66,663

Variable working capital for one operating cycle is Rs.1,91,665.75 or say Rs.1,91,700 — Rs. 1,91,700

12. REQUIREMENT OF FUNDS

(1)	For Capital Expenditure	Rs. 1,91,400
(2)	For Working Capital (for one cycle)	Rs. 2,19,200
		Rs. 4,10,600
	Bank Loan @ 85%	Rs. 3,49,000

13. SALES VALUE

(Less sales commission etc.) — Rs. 1 0,50,000

14. COST ANALYSIS @ 80% CAPACITY UTILISATION

(i)	Fixed cost	Rs. 79,203
(ii)	Variable cost	Rs. 5,83,090
(iii)	Total cost of production	Rs. 6,62,293
(iv)	Sales realisation	Rs. 8,40,000
(v)	Gross surplus	Rs. 1,77,707
(vi)	Net surplus = (Gross surplus - Depreciation - Interest on C.E. - Interest on W.C.)	Rs. 98,147
(vii)	Disposable surplus = (Net surplus + Depreciation	Rs. 1,09,283

The unit has capacity to pay back the loan in 5 years even at 80% capacity utilisation.

TYPICAL COMPOSITION OF AGARBATTI OF MEDIUM QUALITY

	(Percent)
Sandal wood	30
Black Agar	20
Vetives	5
Kapur Kachri	5
Leaves and flowers	10
Olibanum or mytrh	20
Charcoal and other ingredients	10

To this add 25-35 percent of wood gum powder of not less than 80 mesh. Agarbattis are obtainable in different colours, and with different perfumes. The burning time of an agarbatti varies from 15 min to 5 hrs, according to quality and size. Agarbatti is also obtainable in other forms, such as, dashary (sticky paste or powder), deep (cones) and dhoop, tablets, etc.

Agarbatti making is a cottage industry in Mysore state, Chennai and Mumbai provinces. There are about 20 concerns, more than half of which are located in Mysore state, chiefly in Bangalore, Mysore city, Chennai city, Poona, Pandharpur and Tanjore are the other prominent centres of production. Nearly 10 thousand skilled workers, mostly women, are employed in the industry.

PROCESS OF MANUFACTURE

There are mainly two types of batties manufactured.

i) Dipped Varieties

ii) Masala Batties.

Bamboos are cut into the required sizes and then suitably coloured.

1) Dipped Variety:-

For making dipped batties powders of charcoal, gigatu, white chips, etc. are mixed with water to a semi solid paste. This composition is taken on a wooden plank and applied to sticks by rolling with hands. Then the raw sticks are dipped in suitable perfumery compounds diluted with white oil or other solvents like diethyl phthlate and dried.

2. Masala Batti:-

The powders of charcoal, gigatu, white chips, indigenous herbs etc. are mixed along with perfumery compounds consisting essential oils, aromatic chemicals, purified resins and natural fixatives like resins, musk etc. to a semi solid paste with the required quantity of water. This compound is applied to bamboo sticks by hand rolling and dried.

The finished agarbatti sticks are bundled either according to the number of according to weight and wrapped in moisture proof cellophane paper or butter paper and packed in printed cartons which are again wrapped in clear cellophane paper. Finally the cartons are packed in dozens. A typical agarbattis is given here:-

Sandal wood,
Black Agar,
Vetiver,
Kapur Kachri,
Leaves and flowers,
olibanum,
Charcoal and other ingredients.

To this added 25-35 percent wood gum powder of not less than 80 mesh. The purified resin, essential oils are mixed and then ground into a fine paste, some times aniline colours are also added, wood gum is then mixed with paste and kneaded. Pulverizer can be used to grind the various raw materials. The resulting hard paste is coated as bamboo sticks, cut into thin length of the required size and rolled by hand on a smooth plank to suitable thickness.

During rolling, colours, sandal wood dust, fumigating compounds etc. are added to give them even finish and appearance. The rollers are then dried and packed.

The other formulations for different Agarbattis are given below:-

1.

Sandal Wood Flour	:	30%
Black agar	:	20%
Vetiver	:	5%
Camphor powder	:	5%
Flowers and leaves	:	10%
Myrriih	:	20%
Wood or Coal	:	10%

2.

Agar	:	10 gm
Red sand wood flour	:	60 gm
Laban	:	100 gm
Shora	:	80 gm
Silaras	:	5 gm
Gur	:	35 gm
Kapur Kachri	:	50 gm
Rux	:	70 gm
Nagur motha	:	50 gm
Balchar	:	50 gm
Wood Maida	:	125 gm
Rose oil	:	As desired

3.

Agar	:	50 gms
Jata Mansi	:	50 gms
sugandha Bala	:	50 gms
loban	:	500 gms
Talis Patra	:	50 gms
Wood Maida	:	50 gms
Camphor	:	350 gms

Sandal wood flour	:	50 gms
Nagar Motha	:	50 gms
Rose oil	:	As desired

4.

White sandal	:	100 gms
Ral (powder)	:	100 gms
Wood coke (powder)	:	100 gms
Guggal (ground)	:	100 gms

5.

Maida wood	:	150 gm.
Kuchur	:	30 gm.
Tal Patri	:	30 gm.
Dal chini	:	10 gm.
Badi ilaichi	:	20 gm.
Jai Fal	:	20 gm.
Sandal Powder (white)	:	30 gm.
Sandal Powder (Red)	:	20 gm.
Mal Mudi	:	20 gm.
Kuth	:	5 gm.
Kauria loban	:	10 gm.
Water or Airk Gulab	:	As per requirement

MOSQUITO REPELLENT BATTI

Maida (Powder)	:	150 gm.
Wood coke (Powder)	:	30 gm.
Pyrethrum powder	:	20 gm.
Citronella oil	:	10 gm.
White sandal (Powder)	:	150 gm.
Loban	:	50 gm.
Wood coke (Powder)	:	50 gm.
Guggal (Powder)	:	50 gm.
Pyrethrum Powder	:	30 gm.
Citronella oil	:	30 gm.

PERFUMES FORMULATION FOR AGARBATTI:

Yara yara Powder	:	15 gm.
Musk ambrettee	:	15 gm.
Musk Xylene	:	7 gm.
Civet	:	15 gm.
Yara yara Crystal	:	10 gm.
Musk amber	:	5 gm.
Cassia oil	:	15 gm.
Neroli oil	:	20 gm.
Patchouli oil	:	10 gm.
Bergamot oil	:	30 gm.

PLANT ECONOMICS OF AGARBATTI (PERFUMED)

Rated Plant Capacity = 500.00 Kgs./Day

LAND & BUILDING(Land area required 800 sq.mt) = Rented

PLANT & MACHINERY

1. Balance,
2. Wood planks for rolling
3. Grinder equipped with motor
4. Mixers equipped with agitator
5. Trays
6. Racks
7. Packing machine automatic
8. Other miscellaneous machine and equipments

FIXED CAPITAL

1.	Plant & Machinery	Rs.	6,61,000.00
2.	Other Fixed Assets	Rs.	86,100.00
	TOTAL	Rs.	7,47,100.00

RAW MATERIALS

1. Aromatic chemicals & essential oil such as Hydroxy, citronellol, aldehydes, Jasmouium, civet crystals etc.
2. Other important ingredients including colour
3. Packing material cellophane paper, cartons, tubes etc.

TOTAL WORKING CAPITAL/MONTH

1.	Raw Material	Rs.	3,30,000.00
2.	Salary & Wages	Rs.	63,840.00
3.	Utilities & Overheads	Rs.	13,000.00
	TOTAL	Rs.	4,06,840.00

TOTAL CAPITAL INVESTMENT

Total Fixed Capital	Rs.	7,47,100.00
Total Working Capital for 1 Month	Rs.	4,06,840.00
TOTAL	Rs.	11,53,940.00

TURN OVER/ANNUM

By sale of 1,50,000 kgs of Agarbattis Rs. 67,50,000.00

PROFIT SALES RATIO = Profit / Sales x 100 = 23.11 %

RATE OF RETURN = Operating profit / T.C.I x 100 = 135.21 %

BREAK EVEN POINT (B.E.P) = 30.25 %

ADDRESSES FOR NATURAL HERBS AND ROOTS AND OTHER RAW MATERIALS

1. M/s. C.M. Subbaiah Nadar,
Merchants, 30,
Swami sannidhi Lane,
East Mary Street,
Madurai-1 (Tamil Nadu)

2. M/s. C.M. Pornai Swamy Nadar,
Merchants, 30,
Swamy Sannidhi Lane,
East Mary Street,
Madurai-1 (Tamil Nadu)

3. Government Sandalwood Depot,
Satyamangalam, Dist. Periyar
(Tamil Nadu)

4. Government Sandalwood Depot,
Tirupattur, Dist. North Arcot,
(Tamil Nadu)

5. M/s. Shri Ambalal
Parimala Salai,
(Pure Sandalwood Powder)
227, East Adayavalanjan Street,
Srirangam, Tiruchirapalli,
Tiruchirapalli-620006
(Tamil Nadu)

6. Gajanan Nana Trading Company
P.O. Sagar
(Karnataka)

7. Grover Brothers,
79-E, samaldas Gandhi Road,
Kalba Devi,
Mumbai-2 (Maharashtra)

8. B. Ramaiah and Sons
20, Arumugham Mudaliar,
Kalasipalayam Lane,
Bangalore - 560 002
(Karnataka)

9. M. Alavutheen,
Ismail Puram, 12th Lane,
Munichalai Road, Madurai-9
(Tamil Nadu)

10. Kalayan Traders,
13/C, 1st Main Road,
Kalappa Block,
Ramachandrapuram,
Bangalore-21 (Karnataka)

11. M/s. S.H. Kelkar and Co.Ltd.
Lal Bahadur Shastri Marg,
Mulund (W),
Mumbai-80
(Maharashtra)

12. Eastern Aromatics Pvt. Ltd.
Datta Mandir Road,
Bhandup,
Mumabi-78
Maharashtra

13. Aromatic and Industrial Chemicals Pvt. Ltd.
Nirmal, 12th Floor,
Nariman Point,
Mumbai - 21
Maharashtra

14. Industrial Perfumes Ltd.
Hay Bunder Road, Tank Road,
Post Office, Mumbai-33

15. Narden India Ltd.
Maker Chamber-IV, 10th Floor,
222, Backbay Reclamation,
P.O.No.19964, Nariman Point,
Mumbai-21 (Maharashtra)

16. Space Aromes,
29/3-B, Mangaldas Road,
Mumbai-2 (Maharashtra)

17. R.P. Chemical Works,
M.G. Road,
Kannauj (U.P.)

18. J.B. Shah and Company
Pankaj Society,
Near Society Sharkhej Road,
Ahmedabad-7 (Gujarat)

19. Gujarat Aromatics Ltd.
Plot No.297,
G.I.D.C. Industrial Estate,
Ankleswar-393 002 (Gujarat)

20. 'Chica' Ltd., Kannamal Bldg.,
611/612, Mount Road,
Madras (Tamil Nadu)

21. 'Chica' Ltd., Mehta Chambers,
13, Mathew Road,
Mumbai-400 004 (Maharashtra)

22. Aromatics (India) Ltd.
38, Link Road, Malleswaram,
Bangalore-560 003
(Karnataka)

23. Mascneijar Aromatics (India)
Ltd.
G.S.D. Road,
Chennai-600 044 (Tamil Nadu)

24. M/s. Hawarden Traders,
50, South Masi Street,
Post Box No.170,
Madurai-1 (Tamil Nadu)

25. Satyanarayana Traders,
MSIL House,
36, Cummingham Road,
Bangalore-560 052
(Karnataka)

26. Unrise and Co.
43 - A, South Masi Street,
Madurai-560 052
(Tamil Nadu)

27. Sandal and Agarucidar
Wood Powders,
Conservator of Forests,
Belgaum (Karnataka)

28. Aromatics Chemicals
Pefumes etc.
M/s. B.C. Patel,
79, Princess Street,
Mumbai-2 (Maharashtra)

29. M/s. Devar and Company,
143, Princess Street,
Mumbai-2 (Maharashtra).

30. M/s. M.R. Modi,
Princess Street,
Mumbai-2 (Maharashtra)

31. M/s. Mutual Traders,
14, Badrian Street,
Mumbai-1 (Maharashtra)

32. M/s. Nawel Raj and Co.,
208, Govindappa Naicker
Street,
Chennai-1 (Tamil Nadu)
(Bamboo Sticks)

33. Mysore M.S. Agarbatti works,
4, Santhappa Lane, S.G. Park
Cross Road, Bangalore-2
(Karnataka)

Chapter - 7

Automatic Book Binding Unit

There are so many advantages of binding unit under one roof such as quality improvement, reduction in cost, saving of time (most important) reduction in transport charges and easy handling of plant.

The book binding cloth is coated with starch and the product is used for binding the books.

The book binding cloth is a material of oil origin and since the publication trade is increasing, the book binding is gaining popularity.

MANUFACTURING PROCESS

In automatic book binding unit, the operation can be divided into different categories. The most important part in book binding is the folding of full sheets into required size ie according to the given format.

After the printed sheet comes off the press it must usually undergo other operations before it is converted to its product some printed sheets such as simple hand bills letterheads - printed one up & with noblood trim or folds - can be shipped without further processing.

Some sheets are printed with more than one image up or a number of separate images & these must be cut, trimmed, or folded before they can be delivered.

Most printed sheets become a part of something else or need to be processed further such as books, catalogues, advertising folders, brochures, labels, packaging & so forth and to accomplish the conversion they need binding and finishing operations.

Binding & finishing cover a variety and range of operations. The work required to convert printed sheets or webs of paper into books, magazines, folder and so forth is called binding.

The work required to make adiplays, labels, toys, folding boxes, greeting cards & a variety of fancy packaging and advertising materials involves a number of finishing operations.

Most printing is done on large sheets with a number of the same or different subjects on the sheets. Labels are varnished and cut to size after printing.

Printed sheets are folded into signatures of 4 to 64 pages, which are later bound together in various ways to form books. The operations of binding and finishing are as important a part of the converting operation as the printing.

Binding is divided into 8 different types :-

1. Edition binding, which is the binding of quantities of identical books, either case or hardbound or adhesive bound, usually called perfect binding.
2. Job binding or extra binding, which refers to the binding of small quantities and special lots of books.
3. Library binding which is special binding for private and public libraries.
4. Pamphlet and trade binding, which is the binding of leaflets, booklets, magazines and some soft covered books.
5. Manifold or commercial binding, which is the binding of multiple business forms such as purchase orders, sales books and so forth.
6. Mechanical binding which is the binding of individual sheets of paper is a nonremovable form such as a plastic binder by a special binding device.
7. Loose-leaf binding, which is the binding of individual sheets of paper in a removable form in a special binders.
8. Blank book binding and ruling, which is the manufacture of bound books with blank or ruled pages used for accounting record keeping, receipts, picture albums and so forth.

As already mentioned, the folding of full sheet into the required size of the book and according to the printing of pages on the full sheet. It is the most important aspect of book binding unit. In our case, this folding is done with the help of an automatic folding which is having a very high rate of production.

After folding operation, the sheets are arranged in the proper manner. Then these sheets are arranged in the right manner.

After the folding operation on the automatic folding (sheet) unit the arranged pages are gummed with the help of a suitable adhesive. The cloth for book binding is cotton. No other cloth is suitable for this purpose. The other material is starch adhesive. The starch adhesive is made from maize starch.

The range of clothes suitable for book binding is very wide and the strength and wearing qualities vary greatly. Clothes do not deteriorate on exposure to air, therefore the simple test by tearing will indicate at once their wearing qualities.

Any cloth can be used for book binding if it is strong enough & can prevent glue laid on its back from penetrating to its surface. Any cloth can also be used, if it is first lined with paper. Most cloth used in the book production is made specially for the purpose, usually in rolls 36 to 38" wide (the selvage of an inch) and 36 yards long.

The furnish of most book cloth is cotton. Binding cloth may be coloured. The simplest and most common is that in which the entire material has single colour.

The adhesive used in the book binding purposes should be of high quality. So that it can not cause any harm to book by any way.

The binding of folded sheets and application of adhesive is done in next automatic machine.

In some cases, a thin plastic sheet is placed on the cover of the book. This plastic sheet can be placed with the help of a laminating machine.

After the complete book is prepared they are conditioned (or dried) for some time and after that they are packed and sent to the market.

PLANT ECONOMICS OF AUTOMATIC BOOK BINDING UNIT

Rated Plant Capacity = 6,00,000.00 Books/Annum
LAND & BUILDING (Total land 500 sq. mts.) = Rented

PLANT & MACHINERY

1. Steam calendering machine
2. Starch Adhesive making plant
3. Adhesive & Feed Tank
4. Coating machine
5. Gelling Oven
6. Drying & winding equipments
7. Baby Boiler
8. Water Storage Tank
9. Water pump, motor, and other miscellaneous equipments

FIXED CAPITAL

1.	Plant & Machinery	Rs.	9,80,000.00
2.	Other Fixed Assets	Rs.	75,000.00
	TOTAL	Rs.	10,55,000.00

RAW MATERIALS

1. Starch (Maize)
2. Sodium Hydroxide
3. Cotton Cloth
4 Miscellaneous chemicals

TOTAL WORKING CAPITAL/MONTH

1.	Raw Material	Rs.	7,80,000.00
2.	Salary & Wages	Rs.	38,375.00
3.	Utilities & Overheads	Rs.	26,000.00
	TOTAL	Rs.	·8,44,375.00

TOTAL CAPITAL INVESTMENT

Total Fixed Capital	Rs.	10,55,000.00
Total Working Capital for 1 Month	Rs.	8,44,375.00
TOTAL	Rs.	18,99,375.00

TURN OVER/ANNUM

By sale of 6,00,000 meter Book Binding Cloth.	Rs.	1,32,00,000.00

PROFIT SALES RATIO = Profit / Sales x 100 = 19.66 %
RATE OF RETURN = Operating profit / T.C.I x 100 = 136.60 %
BREAK EVEN POINT (B.E.P) = 23.16 %

Chapter - 8

Adhesive (Polyvinyl Butyral Based)

Polyvinyl butyral based adhesive is a phenolic vinyl butyral adhesive. It is a blend of phenolic (thermosetting) and polyvinyl (thermosetting) and polyvinyl butyral (thermoplastic) resin which is predominantly thermosetting.

Regarding adhesion to natural surfaces, poly vinyl butyral is the acetal usually selected for adhesion to natural surfaces. Application to wood confers good hold out, interact adhesion, moisture resistance, flexibility toughness, impact resistance, and protection against discolation.

Application to metal or reinforced plastic facings to paper honey comb structures is remarkable.

Application to textiles, natural and synthetic improves stain and water resistance without noticably affecting feel, drape or colour.

Textile with improved fire resistance dyeability or leather like characteristics have been patented in the USSR and Japan. Aqueous butyral dispersions are adhered to textiles where room temperature drying is significant.

Polyvinyl butyral finds an important role in strengthening high strength plastics. Dupont's aromatic polyamide, kevlar combined with polyvinyl butyral and phenol formaldehyde, laminates into light weight bullet resistant helmets and armor plate. Dupont offers an anti-lacerative sheeting which is a laminate of polyvinyl butyral and oriented polyethylene terephthalate and when adhered to glass provided protection against glass splintering an impact.

FORMULATIONS OF POLYVINYL BUTYRAL BASED ADHESIVE

Formulation No. - 1:-

a.	Polyvinyl Butyral (low hydroxy)	-	2.7%
b.	N - Butyral	-	10.8%
c.	Phenol Resin (Phenol Formaldehyde Resin)	-	51.0%
d.	Methyl Ethyl Ketone	-	35.5%

Polyvinyl butyral based adhesive is applied by a roller or knife and baked for 15 minutes at 200°C and for 1 hr. at 150°C.

Formulation No. - 2:-

a.	Polyvinyl Butyral (low hydroxy)	-	5%
b.	Iso propyl Alcohol	-	14%
c.	Resol/Novolak type resin (Phenol Formaldehyde Resin)	-	31%
d.	Methyl Ethyl Ketone (MEK)	-	50%

Phenol Butyral Adhesive for Metal Bonding:-

Useful in less than 250°F temperature.

		Parts/wt.
Polyvinyl Butyral resin	-	100
Phenol Formaldehyde Resin	-	100
Maleic anhydride	-	10
Methyl Alcohol	-	230
Methyl Ethyl Ketone	-	230

Process - mix well.

MANUFACTURING PROCESS FOR POLYVINYL BUTYRAL BASED ADHESIVE

As per the following formulation :-

a.	Polyvinyl Butyral (low hydroxy)	-	2.7%
b.	N - Butyral	-	10.8%
c.	Phenolic Resin	-	51.0%
d.	Methyl Ethyl Ketone (MEK)	-	35.5%

The first step for the manufacture of polyvinyl butyral based adhesive comprised the addition of polyvinyl butyral resin (low hydroxy) 13.5 kgs.

into methyl ethyl ketone 117.5 kg. contained in a mixer made of stainless steel fitted with an agitator and motor.

The contents of the mixer are well stirred by means of an agitator for about 15 minutes to 1/2 hr. After the polyvinyl butyral is dissolved N - butanol 54 kg. added into the mixer.

A stirring is continued for about 1/2 hour. The viscosity of the adhesive is controlled by the addition of the solvent. Subsequently (phenol formaldehyde 255 kgs.) Phenolic resin is introduced into the mixer/reaction vessel. Resin should be added last.

Thorough mixing (at least half an hour to 1 hour) is conducted till the resin completely goes into solution and a homogenbus solution is obtained.

Final step of the process is the packing of the finished adhesive. Adhesive is packed in plastic containers ranging from 100 gm, 200 gm, 500 gm, 1 kg, 2 kg, 5 kg, 50 kg, capacity as agreed upon with the purchaser. The container should bear the name of the manufacturer, trade name, capacity, etc. printed on it. The containers are next packed in wooden boxes to facilitate easy transportation.

All the raw materials and equipments to produce the final product are easily available throughout the country.

PLANT ECONOMICS OF ADHESIVE (POLYVINYL BUTYRAL)

Rated Plant Capacity = 500.00 Kg./Day

LAND & BUILDING (Total LAND 500 Sq. Mts.) = Rented

PLANT & MACHINERY

1. Mixing Kettle of S.S.filled with Agitator and Motor
2. Weighing Scale (Plat -form Type)
3. Weighing Scale {Small Size}
4. Packing Machine [Semi Automatic]
5. Storage Tanks
6. Lab.Testing Equipments
7. Instrumentation & Process Control
8. Miscellaneous Amount

FIXED CAPITAL

1.	Plant & Machinery	Rs.	4,75,000.00
2.	Other Fixed Assets	Rs.	2,12,000.00
	TOTAL	Rs.	6,87,000.00

RAW MATERIALS

1. Polyvinyl Butyral (Low Hydroxy)
2. N - Butyral
3. Phenolic Resin (Phenol Formaldehyde Resin)
4. Methyl Ethyl Ketone,
5. Packing Material, Pvc plastic containers

TOTAL WORKING CAPITAL/MONTH

1.	Raw Material	Rs.	8,42,562.00
2.	Salary & Wages	Rs.	46,375.00
3.	Utilities & Overheads	Rs.	64,500.00
	TOTAL	Rs.	9,53,437.00

TOTAL CAPITAL INVESTMENT

Total Fixed Capital	Rs.	6,87,000.00
Total Working Capital for 1 Month	Rs.	9,53,437.00
TOTAL	Rs.	16,40,437.00

TURN OVER/ANNUM

By sale of 1,50,000 kgs. of Poly - Vinyl Butyral based adhesive	Rs.	1,50,00,000.00

PROFIT SALES RATIO = Profit / Sales x 100 = 21.55 %

RATE OF RETURN = Operating profit / T.C.I x 100 = 197.09 %

BREAK EVEN POINT (B.E.P) = 20.97 %

Chapter - 9

Adhesive Based on Vinyl Acetate (Fevicol Type)

Fevicol type adhesives come under the category of synthetic resins and latex adhesives and are made from polyvinyl acetate resins. Pclyvinyl acetate is a thermoplastic, odourless, tasteless, non-toxic, essentially clear and colourless resin. It has a noncrystalline and relatively branced rather than linear structure, most grades of resin have a somewhat broad molecular weight distribution. They do not melt, but soften over a temperature range. The resin is unaffected by sunlight. Ultraviolet light and air, further more it will absorb a small amount of water. Polyvinyl acetate is neutral and non-corrosive. The various grades have good heat stability below 100°C. Show slight discoloration at approximately 150°C and decompose at 50°C but brittle at 10° to 150°C.

They found a place in wood adhesives and later were introduced in the familiar household "white glue" polyvinyl acetate is now used in adhesive for book building, paper bags, milk cartons, drinking straws enveloped, gummed tapes, convolute types, folding boxes, multiwall shopping bags, labels and lots of other common products - foils, film and paperboard, cigarette tips, lagging compounds, wood assembly, padding pencils, leathers binding, tile cements etc.

Because of their relatively low cost, ready availability, wide comparatively and excellent adhesive characteristics, many polyvinyl acetate resins, solutions and emulsions are treated as commodity items by the adhesives industry. Most of the acetate grades are primarily a function of molecular weight. Low molecular weight grades are soft and deformable at room temperature, whereas high molecular weight grades are hard and tough. All grades outstanding adhesion to many surfaces, porous and non-porous. The excellent adhesion is due in part to the highly polar acetate groups in the polymer and partially to the unique combination of viscosity tack, tensile strength and other properties that exist during application of the adhesive and during a formation and ageing of the bone.

MANUFACTURING PROCESS

The manufacture of adhesive from synthetic resin is simple and can be started with a small capital investment. The most advantageous factor in this plant is that it can be switched over to any type of adhesives as per market demand.

The equipments used in the manufacturing process is an open jacketed kettle. It is fitted with a thermostat, stirring arrangement jacket for steam heating and a bottom outlet. The vessel is generally made of stainless steel having M.S. (Mild Steel) Jacket. The following steps are taken.

1. Dispersion
2. Polymerization
3. Addition of other ingredients.
4. Packing.

1. Dispersion:

The polymers are charged in the water taken in the kettle. Small amount of soap is added to the mixture and the stirring started. The quantities are added so as to get about 55% solid emulsion.

2. Polymerization:

This step is necessary only when monomer is used. A catalyst (benzyl peroxide) is added. No heating is started. With the thermostat set at some suitable temperature, the stirring is started. When the required temperature has been reached, the heating is stopped and the excess heat of reaction is removed by circulating cooling water through the jacket.

When at the same flow rate the temperature starts falling appreciably the reaction is considered to be near completion.

After the completion, the cooling is also stopped.

3. Addition of other ingredients:

While the emulsion is still quite hot, other ingredients are added and stirred well. The adhesive is finally cooled and taken out from the bottom opening valve.

4. Packing:

Next, the adhesive is packed in plastic containers 1/2, 1, 2, 5, 50 kgs. capacity as agreed upon with the purchaser. The container should bear the name of manufacturer, trade mark and capacity printed on it. The containers are next packed in wooden boxes to facilities easy transportation.

FORMULATION

The cheap and best formulation which is commonly used in India is as follows:

	Part by weight
Polyvinyl acetate emulsion (PVA) (50% solid content)	80
Polyvinyl alcohol (PVA)	10
Dextrin	30
Resol 65%	70
Water	85

Polyvinyl acetate adhesive by emulsion polymerization.

Formula:

Water	42.75% by wt.
Vinyl acetate	55.0 "
Hydroxy Ethyl cellulose	2.0 "
Targitol WPX	0.05 "
Potassium Paroxy disulphate	0.05 "
Sodium bicarbonate	0.15 "

PROCESS:

The cellulose tergitol, and water are heated to 80°C for an hour and then cooled to 30°C to this potassium peroxy disulphate, sodium bisulphate and only 10% of the vinyl acetate is added. Then this reaction mixture is heated 75°C and at this point the remaining vinyl acetate is added increamentally in 4 hours and the reactor is maintained at 80°C. After all the contents are added and the emulsion is heated to 90°C for 30 min. and then cooled.

The solids content is approximately 55 - 57%

Viscosity	3000 cp
pH	5.0

TYPICAL PROPERTIES OF POLYVINYL ACETATE EMULSION (ADHESIVE)

Property	*Percentage*
Total solids	54 - 56%
Viscosity Brook field LVT 60 rpm.	800 - 1200 cp

Ahesive Based on Vinyl Acetate (Fevicol Type)

Sp.gr.	1.11
Avg. Particle size	1.3
Surface tension dynes/cm	50
Retention of filter	
100 mesh rpm	100
Coefficient of Expansion	
per °C. At 20°C	0.00048
at 50°C	0.00052
Avg. wt. pv gallons at	
20°C (lb.)	9.2
Flash point	None

The compositions comprise a mixture of (a) an aqueous emulsion of a vinyl acetate copolymer (b) Polyvinyl alcohol and (c) an acidic metal salt curing agent. The examples shown below illustrate the process of a number of different adhesive formulations typical of this process. The following table presents the complete data for the formulations which were produced. In preparing these formulations, the procedure utilized involved the polymerization of vinyl acetate copolymers with polyvinyl alcohol added to the respective recipes as an emulsifier. The curing agent, in the form of an aqueous solution, was added to the stabilized emulsion just prior to its use as an adhesive.

Each of the above described formulation were successfully employed as adhesives for the bonding of a wide variety of wood, plastic and metal surfaces. The resulting adhesive bonds were, in all cases, superior to the bonds achieved with unmodified polyvinyl acetate-polyvinyl alcohol adhesive blends with regard to such factors as resistance to static loading and heat resistance of the cured films. This superiority was especially noted in the water resistance exhibited by the cured films of the adhesive systems.

For the manufacturing of fevicol based on polyvinyl acetate and polyvinyl alcohol, the main and major step is polymerization which is done in a reactor or kettle. These types of Fevicol exhibit by the modified adhesive compositions when compared with.

1. Polyvinyl acetate-polyvinyl alcohol stabilized emulsions which were devoid of acidic, metal salt curing agents.

2. Polyvinyl acetate-polyvinyl alcohol stabilized emulsions catalyzed with conventional acid catalysts and.

3. Polyvinyl acetate-polyvinyl alcohol stabilized emulsions blended with convention all insolubilizers.

Name of Vinyl Acetate Polymer	Ratio of ViAc: Comonomer	Percent by weight resin solid in emulsion	Grams poly-mer sion form-ulation	Grams poly-vinyl alcohol solids	Curing agent	Gram equi-lents curing agent per 100 gm emsulsion
Copolymer with ethyl acrylate	87:13	50	100	6.0	$Al(NO_3)_3$	0.04
Copolymer with ethyl acid meleate	97:3	50	100	6.0	$Cr(NO_3)_3$	0.05
Copolymer with acrylic acid	98:2	55	100	1.1	$Alcl_3$	0.03
Copolymer with crotonic acid	97:3	45	100	4.0	$Cr(NO_3)_3$	0.08
Copolymer with dibutyl fumerate	80:20	55	100	6.0	$Cr(Cl_4O)_3$	0.08
Copolymer with octyl acrylate	80:20	50	100	6.0	$Cr(Cl_4O)_3$	0.08
Copolymer with acrylamide	96:4	50	100	4.5	$Cr(NO_3)_3$	0.06
Copolymer with N-methylol acrylamide	95:5	50	100	5.0	$Cr(NO_3)_3$	0.01
Copolymer with N-methylol acrylamide	98.81.2	50	100	3.0	$Cr(NO_3)_3$	0.04
Copolymer with N-methylol acrylamide	98.8:1.2	50	100	3.0	$AlCl_3$	0.04
Terpolymer with dibutyl fumarate and acyrlic acid	80:18:2	50	100	6.0	$Cr(NO_3)_3$	0.04

Ahesive Based on Vinyl Acetate (Fevicol Type)

PLANT ECONOMICS OF ADHESIVE

Rated Plant Capacity = 1,20,000 Kg/Annum

LAND & BUILDING (Land Area 250 sq.mt) = Rented

PLANT & MACHINERY

1. Mixing Kettles
2. Weighing scale
3. Testing & Laboratory Equipments
4. Packing machine
5. Other miscellaneous equipments
6. Boiler
7. Electrical and other water installation etc.

FIXED CAPITAL

1.	Plant & Machinery	Rs.	2,56,000.00
2.	Other Fixed Assets		50,000.00
	TOTAL	Rs.	3,06,000.00

RAW MATERIALS

1. Polyvinyl acetate emulsion
2. Polyvinyl alcohol
3 Resol
4. Dextrin
5. Packaging material

TOTAL WORKING CAPITAL/MONTH

1.	Raw Material	Rs.	4,80,500.00
2.	Salary & Wages	Rs.	19,375.00
3.	Utilities & Overheads	Rs.	25,000.00
	TOTAL	Rs.	5,24,875.00

TOTAL CAPITAL INVESTMENT

Total Fixed Capital		3,06,000.00
Total Working Capital for 1 Month		5,24,875.00
TOTAL	Rs.	8,30,875.00

TURN OVER/ANNUM

Receipt through sale 1,20,000 kgs of Fevicol Type Adhesive Rs. 84,00,000.00

PROFIT SALES RATIO = Profit / Sales x 100 = 23.07 %

RATE OF RETURN = Operating profit / T.C.I x 100 = 233.22 %

BREAK EVEN POINT (B.E.P) = 16.28 %

Chapter - 10

Bakery Unit
(Pastries, Bread, Buns, Cake, Toffee etc.)

Pastries, Bread, Cakes, Toffies etc. comes under the bakery product. Now the advancement of age food habits of the ready-made food. Most of all the bakery items are under the category of ready-made food. Now school going children like to have the items like pastries, cakes, breads etc. for their tiffin use office going people like to take breads and pastries products, in our daily break fast. The share of bakery products even daily wages labourers also spend their lunch by taking bread or like that baking product. By the large utilities of baking products in our life takes part the program of progress of bakery unit itself.

Small scale production of baking item can be achieved by carry professional ways of life.

PROCESS OF MANUFACTURE

Danish Pastry
Formula

Ingredients	- lb - ounce - (02)	Methods
Top - grade flour of fair strength make a bay Shortening	- 2 lb - 8 Oz - - 1 Oz -	Sieve flour and rub in the shortening
Salt Sugar	- 1 Oz - - 3.5 Oz.-	Place together in the bay.
Eggs (Ice Cold) Fresh Milk (Ice Cold) Yeast	- 5 Oz - 1lb 4 Oz - 3.5 Oz	Break down the yeast in the cold milk. Add to the bay, mix all to a clear dough but avoid undue toughening.
Butter	- 2 lb	

Bakery Unit (Pastries, Bread, Buns, Cake, Toffee etc.)

Rotary Rack Oven
Diesel Fired

Danish Pastry

When the dough has been mixed, leave it at the side of the slab whilst the 'butter' is manipulated to make it homogeneous.

Pin out the dough and enfold within it the 'butter' as when making puff paste. Pin out, brush off surplus flour and fold in three. Pin out again, cut into two pieces of equal area and place on on top of the other. Finally, pin out once more and again fold in three. Note that in each case all flour adhering to the surface of the pinned-out paste must be brushed off before folding to ensure satisfactory adhesion of the layers.

To clarify all this perhaps it will be best to state the folding in the following manner :

Three folds
two folds - by cutting in two and topping
Three folds.

This paste should now be worked off at once and should not be allowed any resting periods at all until it reaches the prover. Moreover, it should be kept quite cold at all stages again until it reaches the prover.

Ingredients	lb.	oz.	Method
Top-grade flour of			Sieve flour and rub in theshortening.
Make a bay.			
fair strength . .	2	8	
Shortening		1	

Salt		0¼	Place together in the bay.
Castor sugar . .		3½	
Eggs (ice cold) . .		5	Break down the yeast in the cold milk. Add to
Fresh milk (ice cold)	1	4	bay.Mix all to a clear dough.
Yeast		3½	
'Butter'*	2	0	

* 'Butter' in this recipe can mean either all tough, cool butter, a blend of butter and pastry margarine, all pastry margarine, all pastry margarine or a blend of pastry margarine and cake margarine or pastry fat. If pastry fat is used, only 1½ lb. will be required.

Filling for Danish Pastries

Burgermasterpaste.

Cream together 1 lb. ground almonds, 1½ lb. butter or cake margarine, and 1 lb. castor sugar. Add almond essence as required.

Remonce.

Cream together 3/4 lb. ground almonds, 2¼ lb. castor sugar, and 2lb. butter or cake margarine. Add almond essence as required.

Both these fillings can be made with marzipan, making due allowance for the sugar content in rebalancing the recipes.

Bagecreme.

2 pt. milk, 4 oz. cornflour, 6 oz. castor sugar, 4 oz. melted butter or cake margarine, egg colour, vanilla essence.

Make up as for ordinary vanilla custard beating the melted margarine into the mixing as soon as the cornflour has been gelatinized. This custard must be used cold.

When the mixing is ready for proving, danish pastries can be refrigerated, if desired. So retarding fermentation. They can be "held" for up to 4 hour at 36°F. They should then be taken from the reparder, allowed to reach room 'temperature' not usually, then proved and baked at 450°-460°F for 8-9 minutes. Now cool it pack and store for marketing.

Machine-made Short Paste Sugar in Paste

As soon as the paste mixed and rubbed down, take it from the bowl and place it on the side slab or on dusted board. Cover damped, and use as required.

Mention must be made of hand-made short paste. This can be made by rubbing the fats into the sieved flour, making a bay, placing the other ingredients in the centre, drawing in the flour, mixing very lightly together, then rubbing down the paste under the hands.

Often paste is made with twice as much water as the quantity mentioned. In this case, the rubbing down must not be indulged in or the paste will be very tough and spongy. Simply proceed as before, but shake the ingredients together as lightly as possible, then press all together lightly and handle as little possible throughout the mixing process.

Sugar in Paste

Sugar does two things in short paste apart from sweetening it. Firstly, it affects the appearance of the goods when baked. This is because of the natural caramelization of sugar, in the oven colouring the paste . The more sugar, the deeper the colouring. Paste made without sugar does not take on colour so well during baking, therefore it can be baked in a much hotter oven.

Secondly, sugar has a solvent or dispersing action on the gluten of flour, and this accounts for the fact that when larger quantities of sugar are used in paste it is much easier to get ultra-shortness. In fact, by working such paste well by rubbing down under the hands it can be made so shorts as to be most difficult to work at all, and will break simply by the action of the rolling pin. This is not likely to happen with paste containing only 1½ oz. sugar to 1 lb. flour, however.

PROCESS MANUFACTURING OF BREAD

BREAD

Bread manufacturing is a process of mixing of bread ingredients and prepared a proper dough of the Ingredients, after complete making of doughing dough is divided, rounded, moulding and proofing, after proofing the products is further pass through the baking own to complete bake the product. The product i.e. bread is ready for cooling, slicing and packing for marketing.

GENERAL RAW MATERIAL :

1. Wheat Flour
2. Yeast

3. Sugar
4. Salt
5. Water
6. Shortening agent (like vanaspati)
7. Milk or milk powder etc.

There are different types of bread of whose formule are given below:

NORMAL BREAD

INGREDIENTS	PERCENTAGE ON WT. BASIS OF MAIDA
Water	60%
Salt	1%
Sugar	2%
Shortening	2%
Yeast	1.5-2%

MILK BREAD

INGREDIENTS	PERCENTAGE ON WT. BASIS OF MAIDA
Yeast	3.8%-4%
Sugar	3%
Milk	18-20%
Egg	10%
Water	36%

PROCESS

Dissolve the yeast in partly water with the complete addition of sugar in it, stirred the ingredients until it will not formed a homogeneous solution. Temperature of the mixture will be 30° - 35°C.

Now added salt in another pot containing residual water. Mix diet thoroughly to make a homogeneous solution.

Now yeast sugar solution and salt solution is ready.

Take the proper amount of flour, first mixed with sugar yeast solution by mixing machine, after complete mixing added to it salt solution to form proper dough. After complete water, sugar and salt mixing, added the shortening in the dough mixer to make a smooth and soft dough.

Keep the smooth dough for one hour for fermenting the dough. After one hour, the dough has gone to knock-back operation, after knock-baking of the dough is pass through the divider and rounder. From the rounder to it should go to moulder, in the moulder it is kept for final proofing. After final proofing in the mould it will take 40-70 minutes at temperature 40°C) it is pass through baking open where temperature control around 200°C - 300°C and the baking time around 15-30 minutes.

After complete baking of the dough, that is hot form of bread is allow to pass in cooling zone to cool the bread at 30°C, it will take time around 2-3 hours.

After cooling the bread, now pass it through slicing machine and then wrapping the bread of wrapping machine and seal the bread. Now bread is ready for marketing.

MANUFACTURING OF BUNS

Theory and procedure of buns are similar to the breads only ingredients composition are different, even some excess ingredients required.

Formulations of different types of buns are given below:

NORMAL BUNS (SWEET BUNS)

NAME OF THE INGREDIENTS	PERCENTAGE OF INGREDIENTS ON THE WEIGHT BASIS OF MAIDA
Milk	10-12%
Shotening	8%
Sugar	10-15%
Whole Eggs	5%
Yeast	8.5%
Salt	1.0%

BATH BUNS

NAME OF THE INGREDIENTS	PERCENTAGE OF INGREDIENTS ON THE WEIGHT BASIS OF MAIDA
Butter	40%
Sugar	40%
Eggs	50%
Milk	Desired
Yeast	6%

GENERAL PROCESS

Sugar dissolves in part of the water, in sugar solution added all the yeast to make a yeast sugar homogeneous solution. Sodium carbonate, salt are dissolved in other part of water. Now melt the shortening if it is solid form.

Take flour in kneading mixer added yeast sugar solution, mix homogeneously, after complete mixing added salt's solution then added shortening to the whole mixture to form a soft dough. When proper homogeneous dough has been prepared, keep the dough for one hour to make a fermented dough of well in seated volume at temperature 30°C-35°C. Then the knock back operation will start.

After knock back it is pass through the divider and rounder. After warded all the rounded dough put in the mould and keep it for 40 minutes 60 minutes for final proofing. Then the dough is put in the bakery oven at the temperature of 200-300°C.

After complete baking it is taken out and keep it for looking about 2 hours. Now pack it and market the product.

MANUFACTURING PROCESS OF CAKES

In the case of cake manufacturing processing sugar, salt, shortening, baking powder, egg, flour, milk, flavour etc. mixed thoroughly such that air bubbles should be entropped in the batter, then baked in the oven to produce cake.

NAME OF THE INGREDIENTS

1. Flour
2. Shortening
3. Baking Powder

Bakery Unit (Pastries, Bread, Buns, Cake, Toffee etc.)

4. Egg
5. Milk or Milk powder
6. Salt
7. Food Colour
8. Sugar
9. Food Flavour

MANUFACTURING PROCESS

First Shortening (if necessary melt) take in cake mixer then added whole egg to the mixer, mix thoroughly since it forms a homogeneous mixture with full of air bubble, added to it milk or milk powder to form a homogeneous mixture. After complete homogeneous mixing add sugar to it form a homogeneous mixture. Now added to it food colour, flavour and then added to baking powder. As soon as baking powder is added then add flavour to the mixer to complete form a flour batter. Now put the batter to the mould and then pass it through baking oven at temperature of 170°C-225°C at about 25 minutes-40 minutes.

Now, cool it, pack for market.

DIFFERENT FORMULATIONS OF CAKES

ORDINARY YELLOW CAKE

INGREDIENTS	% USED
Sugar	25.5
Fat	13.4
Egg	14.8
Milk	14.8
Flour	29.8
Baking Powder	0.7
Salt	0.6
Flavour	0.4

HIGH RATIO YELLOW LOAVES

INGREDIENTS	% USED
Sugar	29.6
Fat	11.4
Egg	11.4
Milk	22.5
Flour	22.5
Baking Powder	1.3
Salt	0.8
Flavour	0.5

PREPARATION OF TOFFEE

Formula of Toffee

Sugar	-	35 - 40%	40
Glucose Solids	-	30 - 35%	35
Milk Solids	-	5 - 10%	5
Vegetable fats	-	15 - 20%	147
Butter fats	-	5 - 10%	5
Salts	-	0.2 - 0.3%	.3

Manufacturing Process

All the above ingredients in water and boiled to move a homogeneous paste mixture. Now paste mixture is poured on a mold shape tray.

Toffee as originally made was poured on a marble slab to cool and when set it was broken up into conveniently sized pieces and weighed into paper bags. Owing to its hygroscopic nature and tendency to flow and distort, distribution was necessarily confined to a limited area around the point of manufacture. The next development was tray toffee. The rectangular trays about 14 in by 8 in. and 3/4 in. deep. A piece of waxed paper was placed on delivered to the shops. Here it was broken up by the retailer and weighed out into bags at the point of sale. This method of handling extended the distribution area.

PROJECT FOR 'A' TYPE BAKERY UNIT

This unit is meant for Institutions/Co-operative Societies. The Unit is expected to produce different types of Bakery products, the details of which are given below :

Details of the Scheme

(1)	Name of products	:	Different types of Bakery Products.
(2)	Type of unit	:	For Institutions / Co-operative Societies
(3)	Estimated Annual Capacity	:	Various products of Bakery items : sales valued at Rs.7.00 (Lakhs)
(4)	Estimated work period	:	300 days in a year
(5)	Estimated area of place	:	500 sq. ft. for workshed
(6)	No. of persons required (employment)	:	8 persons
(7)	Turnover cycles	:	20 cycles in year or 15 days per cycle
(8)	Cost of the Shed	:	Workshed 200 sq.ft. @ Rs.200 per sq.ft. Rs.40,000.

Bakery Unit (Pastries, Bread, Buns, Cake, Toffee etc.)

Details of Equipment / Machinery

(a)	Oven/Bhatti 8' 10'	Rs.	12,500
(b)	Tools and Equipments		
	(i) Maxing machine with 1/2 H.P. Motor	Rs.	12,500
	(ii) Slicing machine with 1/2 H.P. Motor	Rs.	12,500
	(iii) Bread moulds, mixing vessees, Roller biscuits, container and other small tools, weighing balance etc.	Rs.	15,000
	(iv) Furniture and fixtures-racks, table fan, etc.,	Rs.	10,000
	(v) 2 cycle vans	Rs.	8,000
		Rs.	70, 500
	Total Capital Expenditure	Rs.	1,10,500

Final product

Various products of Bakery items valued at Rs. 6,95,000

or say Rs.7,00 (Lakhs)

Working Capital Requirement

(i)	**Fixed Working Capital**		
	(a) Salary for Manage	Rs.	30,000
	(b) Administrative expenditure	Rs.	2,400
	(c) Advertisements	Rs.	2,400
	(d) Insurance	Rs.	1,400
		Rs.	36,200

(Fixed cost for one operating cycle Rs. 1,800 (20 cycles) in a year).

(ii)	**Variable Working Capital**		
	(a) Raw material	Rs.	4,12,500
	(b) Wages for 8 workers	Rs.	96,000
	(c) Transport	Rs.	3,000
	(d) Electricity	Rs.	3,750
		Rs.	5,15,250

(Variable cost for one cycle (20 cycles in a year) Rs. 25,763 or say Rs.25,800)

(iii) Depreciation

(i) Workshed Rs.40,000	Rs.	4,000
(ii) Equipments and Bhatti Rs. 70,500 (10% on both item)	Rs.	7,050
	Rs.	11,050

(iv) Funds Required

(a) Capital Expenditure	Rs.	1,10,500
(b) Working Capital for one cycle	Rs.	27,600
	Rs.	1,38,100
(c) Bank Loan (85%)	Rs.	1,17,400

(v) Cost Analysis (80% Capacity Utilisation)

(1) Fixed costs (Sal + Stay + Ad + Ins.)	Rs.	36,200
(2) Variable costs 80% of capacity utilisation (Wages + Raw Material + Trans + Elect.)	Rs.	4,12,200
(3) Cost of production (1+2)	Rs.	4,48,400
(4) Estimated Sales realisaion (80% of Rs.7,00,000)	Rs.	5,60,000
(5) Gross surplus	Rs.	1,11,600

(VI) Interest and Depreciation

(1) Interest on Term Loan	Rs.	17,700
(2) Interest on Working Capital on W.C. of Rs.28,000	Rs.	5,000
(3) Depreciation	Rs.	11,000
	Rs.	33,700

(VII)	Net Surplus	Rs.	77,900
(VIII)	Disposable Surplus : N.S. + Depreciation	Rs.	88,900

The project can pay back the loan in 4 years even at capacity utilisation of 80%.

Bakery Unit (Pastries, Bread, Buns, Cake, Toffee etc.)

PLANT ECONOMICS OF BAKERY UNIT, BUNS, CARE, TOFFEE ETC.

Rated Plant Capacity = 1243.70 KGS/Day

LAND & BUILDING (Land Required 500 sq.mt.)= RENTED

PLANT & MACHINERY

1. Auto Sifter
2. Dough Kneader
3. Dough Grinder
4. State Convert
5. Dough Rounder
6. Dough Moulder
7. Diesel Rotary Rock oven
8. Cooling rack
9. Trolley
10. Automatic Slice
11. Cream Milk
12. Dies and Mold
13. Electrically Heating Kettle
14. Cooling Chamber
15. Packing, and sealing Machine
16. Miscellaneous Machine

FIXED CAPITAL

1. Plant & Machinery	Rs.	9,43,500.00
2. Other Fixed Assets	Rs.	3,20,000.00
TOTAL	Rs.	12,63,500.00

RAW MATERIALS

1. Flour
2. Shortening
3. Salt
4. Sugar
5. Egg
6. Milk Solid
7. Yeast
8. Butter
9. Glucose

TOTAL WORKING CAPITAL/MONTH

1. Raw Material	Rs.	4,28,933.00
2. Salary & Wages	Rs.	54,240.00
3. Utilities & Overheads	Rs.	46,000.00
TOTAL	Rs.	5,29,173.00

TOTAL CAPITAL INVESTMENT

Total Fixed Capital	Rs.	12,63,500.00
Total Working Capital for 1 Month	Rs.	5,29,173.00
TOTAL	Rs.	17,92,673.00

1. Pastry Products: 120000 Kgs.
2. Paste 30000 Kgs.
3. Bread/Bun 99540 kgs.
4. Toffee 123570 kgs.

TOTAL	Rs.	1,07,50,200.00

PROFIT SALES RATIO = Profit / Sales x 100 = 36.60 %

RATE OF RETURN = Operating profit / T.C.I x 100 = 219.46 %

BREAK EVEN POINT (B.E.P) = 19.40 %

Chapter - 11

Ball Pen

Ball pens are manufactured generally from plastic in different varieties to meet with demand of different classes of people. Majority of people in India like medium class ball pen. Plastics are accepted by engineers as important new materials supplementing metals, wood ceramics, glass and rubber as well as competing with them for some industrial applications some of the plastics are more transparent then glass and weight less than half its weight. For easy of fabrication and adoptability to mass production methods the range of plastics offer the greatest scope to manufacturers.

These are derived from petroleum oil, salt, as air and water during the last 5 to 10 year considerable progress has been made in plastic moulding.

There are now more firms engaged in the moulding branch of this industry.

Polystyrene is strically a vinyl resins being also named polyvinyl benzene polystrene resins are produced 60% as homopolymers. 30% as copolymers with cryslonitril but adiene, polysters, divinyl. Benzene or acrylate esters and 10% as terpolymer white acrylositrile and butadiene.

PROCESS OF MANUFACTURE

Ball pens are manufactured from polystyrene plastics and are manufactured by injection moulding technique. The most widely used method is the injection moulding process. The thermoplastic materials used for this process are chiefly polystyrene, polythene and cellulose acetate.

Principle of Injection Moulding :

The principle involved in injection moulding lies in softening of the moulding materials is a heated cylinder and then pushing the matter mass by means, of a piston through a conical shaped nozzle into a mould that is kept closed during the moulding operation for shaping. The pressure by the piston is maintained until solidification takes place in the mould. The piston is then withdrawn, the mould is opens and the finished moulding is ejected, it is essentially a process of loading heating injection and cooling.

The amount of materials to be fed into cylinder is controlled by a measuring device which is usually operated by the length of the stroke of the piston in the previous cycle. This ensure that the same quantity of materials is contained in the heated cylinder at the commencement of each stroke.

The hopper usually contains moulding powder for approximately one hour operation. When the piston has been operation, when the piston has been withdrawn from its previous cycle the materials has dropped into the piston cylinder. On its forward stroke. The piston exerts maximum pressure on the materials in the heating cylinder which causes the plasticized materials to fill the moulds.

Injection moulding machines are self contained so far as the heating and pressure pump unit are concerned and control system. Which makes possible automatic, semi automatic or manual operation, the heating is accomplished directly by electrical heaters. The most widely used method of improving heat transfer from the cylinder to the plastic materials, is to provide a torpedo shaped buffle with the cylinder. The function of torpedo is to spread the plastic materials out into a thin annular layer between the other surface of cylinder. The resulting then section will be heated more rapidly. To produce ball pens on small scale, hand operated injection moulding machines are generally used. As they cost less and are easy to install and operate.

These machines consume very less electricity and in most cases domestic current can be used. These hand operated injection moulding machines are made in various capacities.

Ball pen case be made in three parts or two parts as desired and accordingly the die can be changed. Here is described the ball pen with two pieces.

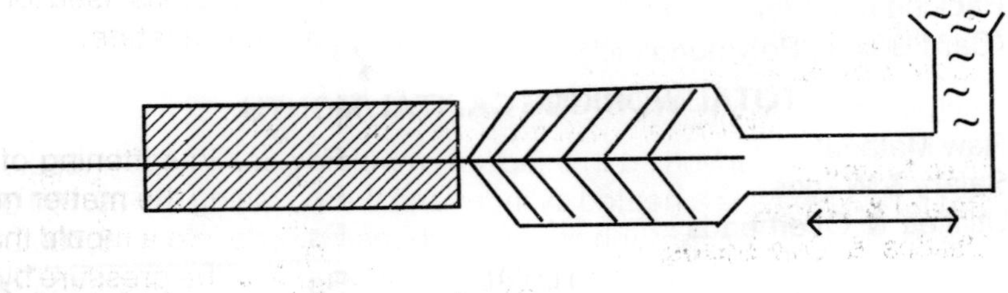

Die or mould can be made of the required shape. Polystyrene plastic is fed to the machine and this is heated up. Now for the threading in the core that can be done in both. By the moulding itself of afterwards by machine. By moulding threading can be obtained with great case. And is less time consuming. Threading is in opposite direction for the mate male and female part of the pen. Accordingly, die is made. Now heated plastic is fed through nozzle with pressure to the mould. For different colours of pens, colours dyes can be added.

Now, mould is cooler so that ball pen in the mould is cooled down quickly and is ejected out while injection instructions should be followed given.

In the similar way other parts can be formed by changing the die, as in:-

PLANT ECONOMICS OF BALL PEN MANUFACTURING

Rated Plant Capacity = 500.00 Pen/Day

LAND & BUILDING (Land Area 150 sq.mt.) = Rented

PLANT & MACHINERY

1. Injection moulding machinery
2. Moulds and Dies
3. Other Misc.

FIXED CAPITAL

1. Plant & Machinery	Rs.	1,05,000.00
2. Other Fixed Assets	Rs.	27,500.00
TOTAL	Rs.	1,32,500.00

RAW MATERIALS

1. Polystyrene plastic required
2. Other Raw Materials
3. Colours
4. Packing material
   (Card Boxes, Polythene etc.)

TOTAL WORKING CAPITAL/MONTH

1. Raw Material	Rs.	11,600.00
2. Salary & Wages	Rs.	20,160.00
3. Utilities & Overheads	Rs.	8,700.00
TOTAL	Rs.	40,460.00

TOTAL CAPITAL INVESTMENT

Total Fixed Capital	Rs.	1,32,500.00
Total Working Capital for 1 Month	Rs.	40,460.00
TOTAL	Rs.	1,72,960.00

TURN OVER/ANNUM

By sales of 150000 ball pens	Rs.	7,50,000.00

PROFIT SALES RATIO = Profit / Sales x 100 = 28.46 %
RATE OF RETURN = Operating profit / T.C.I x 100 = 123.42 %
BREAK EVEN PCINT (B.E.P) = 47.03 %

Note : Ball Pen industry may be setup in cottage scale and all the machinery and raw materials are easily available throughout the country with the plastic processing machinery suppliers.

Chapter - 12

Bread Manufacturing

At this present time, the bakery product industry represents a major of the food industry because of its high volume of production and large number of employees.

In the past because of the short shelf life of bread each community had its bakery which produced bread on daily basis and sold it directly to the consumers. With the introduction of preservation and improved mechanical method of making bread, these appeared increasing number of whole sale baking companies which produce bread in massive quantities and sold it to retailers over a wide distribution area. The whole sale type bakery now dominates the multi-millions rupees baking industry today.

Now-a-days, continuous bread making process is of particular interest to the large wholesale bakeries have been an important development in baking industry besides producing bread at greatly increased rate the continuous process provides much chosen control of the characteristics of the finished bread product.

PROCESS OF MANUFACTURE

The process of manufacture of bread starts with mixing and formation. Mixing and fermentation of dought is carried out by two methods (i) straight dought method and (ii) sponge dough methods.

SPONGE DOUGH METHOD

Flour is conveyed automatically to the scale hopper above the mixer about 60% of the flour required for a batch is scaled into the mixing bowl. Yeast suspened in water and the yeast food are added on top of the flour. The required amount of water is added into the bowl and these ingredients are then mixed into a sponge. Here mixing process a homogenous mass of the wheat gluten. If the flour requires supplimentation with enzymes, they are added to the sponge. The sponge then dumped from the mixer into greased through a conveyer to the fermentation room where temperature is maintained at about 80°F and the relative humidity at 75-80°, sponge fermentation time is variable but ranges from 3.5 to 4 hours. As the fermentation proceeds, there is a sudden increase in the volume of the sponge. After full fermentation of sponge, it is again sent to the mixer. Here non fat dry milk, sugar, salt shortening and other ingredients are added. The remaining flour and water are scaled and metered into the mixer and the dough is mixed.

PROOFING AND BAKING :

The pannel dough must be permitted to rise (proof) in the pan to secure the volume required of finished bread during this periods, the dough expands to about size times to its original volumes. Proofing can be done in continuous proofers where the pans are conveyed through a temperature and humidity controlled cabinet (about 100°F and 80-90% a relative humidity) and then to the areas. It can also be done by loading the pans on the sacks which are shield or conveyed by monorail into a proof box. Proofing requires about, one hour. From the proof box the dough does to the oven. If a continuous proofer is used, the transfer to the oven is entirely mechanical. If proofing is done on rack, the straps of the pans must be transferred to the oven by hand. Most ovens are traveling ovens therein the pans of proof dough are loaded at one end and the baked leaves come out to the other. The oven may consist several chambers with variation in temperature from one chamber to another currently pound leaves of bread are baked for about 20 minutes at an average temperature of 450°.

COOLING SLICING & WRAPPING :

The bread is depend automatically and conveyed by belts through the bread cooler. From the bread cooler, the bread goes to the slicer and wrapper. The bread is sliced by rapidly moving razor, sharp bands and may be wrapped in waxed paper or transparent films such as cellophane or polyethylene.

FORMULAE :

(I) BREAD WITH OR WITHOUT ASCORBIC ACID :

INGREDIENTS	% OF FLOUR (WT.BASIS).
Flour	100
Water	66
Sugar	8.00
Yeast	3.00
Shortening	3.25
Salt	2.01
Milk (Dry)	1.00 +
Yeast food	0.525
Monocalcium Phosphate	0.145
Sodium Propionate	0.10
Oxidizing agents	-
(Potassium bromate & Potassium iodate)	0.009
Variable.	

(II) STANDARD BREAD

Flour	5000
Water	150
Milk solid	100
Acidulant	6
Yeast	100
Salt	75
Sugar	400
Monoglycerides	1.25
Water	3.450
Potassium bromate (based upon Flour wt)	60
Potassium iodate (based upon flour wt.)	15
PPM (Part per million)	25

(iii) CONTINUOUS DOUGH FORMULA

Ingredients	% Flour (Wt. Basis)
Flour	100
Water	66-70
Yeast	3
Sugar	7
Salt	2
Milk	1
Liquid shortening	3.3
Ammonium sulfate (Yeast food)	0.08
Calcium Phosphate	0.4
Atmul (softher)	0.1
Functional Additings	Variable.

(IV) A BREAD DOUGH IS MADE FROM THE FOLLOWING FORMULATION.

Ingredients	Amount % wt. Based on Wt.Flour
Flour	100
Water	67.0
Sugar	8.0
Salt	2.25
Calcium Propionate	0.1
Calcium acid phosphate	0.1
Yeast food	0.5
Yeast	2.5
Shortenging Blend	3.0

PLANT ECONOMICS

Rated Plant Capacity = 1243.70 Kgs/Day

LAND & BUILDING (Land Area 500 sq.mt) = Rented

PLANT & MACHINERY

1. Auto Siffter
2. Dough Kneader
3. Dough Grinder
4. State Convet
5. Dough Rounder
6. Dough Moulder

7. Diesel Rotary Rock oven
8. Cooling rack
9. T Rolly
10. Automatic Slice
11. Cream Milk
12. Dies and Mold
13. Electrically Heating Kettle
14. Cooling Chamber
15. Packing, and sealing Machine
16. Miscellaneous Machine

FIXED CAPITAL

1. Plant & Machinery		Rs.	9,43,500.00
2. Other Fixed Assets		Rs.	3,20,000.00
	TOTAL	Rs.	12,63,500.00

RAW MATERIALS

1. Flour
2. Shortening
3. Salt
4. Sugar
5. Egg
6. Milk Solid
7. Yeast
8. Butter
9. Glucose solid
10. Packaging Materials

TOTAL WORKING CAPITAL/MONTH

1. Raw Material		Rs.	4,28,933.00
2. Salary & Wages		Rs.	54,240.00
3. Utilities & Overheads		Rs.	46,000.00
	TOTAL	Rs.	5,29,173.00

TOTAL CAPITAL INVESTMENT

Total Fixed Capital		Rs.	12,63,500.00
Total Working Capital for 1 Month		Rs.	5,29,173.00
	TOTAL	Rs.	17,92,673.00

TURN OVER/ANNUM

1. Pastry Products: 120000 Kgs.
2. Paste 30000 Kgs.
3. Bread/Bun 99540 kgs
4. Toffee 123570 Kgs

TOTAL Rs. 1,07,50,200.00

PROFIT SALES RATIO = Profit / Sales x 100 = 36.60 %

RATE OF RETURN = Operating profit / T.C.I x 100 = 219.46 %

BREAK EVEN POINT (B.E.P) = 19.40 %

Chapter - 13

Cane and Bamboo Industry

BACKGROUND OF THE INDUSTRY

Bamboo and Cane are remarkable natural materials. They are renewable resources which India has in abundance. Special features such as pliability and liner strength have been used to advantage by craftsmen and local apprentices in many creative ways. The skills developed over the centuries have been passed on, like other crafts, without the assistance of formal instruction. It may seem that all the possibilities of using these materials must have been exhausted because of the long and close interaction of people with the environment where bamboo and cane are found in magnificent abundance. However, it is almost certain that this is not so. The needs of products and things change with time, equally the techniques of handling the material. Sometimes the original craftsmen, provide new vistas for design and marketability of the products as well.

BAMBOO

Bamboo is a cultural feature of south east Asia. No country in the region is without an indigenous bamboo flora. Bamboo substitutes timber in many respects. It is the most versatile forest produce. At least one third of the human race uses bamboos for several purposes.

The bamboo though apparently soft, is very resilient, upright and unwavering and is a paragon of virtues. Bamboo is a fast growing species attaining havestable maturity in a brief spell of five years.

CHARACTERISTIC USES

Due to its fast growth, easy propagation, soil binding property and short period in which they attain maturity, bamboo is an ideal species for use in afforestation, soil conservation and social forestry programmes. Bamboos find a large number of fascinating uses in the rural sector. They are used for walling, huts, thatching and roofing.Besides land scaping, they can also be used for medicinal purposes and for food material (Thailand earns approximately U.S. $ 30,000,000 through export of about

18 percent of Japan's canned bamboo shoot requirement). Some of the traditional uses are in agricultural implements, anchors, arrows, protection shields, baskets, beds, boots, bows, bridges, brooms, brushes, cart-yokes, chairs, combs, utensils, dustpans, spears, fences, fishtraps, fishing rods, flutes, fuel (high thermal efficiency - its dust from paper mills can be converted into fuel briquettes), furniture, hats, handicrafts, kites, ladder, lamp stands, trays, sportsgoods, toys, chicks for door and windows, tool handles, umbrella handles, walking sticks,decoratives, ceiling, room divider, sales emporium furnishing, hotel decoration items, and other numerous types of handy fancy decorative articles.

CONSUMPTION PATTERN OF BAMBOOS IN INDIA

Sr. No.	Uses	Percentage of Consumption
(i)	Pulp	35.00
(ii)	Housing	20.00
(iii)	Non-residential	5.00
(iv)	Rural uses	20.00
(v)	Fuel	8.50
(vi)	Packing including basket	5.00
(vii)	Transport	1.50
(viii)	Furniture	1.00
(ix)	Other wood working industries	1.00
(x)	Others including ladders, mats etc.	3.00

CANES

Canes are long, slender stems of certain travelling or climbing palms. They are rated as minor forest products, inspite of the fact that they are probably the most important forest products, after timber. They are found in evergreen forests of the tropical and sub-tropical regions, of which 30 species occur in India, distributed chiefly in the Himalayas, Assam, Arunachal Pradesh, Nagaland, Manipur, Mizoram, Meghalaya, Kerala, Karnataka, Tamil Nadu and the Andamans. Canes are usually cylindrical and of uniform thickness strawyellow to brown in colour and are more or less covered by spiny leaves. The diameter varies from 3 mm. to about 60 mm. The surface is hard, smooth and shiny due to deposit of silica.

Canes have been exploited by man for centuries. Their properties of toughness, strength, flexibility and elasticity have made them useful for mass purposes. Whole canes are used for furniture, hats, baskets, walking sticks, fishing rods etc. Cane splits are used for basketry, rattaining furniture and extensively for tying and binding.

Cane and Bamboo Industry

Cane and Bamboo Industry is a traditional village industry eminently capable of providing large scale employment mainly to weaker sections of the society and its need comparatively low investment. As the products are value added, the turnover per unit of investment is very large in this industry. This industry also has very high export potential on account of many varieties of superfine articles being produced by thousands of highly skilled artisans engaged in this industry.

Level of Technology and Requirement of Technology

At present technology level for the items manufactured under the Forest Based industries is either traditional or low level which results in considerable waste. This has resulted in loss of time, disproportionate output of final products of quality that are sometimes unaccepable in the market.

There is a distinctive gap between growers/traders of raw materials and product manufacturers. Semi processing units may render essential quality inputs even from inferior raw materials to the production units for achieving finai products of correct dimensions, quality and visual acceptance and thereby better survival in Inland and International market. Interior raw materials, dimensionally defective, back dated process technique, poor finish etc. redered unacceptability of the products and hence some of the possible new areas may be opted. Of course, there are opportunities for adoption of simple, better, easy to operate machines and improved technologies which may return more production with less time and human physical hardship and quality acceptable to consumers, creating avenues for more employment and better market return.

I. PROJECT PROFILE FOR MANUFACTURE OF CANE AND BAMBOO ARTICLES

This unit is meant for Institutions/Co-operative societies. The details of the scheme are given below :

1.	Type of unit	:	Manufactaure of Cane and Bamboo Articles.
2.	Name of the product	:	Utility and fancy bamboo and cane made articles, articles made out of pliable reed like vegetative materials having properties similar to cane and bamboo species.
3.	Number of persons required for working	:	21 persons including one supervisor.
4.	Annual capacity	:	Estimated annual sales is assumed at Rs. 8.00 lakhs.
5.	Estimated work period	:	Minimum 300 days in a year with 8 hours of work per day.

6. Cost of the Project

I. CAPITAL EXPENDITURE

(a)	Workshed 800 sq. ft. pucca construction	Rs. 1,60,000
(b)	Tools and Equipments	
	(i) Hacksaw frame with blade	
	(ii) Knives	
	(iii) Axe or bamboo splitter	
	(iv) Hammer	Rs. 45,000
	(v) Five splitter	
	(vi) Hand drill with bits	
	(vii) Scale (metal)	
	(viii) Blow lamp eye	
	Total	Rs. 2,05,000
Capital Expenditure -Term Loan		Rs. 2,05,000

7. Raw Material

(i)	Bamboo 15 nos per day per whole bamboo for 300 days	Rs. 1,89,000
(ii)	Colours, nails, thread etc.	Rs. 30,000
		Rs. 2,19,000

8. Salary and Wages / Year

(i)	Wages for 20 artisans for 300 days	Rs. 3,60,000
(ii)	Salary for 1 supervisor	Rs. 30,000

9. Overhead Charges

(i)	Interest on Capital Expenditure	Rs. 32,800
(ii)	**Insurance**	
	(a) Stock in hand-raw material	Rs, 2,190
	(b) Capital expenditure	Rs. 2,050
		Rs. 4,240
(iii)	**Depreciation**	
	(a) Building	Rs. 8,000
	(b) Tools and equipment	Rs. 4,500
		Rs. 12,500

(iv) **Indirect Expenses**

(i)	Octroi and freight charges	Rs.	15,000
(ii)	Packing and forwarding charges	Rs.	10,000
(iii)	Office expenses such as postage, printing and stationeries	Rs.	6,000
(iv)	Publicity and promotional expenditure for propaganda	Rs.	12,000
		Rs.	43,000

II. Working Capital Requirement

I. Fixed Working Capital Needs

(1)	Salary	Rs.	30,000
(2)	Office expenses	Rs.	6,000
(3)	Interest of C.E.	Rs.	32,800
(4)	Insurance	Rs.	4,240
(5)	Publicity and propaganda	Rs.	12,000
		Rs.	85,040

Fixed cost for one operating cycle (25% of total) Rs. 21,260 or say Rs. 21,000 — Rs. 21,000

II. Variable Working Capital Needs

(1)	Raw material	Rs.	2,19,000
(2)	Wages	Rs.	3,60,000
(3)	Interest on working capital	Rs.	31,000
(4)	Packing and forwarding charges	Rs.	10,000
(5)	Freight and octroi	Rs.	15,000
		Rs.	6,35,000

Variable working capital for one operating cycle is Rs. 1,58,750 or say Rs. 1,58,800

10. Requirement of Fund

(1)	For Capital Expenditure	Rs.	2,05,000
(2)	For Working Capital (for one cycle)	Rs,	1,79,800
		Rs.	3,84,800
	Bank loan @ 85%	Rs.	3,27,000

11. Sales Value

(Les Sales Commission etc.) — Rs. 9,00,000

12. Cost Analysis @80% Capacity Utilisation

(i) Fixed Cost — Rs. 52,240

(ii)	Variable cost	Rs. 4,84,000
(iii)	Total cost of production	Rs. 5,36,240
(iv)	Sales realisation (excluding commission)	Rs. 7,20,000
(v)	Gross surplus	Rs. 1,83,760
(vi)	Net surplus = (Gross surplus-Depreciation - Interest on C.E. - Inerest on W.C.)	Rs. 1,07,460
(vii)	Disposable surplus = (Net surplus+ Depreciation)	Rs. 1,19,960

The unit has capacity to pay back the loan in 5 years even at 80% capacity utilisation.

II. Project Profile for Broom Making Unit

This unit is meant for Institutions/Co-operative societies. The details of the scheme are given below :

1.	Type of activity	:	Broom making unit.
2.	Annual capacity	:	Annual capacity is assumed at sales value of Rs. 8.00 lakhs worth of products.
3.	Number of persons required for working	:	8 full time and 4 part time workers as and when required.
4.	Name of the product	:	(i) Brooms of different shapes, sizes and materials (long and short handle)
	By product	:	(ii) Baskets from midribs, cheaper quality.
5.	Estimated work period	:	300 days in a year with 8 hours of work per day.

6. Cost of the Project

I. Capital Expenditure (Term Loan)

(a)	Area of workshed 800 sq. ft. pucca building for workshed	Rs. 1,60,000
(b)	Godown for storing raw material 800 sq. ft. pucca building	Rs. 1,60,000
(c)	Tools and Equipmens	
	(i) Knives, metal combs, branch cutter etc.	Rs. 35,000
	(ii) Carding machine	

	Rs. 3,55,000
Total Capital Expenditure -Term loan	Rs. 3,55,000

7. Raw Material (per annum)

(i) Full length leaves 1,000 bdls	Rs. 1,20,000
(ii) Nylon ropes/thread 250 kg	Rs. 28,750
	Rs. 1,48,750

8. Salary and Wages

(i) Wages for 8 full time workers	Rs. 1,44,000
(ii) Wages for 4 part time workers	Rs. 54,000
	Rs. 1,98,000

Salary for Managerial Staff

(i) Supervisor	Rs. 36,000
(ii) Store-keeper	Rs. 36,000
	Rs. 72,000

9. Overhead Charges

(i) Interest on Capital Expenditure	Rs. 56,800
(ii) **Insurance**	
(a) Stock in hand of raw material	Rs. 1,487.50
(b) Capital expenditure	Rs. 3,550.50
	Rs. 5,038.00
(iii) **Depreciation**	
(a) Building	Rs. 16,000
(b) Tools and equipment	Rs. 3,500
	Rs. 19,500
(iv) **Indirect Expenses**	
(a) Freight and octroi	Rs. 15,000
(b) Packing and forwarding charges	Rs. 10,000
(c) Office expenses such as postage, printing and stationeries	Rs. 6,000
(d) Publicity and other promotional expenditure	Rs. 12,000
	Rs. 43,000

II. Working Capital Requirement

I. Fixed Working Capital Needs

(1) Salary	Rs. 72,000
(2) Office expenses	Rs. 6,000

(3) Interest of C.E.	Rs.	56,800
(4) Insurance	Rs.	5,038
(5) Publicity and other promotional expenditure	Rs.	12,000
	Rs.	1,51,838

Fixed cost for one operating cycle (25% of total) is Rs. 37,959.50 or say Rs. 38,000	Rs.	38,000

II. Variable Working Capital needs

(1) Raw material	Rs.	1,48,750
(2) Wages	Rs.	1,98,000
(3) Interest on working capital	Rs.	23,600
(4) Packing material and forwarding charges	Rs.	10,000
(5) Freight and octroi	Rs.	15,000
	Rs.	3,95,350

Variable working capital for one operating cycle is	Rs.	98,800

10. Requirement of Funds

(1) For Capital Expenditure	Rs.	3,55,000
(2) For Working Capital (one cycle)	Rs.	1,36,800
	Rs.	4,91,800
Bank loan @85% upto	Rs.	4,18,000

11. Sales Value

(Less sales commission etc.)	Rs.	7,50,000

12. Cost Analysis (80% Capacity Utilisation)

(1) Fixed cost	Rs.	95,038
(2) Variable cost	Rs.	2,97,400
(3) Total cost of production	Rs.	3,92,438

(4)	Sales realisation (excluding commission)	Rs.	6,00,000
(5)	Gross surplus	Rs.	2,07,562
(6)	Net surplus = (Gross surplus-Depreciation -Interest on C.E. - Interest on W.C.)	Rs.	1,07,662
(7)	Disposable surplus = (Net surplus+ Depreciation)	Rs.	1,27,162

Chapter - 14

Processing of Cereals and Pulses Industry

Introduction

The traditional cottage indusry of processing of cereals and pulses occupied a prominent place amongst the Industries for processing of agricultural produces. Compared to processing on huller, the hand pounding of paddy gives higher per centage of recovery of rice, higher nutritional value and provides wholesome food. The conversion of paddy into rice, khil etc., wheat to flour, bakery products processing of pulses and their various products like papad, wadi and different types of spices etc., have capacity of generating large scale employment opportunities in the rural areas especially for the women folk. All out efforts were made by KVIC to evolve and introduce improved implements, both hand-operated and power-operated with a view to meeting partially the threat posed by the unauthorised proliferation of hullers and improving the economic viability of the programme keeping in view its capacity to generate employment opportunities.

The agro-based industries which are perhaps the oldest known occupations since the commencement of civilised life on Earth have great significance for rural areas since they can form an effective instrument in forging a firm linkage between agriculture and industry. They hold out the promise for transforming our countryside by bringing about substantial improvement in the quality of living of our rural masses. The P.C.P. Indusry therefore occupies a pivotal position in the country's economy.

The Industry serves as an important vehicle for delivery of higher standards of nutrition to the people and therefore deserves a special consideration for effective growth and propagation of the programme in the rural areas. P.C.P. Industry is a traditional industry. It required limited capital, whereas return to the capital is quite high.

I. Project for Paddy Processing Unit

It is well known that the hullers which have proliferated in the countryside for processing of paddy are wasteful as on an average, 4 to 6 percent less rice is obtained compared to that obtained in handpounding. In hullers the husk and bran get mixed up and renders bran unfit for cattle consumption or further processing. The per centage of broken rice is also high in hullers which give more polish and adversly affect the nutritional ingredients of rice. To tackle this problem, KVIC developed decentralised paddy dehusker and polisher which can ensure higher yield of rice recovery, less brokens and availability of bran and husk separately.

Details of the scheme

(1)	Name of product	:	Processing of paddy for obtaining rice
(2)	Type of unit	:	Institutions/Co-operatives
(3)	Estimated annual capacity of unit	:	Of 5,000 Qtls.
(4)	Estimated area of work place	:	100 sq. ft. of land.
(5)	Estimated work period	:	300 days in a year
(6)	Number of persons employment	:	12 persons
(7)	Turnover cycle	:	10 cycle in year
(8)	Capital Expenditure		
(i)	Workshed		Rs. 45,000
(ii)	Drying yard		Rs. 6,250
(iii)	Machinery and Equipments		Rs. 72,000
			Rs. 1,23,250

Working Capital Requirement/Year

Fixed Working Capital

(1)	Salary for Manager	Rs. 30,000
(2)	Rent	Rs. 6,000
(3)	Advertisement	Rs. 4,800
(4)	Insurance	Rs. 2,930
(5)	Stationery and Printing	Rs. 3,125
		Rs. 46,855

(Fixed W. C. for one operating cycle Rs. 4,686 or say Rs. 4,700)

Variable Working Capital

(1)	Raw material	Rs. 15,62,500
(2)	Electricity	Rs. 31,250
(3)	Wages for 12 workers	Rs. 1,08,000
(4)	Transport	Rs. 65,000
(5)	Misc. Expenses	Rs. 60,000
		Rs. 18,26,750

(Variable W. C. for one operating cycle Rs. 1,82,500 or say Rs. 1.83 lakhs)

Depreciation

(1)	Workshed	Rs. 4,500
(2)	Drying yard	Rs. 625
(3)	Machinery	Rs. 7,200
		Rs. 12,325

Funds Required

(a)	For Capital Expenditure	Rs. 1,23,250
(b)	Working Capital for one cycle	Rs. 1,87,700
		Rs. 3,10,950
(c)	Bank Loan (85 %)	Rs. 2,64,300

Production Costs (80 % Capacity Utilisation)

(a)	Fixed costs (Sal. + Insurance + Stationery + Ad)	Rs. 46,855
(b)	Variable costs (Wages + Raw Material + Electricity + transportation + others) 80 % of the total	Rs. 14,61,400
(c)	Total production cost (a + b)	Rs. 15,08,255
(d)	Sales (80 % of the total)	Rs. 17,30,000
(e)	Gross surplus (d - c)	Rs. 2,21,745

Interest and Depreciation

(a)	Interest on Term Loan	Rs. 19,720
(b)	Interest on Working capital	Rs. 33,786
(c)	Depreciation (10 % on C. E.)	Rs. 12,325
		Rs. 65,831
	Net Surplus	Rs. 1,55,914
	Disposable surplus, i.e. net surplus + depreciation	Rs. 1,68,239

The project can therefore pay back the loan in less than 4 years even at a capacity utilisation of 80%.

II. Project for Dal / Pulses Unit

This unit is meant for Registered Institutions / Co-operative Societies. The unit is expected to produce Dal/Pulses, the details of which are given below :

Details of the scheme

(1)	Name of production unit	:	Pulses Unit
(2)	Type of unit	:	For Institutions / Co-operative Societies
(3)	Estimated Annual Capacity	:	3,000 quintals
(4)	Estimated work period	:	250 days in a year
(5)	Estimated area of work place	:	300 sq. ft. of workshed
(6)	No. of persons required	:	11 persons
(7)	Turnover cycles	:	10 cycles in year

Capital Expenditure

(i) Workshed 300 sq. ft. @ Rs. 2,000 per sq. ft.	Rs.	60,000
(ii) Drying yard of 30 sq. ft.	Rs.	10,000
(iii) Machinery and Equipments		
(a) Roller	Rs.	4,000
(b) Varam Machine	Rs.	2,500
(c) Chalni 3 sets	Rs.	5,000
(d) Patka Machine	Rs.	5,000
(e) Winnowing' Fan	Rs.	6,000
(f) Electric Motor for all Machines 10 H.P.	Rs.	12,250
(g) Installation of Machine	Rs.	5,000
(h) Weighing Balance	Rs.	3,500
(i) Transportation	Rs.	5,000
	Rs.	48,250
Total Capital Expenditure	Rs.	1,18,250

Raw Material Requirement

(1) Different varieties of. pulses required 3,000 qtls. per annum	Rs. 36,00,000

Wages / Salaries

(i) Manager	Rs.	30,000
(ii) Skilled workers-4	Rs.	40,000
(iii) Semi-skilled workers-6	Rs.	45,000
	Rs.	1,15,000
Final products sale value	Rs.	41,40,000

Term Loan (C. E.)

(1)	Building	Rs. 60,000
(2)	Drying Yard	Rs. 10,000
(3)	Machinery	Rs. 48,250
		Rs. 1,18,250

Working Capital Requirement

(1) Fixed Working Capital

(i)	Salary for Manager	Rs. 30,000
(2)	Rent	Rs. 6,000
(3)	Marketing and Advertisement	Rs. 4,800
(4)	Stationery	Rs. 3,000
(5)	Insurance 1 % on (C. E. + stock) (Rs. 1,182 + Rs. 3715)	Rs. 4,897
		Rs. 48,697

(Fixed working capital for one operating cycle (10 cycles) Rs. 4,869 say Rs. 4,900)

(II) Variable Working Capital

(1)	Raw material	Rs. 36,00,000
(2)	Wages	Rs. 85,000
(3)	Electricity charges	Rs. 21,000
(4)	Transport charges	Rs. 45,000
(5)	Miscellaneous	Rs. 7,500
		Rs. 37,58,500

(Variable working capital (10 cycles) for one operating cycle Rs. 3,75,850 or say Rs. 3.76 lakhs)

Depreciation

(1)	Building and Drying Yard	Rs. 6,000
		Rs. 1,000
(2)	Machinery	Rs. 4,825
		Rs. 11,825

Funds Required

(a)	Term Loan for C. E.	Rs. 1,18,250
(b)	Working Capital for one cycle	Rs. 3,80,900
		Rs. 4, 99,150
(c)	Bank Loan (85 %)	Rs. 4,24,300

Cost Analysis (80 % Capacity Utilisation)

(a) Fixed costs (Sal + Rent + Market + Ad + Sta. + Ins.)	Rs. 48,697
(b) Variable costs (80% of Wages + Raw Material, Elect., Trans., Misc.)	Rs. 30,06,800
(c) Cost of production (a + b)	Rs. 30,55,497
(d) Sales realisation (80 %)	Rs. 33,12,000
(e) Gross Surplus (d - c)	Rs. 2,56,503

Interest and Depreciation

(a) Interest on Term Loan	Rs. 18,920
(b) Interest on Working capital	Rs. 68,560
(c) Depreciation	Rs. 11,825
	Rs. 99,305
Net Surplus (Gross surplus - Interest and Depreciation)	Rs. 1,57,198
'Disposable Surplus	Rs. 1,69,023

The project can pay back the loan in 6 years even at 80 % capacity utilisation.

III. Project for Murmura Unit

This unit is meant for co-operative societies/institutions. The unit is expected to produce Murmura, the details of which are given below :

Details of the scheme

(1) Name of product	:	Murmura
(2) Type of unit	:	Co-operative Societies /Institutions
(3) Estimated annual capacity of production	:	1,200 qtls. of Murmura and 700 qtls. of by - products.
(4) Estimated working period	:	250 days in a year
(5) Estimated area of working place	:	300 sq. ft. of covered area (semi-pucca and 45 sq. mt. of drying yard.)
(6) No. of persons required	:	14 persons
(7) Turnover cycles	:	10 cycles per annum

Capital Expenditure

(a) Workshed for 300 sq. ft.	Rs.	22,500
(b) Drying yard 45 sq. mts.	Rs.	10,000
(c) Machinery and Equipments		
(i) Bhatti 5 Nos.	Rs.	7,000
(ii) Multipurpose sheller with 5 H. P. Motor both for dehusking and polishing	Rs.	22,000
(iii) Tools, Equipments, Pans, etc.	Rs.	10;000
(iv) Electrification and Installation	Rs.	2,500
(v) Parboiling unit	Rs.	15,00
	Rs.	89,000

Raw Material Requirement

(i) Paddy 2000 qtls.	Rs.	8,00,000
(ii) Fuel charges	Rs.	64,000
(iii) Sand	Rs.	4,000
(iv) Salt	Rs.	3,000
	Rs.	8,71,000

Wages / Salaries

(i) Manager	Rs.	30,000,
(ii) Skilled workers	Rs.	50,000
(iii) Semi-skilled workers - 8	Rs.	60,000
	Rs.	1,40,000

Final Product

(i) Murmura 60%	1200 qtls.
(ii) By-products 35%	700 qtls.
(iii) Wastage 5 %	100 qtls.
	2000 qtls.

Fixed Working Capital

(1) Salary of Manager	Rs.	30,000
(2) Rent	Rs.	6,000
(3) Printing and Stationery	Rs.	1,250
(5) Insurance	Rs.	1,760
	Rs.	39,010

(Fixed working capital for one operating cycle is Rs. 3,900 or say Rs.0.04 lakhs)

Variable Working Capital

(1) Raw material	Rs.	8,71,000
(2) Wages	Rs.	1,10,000
(3) Electricity	Rs.	12,500
(4) Transportation	Rs.	12,500
(5) Misc. expenses	Rs.	6,250
(6) Market Tax and purchase Tax etc.,	Rs.	6,250
	Rs.	10,18,500

(Variable W. C. for one operating cycle Rs. 1,01,800)

Depreciation

(1) Workshed	Rs.	2,250
(2) Drying Yard	Rs.	1,000
(3) Machinery	Rs.	5,650
	Rs.	8,900

Funds Required

(1) C. E.	Rs.	89,000
(2) Working Capital for one cycle	Rs.	1,05,700
	Rs.	1,94,700
(3) Bank Loan (85 %)	Rs.	1,65,500

Cost Analysis (80 % Capacity Utilisation)

(1) Fixed costs (Sal + Rent + Print + Stoc + Ins.)	Rs.	39,010
(2) Variable Costs (Wages + Raw Material + Elect. + Trans. + Misc. + Taxes 80% of the total)	Rs.	8,14,800
(3) Cost of production (1 + 2)	Rs.	8,53,810
(4) Estimated Sales (80 % of the total) (Total Sales estimated are Rs. 12.5 lakhs)	Rs.	10,000,000
(5) Gross Surplus (4 - 3)	Rs.	1,46,190

Interest and Depreciation

(1) Interest on Term Loan	Rs.	14,240
(2) Interest on Working capital	Rs.	19,030

(3) Depreciation	Rs.	8,900
	Rs.	42,170
Net Surplus	Rs.	1,04,020
Disposable Surplus = Net Surplus + Depreciation	Rs.	1,12,920

The project can pay back the loan in 4 years even at a capacity utilisation of 80 %.

IV. Project for Poha Making

This unit is meant for Institutions/ Co-op. Societies/Entrepreneurs. The unit is expected to produce poha, the details of which are given below :

Details of the scheme

(1) Name of product	:	Poha
(2) Type of unit	:	For Institutions/Co-operatives/ Entrepreneurs
(3) Estimated Annual Capacity	:	Production value Rs. 6,60,000
(4) Estimated working days	:	250 days
(5) Estimated area of work place	:	300 sq. ft. for workshed
(6) Number of persons - Employment	:	6 persons
(7) Turnover cycles	:	10 cycles in a year 25 days per cycle

Cost of the project

(i) Workshed 300 sq. ft.		Rs.	60,000
(ii) **Machinery and Equipments**			
(i) Poha roller machine		Rs.	20,000
(ii) Electric machine 7.5 H. P. with starter		Rs.	12,250
(iii) Iron plate and pan 2 Nos.		Rs.	1,875
(iv) Oven Bhatti		Rs.	1,875
(v) Weighing balance		Rs.	3,750
(vi) Water Tank		Rs.	2,500
(vii) Installation and electrification		Rs.	1,875
(viii) Sieves (Chalni)		Rs.	650
		Rs.	44,775
	or say	Rs.	45,000
Total Capital Expenditure		Rs.	1,05,000

Raw Material Requirement

(i) Raw material	Rs.	3,75,000
(ii) Fuel	Rs.	31,250
(iii) Miscellaneous	Rs.	12,500
	Rs.	4,18, 750

Estimated Production

(i) Finished Goods	600 qtls.
(ii) Bran	50 qtls.
(iii) Husk	320 qtls.
(iv) Shortage	30 qtls.
	1000 qtls.

Sales Realisation

(1) Annual Sales of finished goods for 60 qtls.	Rs.	7,20,000
(2) Bran 50 qtls.	Rs,	15,000
(3) Husk 320 qtls.	Rs.	9,600
	Rs.	7,44,600
or say	Rs.	7,45,000

Working Capital Requirement

(a) Fixed Working Capital		
(i) Manager's salary.	Rs.	30,000
(ii) Repairs and Maintenance	Rs.	2,500
(iii) Advertisement Expenditure	Rs.	2,400
(iv) Rent	Rs.	4,800
(v) Insurance	Rs.	1,795
	Rs.	41,495

(Fixed cost for one operating cycle @ 10% cost of fixed Rs. 41,495 = Rs. 4,150 or Say Rs. 4,150)

(B) Variable Working Capital

(1) Raw material	Rs.	3,75,000
(2) Wages for 6 workers	Rs.	60,000
(3) Fuel	Rs.	31,250
(4) Oil	Rs.	12,500
(5) Electricity	Rs.	1,250
(6) Transportation and Travelling	Rs.	6,250
	Rs.	4,86,250

(Variable W. C. Rs. 48,625 for one operating cycle)

Depreciation

(1) Workshed	Rs.	6,000
(2) Machinery and Equipment	Rs.	4,500
	Rs.	10, 500

Funds Required

(a) C. E.	Rs.	1,05,000
(b) Working Capital for one cycle	Rs.	52,775
	Rs.	1,57,775
(c) Bank Loan (85 %)	Rs.	1,34,100

Cost Analysis (80 % Capacity Utilisation)

(1) Fixed costs (Sal + Repairs + ad + Rent + Ins.)	Rs.	41,495
(2) Variable Costs 80% of (Raw Material + Wages + Fuel + Elect. + Trans. + Travel + others)	Rs.	3,89,000
(c) Cost of Production (a + b)	Rs.	4,30,495
(d) Estimated Sales (80 % of the total)	Rs.	5,28,000
(e) Gross Surplus (d - c)	Rs.	97,505

Interest and Depreciation

(1) Interest on Term Loan	Rs.	16,800
(2) Interest on Working Capital	Rs.	9,500
(3) Depreciation	Rs.	10,500
	Rs.	36,800
Net Surplus	Rs.	60,705
The disposable surplus, i.e. net surplus + depreciation is	Rs.	71,205

The project can pay back the loan in 5 years even at 80% capacity utilisation.

V. Project for Papad Making

Introduction

In India Papad making has been traditionally a household industry. But in recent years, it has developed into a small scale village industry. Papad is a thin, popular food product, circular in shape, rolled from a dough made out of pulses flour with salt and spices added. The recipes for papad vary from region to region. With the changing pattern of living and increasing urbanisation, the demand for papad in the market is growing fast and is rapidly expanding. Essentially a labour intensive activity employing mainly starchy and proteinous materials has a low shelf life and has to be consumed as early as possible from the date of production.

Papad making normally does not require any machinery. If suitable quality of pulses flour is made available, papad can be rolled by hand out of the dough prepared by manual labour. The papad thus prepared is dried in the sun and packed in polythene bags. Such well packed papad has a better shelf life and can be transported over long distances for distribution to the consumers.

Papad making is a family occupation with the skill handed over from generation to generation. However, when practised as a commercial venture Papad making may require suitable training in order to ensure the required standards in quality, both physically and chemically. Even the packing has to be done scientifically so that the shelf life is protected.

The process of papad making includes :

(1) Dough Making,

(2) Pounding of dough,

(3) Rolling and drying of Papad

To begin with, Fine urad dal flour (11 kg.), Black Pepper (coarsely powdered) 250 gm.) and Asefoetida (25 gm.) are to be mixed with flour and to be prepared with the help of water solution in which soda- bi-carbonate and salt are dissolved. The dough made out of boiled and cooled water has a better keeping quality. The water solution should be added gradually so as to ensure stiff consistency for the dough. Soda-bi-Carbonate and salt are to be mixed in water and allowed to remain for 8 hours.

The upper portion is to be decanted and used as a water solution. In the next stage pounding of dough with little oil is necessary for elastic consistency of the dough. The desired quantity of dough can be pounded on an iron plate with an 18" iron pestle. It is to be taken in small quantity of 2 to 3 kg. for pounding. Sufficient pounding.of dough is most essential to ensure fluffyness to the finished product. Generally adequate pounding of the above mentioned quantity takes 20 minutes.

Before rolling of papad small quantity is stretched with hand. Stretching and proper kneading makes the dough lighter too. It is then rolled in to sticks of 9"length and 2" diameter, cut into small pieces of desired size and rolled with rolling pan. While rolling papad a few drops of oil should be applied on the rolling plate for easy rolling and to get an even and thin surface for papad.

Rolled papads are to be spread on palm leaf mats or plastic sheet for drying in the Sun.

The Papad should be dried properly since more percentage of moisture will deteriorate its quality very soon and if overdried, the Papad will become brittle. After drying oil, it is stored in closed containers and kept in dry place so as to ensure better quality. Papad can be roasted directly on fire by turning or can be fried in edible fat and consumed with meals. Roasted Papad tastes better.

Varieties in Papad (Formulae for Papad making)

(1) **Urad (Ordinary quality)**

(a)	Urad flour	11 kg.
(b)	Black pepper powder	250 gm.
(c)	Soda- bi-carbonate (coarsely powdered) 250 gm.	
(d)	Asafoetida (powder)	25 gm.
(e)	Salt	850 gm.
(f)	Water	5 litres

(2) **Moong (Ordinary quality)**

(a)	Moong flour	5 • kg.
(b)	Urad flour	5 • kg.
(c)	Soda-bi-carbonate	350 gm.
(d)	Black pepper powder	250 gm.
(e)	Asafoetida (powder)	25 gm.
(f)	Water	4 • litres
(g)	Salt	850 gm.

(Note: To mix Urad and Moong flour)

(3) **Garlic**

(a) Urad flour	11 kg.
(b) Garlic (with covers) (covers to be taken out while mixing)	300 gm.
(c) Green chillies	500 gm.
(d) Soda- bi-carbonate	350 gm.
(e) Salt	850 gm.
(f) Water	4 litres

(In Garlic Papad, Asafoetida and Black pepper are not consumed)

(4) **Red Chillies**

(a) Urad Flour	11 kg.
(b) Red Chillies Powder	350 gm.
(c) Asafoetida	25 gm.
(d) Soda- bi-carbonate	350 gm.
(e) Salt	850 gm.
(f) Water	5 litres

(5) **Urad Special**

(a) Urad flour	11 kg.
(b) Black pepper powder	500 gm.
(c) Asafoetida	25 gm.
(d) Soda- bi-carbonate	350 gm.
(e) Salt	850 gm.
(f) Water	5 litres

(6) **Moong Special**

(a) Moong flour	5 • kg.
(b) Urad flour	5 • kg.
(c) Black pepper powder	500 gm.
(d) Soda-bi-carbonate	350 gm.
(e) Asafoetida	25 gm.
(f) Salt	850 gm.
(g) Water	4½ litres

(7) Punjabi Special

(a) Urad flour	11 kg.
(b) Asafoetida (powder)	25 gm.
(c) Black pepper powder	500 gm.
(d) Black pepper (chaff)	300 gm.

(e) Soda- bi-carbonate 350 gm.
(f) Water 5 litres
(g) Salt -80 gm.

Role of KVIC in papad making

(i) Scenario of Papad Industry: Under PCP Industry of the KVIC, papad is a value added product and has a tremendous market as it forms a popular food item in Indian dietary. As the investment is minimum and the product is a moving item and return is quick, women beneficiaries are attracted to the Papad scheme. This activity has a very good capacity to generate employment opportunities in rural areas at low capital cost. Due to change in food patterns and increasing urbanisation, demand for papad in the market, at home and abroad is growing fast. Thus export potentiality of papad is a significant factor.

During the rainy season Papad production is being hampered. Therefore research has been carried out for continuous production of Papads so that production as well as employment opportunities need not be discontinued. Under the KVIC the programme implementing agencies distribute dough to the artisans who carry out rolling of Papad at their residence. A vigil and supervision are required so that rolling and drying operations are carried out in hygienic conditions.

The Papad making activity provides work mostly to the women folk at their door steps so that they can work even while attending to their household chores, earn some money and help their family members to raise their standard of living.

(ii). Training: Artisan course for Papad making having a duration of 2 months has been introduced by the Khadi and V.I. Commission from 1984 and KVIC is going to start training programme through some of the production centres situated in different States.

During the training period stipend @ Rs, 350 per month is paid to the trainees.

iii) Research and Development Technologies (Papad press)

There are four methods in vogue.

(1) CFTRI Technology.
(2) JBCRI Technology.
(3) HASH Technology.
(4) Improved Technology.

The details are given below :

In Papad making Industry, a process has been devised for drying Papad during monsoon.

In this process, on fire (like stove), iron pan is placed. On the iron pan a basket of 2 ft. height is kept on which wet cloth is covered, on which rolled papad is placed for drying. About 20-30 minutes are required for drying.

(iv) Scheme and project for Papad Industry/Quality Control in Papad making: With considerable varieties now being made at the cottage industry scale and the volume of production increasing, papad is finding a good export market in the West Asian Countries, U. K., USA, Russia, Malaysia etc. This product as mentioned earlier, is usually made from a blend of cereal flour, edible vegetable oil, and alkaline and mucilegenous additives. The dough is rolled into thin discs of varying diameters which are then dried and sold either by numbers or by weight after being suitably packed.

Papad under the KVI Sector is manufactured and dried under hygienic conditions.

Papad has only edible quality ingredients, which are free from insect infestation, extraneous matter and fungal growth.

(a) Rice flour, (b) Wheat flour, (c) Barley flour, (d) Maize flour, (e) Sorghum flour, (f) Potato flour, (g) Edible tapioca flour or Sago, (h) Blackgram (Phaseolus, Mungo), (i) Flour made from decucicled blackgram, (j) Green gram (Phaseolour aureus a Roxh) flour-made from decuticled green gram, (k) Horse gram (Dolichos biflorus) flour, (l) Dal arhar (Cajahus Cajan sp.) flour, (m) Flour of other decutivled pulses except Kesari dal (Lathyrus sativus), (n) Edible common powdered salt, (o) Edible vegetable oils, (p) Spices (extracted ones are not be used), (q) Harmless vegetable juices obtained from banana stem, gourds, Okra (Bhindi) , cissus or Vitis Guardrangularies etc., (r) Sodium bicarbonates or Food grade sodium bicarbonate or filtered water extract of Papad Sajjikhar (s) Pulp of jack fruit and, (t) water-potable.

Papad should be in the form of thin circular discs having a diameter ranging from 5 to 25 cm. The mean variation in diameter of Papad in any package should not exceed 10 per cent of the declared size.

The thickness of the disc may range between 0.3 to 1.2 mm except in the case of Papad made from sago. The thickness of Papad can be between 1.0 to 1.5 mm. The mean variation in the thickness of Papad in any package shall not be more than 0.3 mm. Papad should be of pleasant taste and smell and be free from rancid, bitter and alkaline or soapy taste.

In the raw form Papad should be pliable and should not crumble. It should be free broken or frayed edges, excessive number of holes, adhering dirt foreign matter, insect infestation or fungal growth and any other harmful ingredients.

Spiced Papad in the raw form shall have an aroma and taste characteristic of the spices used. On frying Papad should be brittle (break easily) and crisp to bite. They should not give leathery, gritty, sticky or soggy feeling.

Papad shall be packed either by count (25,50 or 100 a package) or by weight (package weighing 250 g. or 500 g. or 1 kg.) or in any other manner as agreed to between the purchaser and the supplier. The material used for packaging of Papad shall be moisture proof and non toxic.

Packing of Papads

The moisture absorption characteristics of Papads greatly depend on the various commonly used additives. To prevent fungal spoilage in Papads, the moisture content should never exceed the critical limit of 12 per cent on dry weight basis, and it was found that a level of common salt above 8 per cent should be avoided as it affects the organoleptic quality, crystallises on surface at lower PH, and increases the moisture pick up significantly at high PH, thereby tendering Papads susceptible to fungal spoilage.

If need be, addition of an antifungal agent i.e. calcium propionate can be used at the rate of 01. to 0.2 per cent on the weight of the flour, during dough making.

Studies on packaging have revealed that 340 gm pack of 200 guage low density polythylene (LDPE) or 170 gm unit pack of 400 gauge (LDPE) has a shelf-life of more that 4 months at 92 per cent RH and 38°C, corresponding to a shelf-life of nearly 12 months under normal conditions of storage. 350 gauge high density polythylene is 2-2• times protective as the 400 gauge LDPE against increase of moisture.

Fumigants such as methyliodides ethylene oxide and acrysonitrile are effective at dosages of 32-64 mg/1 in controlling insect infestation and mould attach in Papads with 18 per cent moisture content.

'A' type Papad Making unit

This unit is meant for Institutions/Co-operative Societies. The unit is expected to produce different varieties of Papads, the details of which are given below

(1) Name of the Product	:	Different varieties of Papad
(2) Type of unit	:	'A' type Papad making unit meant for institutions/ co-operative societies.
(3) Estimated annual capacity of production	:	600 qtls. of finished product of different varieties of Papad @ 50 qtls. per month valued at Rs. 9,80,000.
(4) Estimated work period	:	250 days in a year with 8 hours of work per day.
(5) Estimated area of work place	:	400 sq. ft. covered area.
(6) No. of persons required for working	:	63 persons (60 women workers and 3 office staff).
(7) Turnover cycles	:	10 cycles in a year.

Capital Expenditure

(I) Building (i) Store room 25' x 10' = 250 sq. ft.		
(ii) work hall 15' x 10' = 150 sq. ft.		
Total sq. ft. is 400. @ Rs. 200 per sq. ft.	Rs.	80,000
(II) Machinery and Equipments		
(i) Garlic processing machine with power-1	Rs.	3,125
(ii) Wax packing balance (big) 1	Rs.	625
(iii) Weighing balance (big) 1	Rs.	4,375
(iv) Weighing balance (small)	Rs.	1,875
(v) Weights	Rs.	2,500
(vi) Iron plate - table (5' x 4') 1	Rs.	2,500
(vii) Iron pestle	Rs.	625
(viii) Small drums	Rs.	250
(ix) Big drums	Rs.	570
(x) Water storage tanks	Rs.	1,250
(xi) Aluminium utensils (big)	Rs.	1,250
(xii) Aluminium utensils (small)	Rs.	315

(xiii)	Electrification and installation charges	Rs.	1,250
(xiv)	Furniture and fixtures	Rs.	3,750
		Rs.	24,260

Total Capital Expenditure
(Rs. 24,260 + 80,000) Rs. 1,04,260

Raw Material Requirement

(i)	41,250 kgs. of Atta and Masala	Rs.	3,30,000
(ii)	640 kgs. of oil	Rs.	21,760
(iii)	Packing materials	Rs.	16,138
		Rs.	3,67,898

Wages / Salaries

(i)	Manager-cum-Accountant 1	Rs.	28,800
(ii)	Production supervisor 1	Rs.	24,000
(iii)	Attendant 1	Rs.	18,000
(iv)	Processing charges to women workers on piece rate basis @ Rs. 0.80 per kg. for materials for 41,250 kgs.	Rs.	33,000
(v)	Dough making charges to women workers on piece rate basis @ Rs. 4 per tin of 11 kgs. raw materials or 3750 tins.	Rs.	15,000
(vi)	Rolling charges to women workers on piece rate .basis on finished © Rs. 4 per kg. for 63,750 kgs. of Papad including wastage.	Rs.	2,55,000
(vii)	Wages to women workers for packing @ Rs. 30 per day for worker for 250 days for 5 workers for packing (250 x 30 x 5)	Rs.	37,500
		Rs.	4,11,300
		Rs.	4,11, 300

Capital Requirement and Economics of the Scheme

I. Fixed Working Capital

(1)	Salary to Manager	Rs.	28,800
(2)	Salary to Supervisor	Rs.	24,000
(3)	Salary to Attendant	Rs.	18,000
(4)	Printing and Stationery	Rs.	5,000
(5)	Other administrative Expenses.	Rs.	5,000
(6)	Insurance	Rs.	2,243
		Rs.	83, 043

(Fixed,cost for one cycle Rs. 8,304 or say
Rs. 8,300 (10 cycle in a year)

II. Variable Working Capital

(1) Raw Materials	Rs.	3,67,898
(2) Wages	Rs.	3,40,500
(3) Transport	Rs.	15,000
(4) Electricity charge	Rs.	3,759
(5) Cleaning and processing Loss	Rs.	1,000
	Rs.	7,28,148

(Variable cost for one @ cycle Rs. 72,815 or Rs. 72,800)

Depreciation

(i) Building	Rs.	8,000
(ii) Machinery	Rs.	2,425
	Rs.	10,425

Funds Required

(a) Capital Expenditure	Rs.	1,04,260
(b) Working Capital for one cycle	Rs.	81,100
	Rs.	1,85,360
(c) Bank Loan (85 %)	Rs.	1,57,600

Cost Analysis (80 % Capacity Utilisation)

(i) Fixed costs (Sal - Print + Ins.)	Rs.	83,043
(ii) Variable Costs (Wages + Raw Material + Trans. + Elect.) 80% of the total	Rs.	5,82,518
(iii) Cost of production (i + ii)	Rs.	6,65,561
(iv) Estimated Sales Realisation (80%)	Rs.	7,84,000
(v) Gross Surplus (iv - iii)	Rs.	1,18,430

Depreciation and Interest

(1) interest on Loan	Rs.	16,700
(2) Interest on Working Capital	Rs.	14,600
(3) Depreciation	Rs.	10,425
	Rs.	41,725

Net Surplus	Rs.	76,714
The disposable surplus, i.e. net surplus + depreciation is	Rs.	87,139

The project can pay back the loan in 4 years even at capacity utilisation of 80%.

(1) C.F.T.R.1. Technology

(A) Title : Papad press
(B) Product : Papad
Co-product

(C) **Machine usage**

For making papad (120/hr) from dal flours and also from horse gram flour which is rather hard and strenuous to be rolled by the traditional method.

(D) **Market Information**

There is a good domestic market for Papad. Popularity of Papad is ever increasing and the demand for these products is bound to increase. Hence it is relevant to produce simple machines for making convenient foods.

(E) Raw material : Pulses

(F) **Operation procedure**

The Machine has two discs. The upper disc is movable and the lower disc is stationary. The upper disc is connected through a toggle mechanism to a hand ever. When the lever is operated the upper disc comes down and presses against the lower disc, thus flattening a dough ball kept on the bottom disc. The thickness of the Papad can be adjusted by adjusting the clearance between the disc.

(G) **Major Equipment/Machineries (Indigenously Available)**

The press is made of mild steel and weighs about 12 kg. and measures 30 x 47 cm. when handle is removed.

(H) **(a) Premium for process release**

Rs. 4,000 (leg operated/hand operated press)

(b) Mode of Payment

Demand draft in favour of Director, CFTRI, Mysore.

(I) **Service available after process release**

(1) Supply of design drawings (detailing process knowhow)

(2) Technical discussions on the process released.

(3) Certification of equipment fabricated as per design drawing of CFTRI at the works established by the Licence (Expenses of Scientist deputed to be borne by licencees).

(J) **Other Services available related to process release**

(1) Preparation of pre-investment / survey / feasibility / detailed project report.

(2) General/ Advisory/ Engineering consultancy for setting up the production unit.

(3) Product quality assessment.

(2) **JBCRI Technology**

(i) Particulars	:	Papad making machine
(ii) Technical Details		
(a) Length (Cm)	:	48
(b) Width (Cm)	:	41
(c) Height (Cm)	:	15 .
(d) Total Weight (Kg.)	:	34,600
(e) Electric power required	:	Nil
(f) Production capacity	:	1600 Papad
(g) (8 hours) (depends on skill of operator)		
(h) Cost	:	Rs. 2000
(i) Used for	:	Papad making
(j) Construction	:	M. S. and Nylon
(k) Major material of	:	Chrome plated
(l) Wage earning capacity	:	Rs. 40 per kg. per labour.
(m) Time required for training	:	One week
(n) Employment generation	:	2 persons for one machine.

(3) **Hash Technology**

(i) Machine Body	:	Electric Motor switch with attractive sunmica cabinet
(ii) Length	:	19" 480 M.M.
(iii) Breadth	:	18" 450 M.M.
(iv) Weight	:	Approximate 94 kg.
(v) Height	:	22" 550 M.M.
(vi) Electric Motor	:	0.5 H.P. (Single phase)
(vii) Productivity	:	60 to 70 kg. in 8 hours
(viii) Electrical expenses	:	Approximate 4 units in 8 hours

(ix)	Guarantee	:	One year guarantee on manufacturing damage.
(x)	Items which can be prepared	:	Papad, Puri, Papadi, Methli, Phaphde.
(xi)	Maximum size of Papad	:	11"

Stages of Papad Making

(1) Addition of ingredients
(2) Application of Oil
(3) Beating of dough
(4) Pressing / Rolling

Drying Method

Replace upper P.V.C. plastic sheet and reverse the other sheet of Papad on clean cloth. Papad is now ready. 20 P.V.C. plastic sheets are supplied with machine without extra cost.

(4) Improved Technology

(a)	Name of the Manufacturer	:	Radheshyam Patidhar P.O., Kajuriya Sarang Dist. Mandsaur (M.P.)
(1)	Machine Body	:	Hand Operator
(2)	Length	:	18"
(3)	Breadth	:	12"
(4)	Height	:	13"
(5)	Production capacity	:	3 kg. per hour
(6)	Guarantee period	:	One year
(7)	Items which can be prepared	:	Papad
(8)	Price	:	Rs. 2200/- Ex. Factory.

(b) M/s Jatindra Papar Warian,
Gram Udyog Samiti, Katra Kanian,
Amritsar, Punjab has developed dough beating machine with 1 H.P. electric Motor.
Cost of Machine: Rs. 6000/-
Capacity : 75 to 100 kg. per hour depending on the type of dough to be beaten.

Chapter - 15

Confectionery Industry Semi Automatic Plant (Toffee, Candy, Chewing Gum, Bubble Gum etc.)

Confectionery or sweetmeats are preserved edible delicacies consisting of a solid or crystalline phase and a liquid or non-crystalline phase the relative proportion of which determine the type of confectionery. The principal types of confectionery are hard boiled goods, caramel and toffee, ratin goods, confits or dragees, and lozenges.

Sugar is the principal ingredient of confectionery. There are about 60 important confectionery factories in the country. Mainly in U.P. Bihar, Mumbai, Punjab, and Bengal. In addition, a large number of small concerns are producing sugar confectionery with indigenous equipments.

FORMULATIONS FOR CHEWING GUM/BUBBLE GUM

Gum Base

Here is given formulation for the preparations of the chewing gum/ bubble gum. This formulation is the best among all other formulations used in the country. It is widely used in India due to wonderful demand and consumption of it. And this formulation is much feasible and economical. Formulation is based on percent by weight.

	Ingredients	% by wt.
1.	Elastomer (Synthetic gum)	10
2.	Elastomer Solvent (Ester gum)	12
3.	Hydrophilic plasticizers (Polyvinyl Acetate)	30
4.	Oleaginous plasticizers (Cocoa butter)	21
5.	Emulsifier (Glyceryl monostearate)	12

6.	Filler ($CaCo_3$)	10
7.	Pigments (TiO_2)	3
8.	Additives (flavour)	2

FOR CHEWING GUM

	Ingredients	By wt. %
1.	Gum Base	21
2.	Corn Syrup 44 Be	16
3.	Powder free	0.5
4.	Powdered Sugar (Sucrose)	51
5.	Dextrose	9
6.	Peppermint Oil	2
7.	Lecithin	0.5

MANUFACTURING PROCESS

Manufacturing process of chewing gum is mainly in two sub parts.

(1) Gum base preparation.

(2) Chewing gum preparation.

(1) **Gum base preparation**

This long process having three sub group mixing process.

First group :- 1. Natural or Synthetic gum or elastomers

UNIPLAST SWEET FORMING

Suitable for solid as well as liquid Filled Sweets
Seamless Sweet Foaming, output upto 1000 kgs/H/r.
Powerload 3 H.P.

2. Elastomer solvent.
3. Additives.

Second Group :- 1. Hydraulic plasticizer.
2. Hydrophobic plasticizer.
3. Filler.
4. Pigments.

Third group :- 1. Oleoginous plasticizers.
2. Emulsifiers.

First of these, the groups is blended separately in the dry solid blender and then fed it to the high intensive mixer.

Second group is also blended in the dry solid blender then first and second mixer is fed to the intermediate intensity mixer for the fine mixing. Third group also blended separately in the dry blender and then this third group and mixer after intermediate intensity mixes is fed to the rapid efficient mixer. This rapid efficient mixer is used to provide essentially no shearing action but a very rapid folding action.

Chewing Gum Preparation

The gum base is melted at 270°F and placed in dough mixer kettle, with the blades. The corn syrup and lecithin are mixed for 2 minutes at the temperature of 200°F. At the same time the mixer is folding well, powdered free sacharin is added and for another three minutes it is mixed at 200°F. After it the sucrose, dextrose and flavour oil are added and with in this time the mixture is mixed for 5 minutes The gum is taken out from the mixing kettle and cut it into 25 lb loaves and then cool it 90°F -120°F. Then roll it to a thickness of 0.178 cm on a standard Gimpel machine and scored into strips 7.26 cm wide and 41.9 long, and cooled for 12 to 18 hours. The chewing gum product have a pleasant sweet taste for upto 30 minutes.

Formulation

1. English Toffee Nougats

Corn syrup	38 lbs
Nulomoline	10 lbs
Dairy Butter (Salted)	5 lb
Coconut Butter (86°F mp)	10 lb
Brown Sugar	15 lb
Fine Granulated Sugar	20 lb
Salt	503

Flavour with a canbinatias of clove oil, Almond oil and vanilla.

Place the following ingredients in a caramel cooking kettle, Nulonoline, corn syrup, butter, coconut butter & condensed milk. Give the steam valve a few turns and allow the batch to mix until the fats are melted & mixed with the other ingredients. Then add the brown and white sugar, turn the steam on full and cook the batch as rapidly as possible to a firm ball.

This toffee can be cooked quite successfully, using as much as 110 pounds of steam pressure. After the batch has been cooked to the desired consistant, turn of the heat. Add the salt & flavour and mix thoroughly. Spread the batch at once to cool. Then gradually fold it together so as to secure an even temperature throughout the batch. It is now ready to pass through drop rolls.

After the toffee ruggets are cold, place them in a pan. Spray them with coconut butter. Then add product sugar that has been flavoured with mint oil. Allow the candies to revolve. Spread them and to set. Then pack.

CONFECTIONERY MACHINES

TOFFEE COOKER
BATCH SIZE 50 KGS.

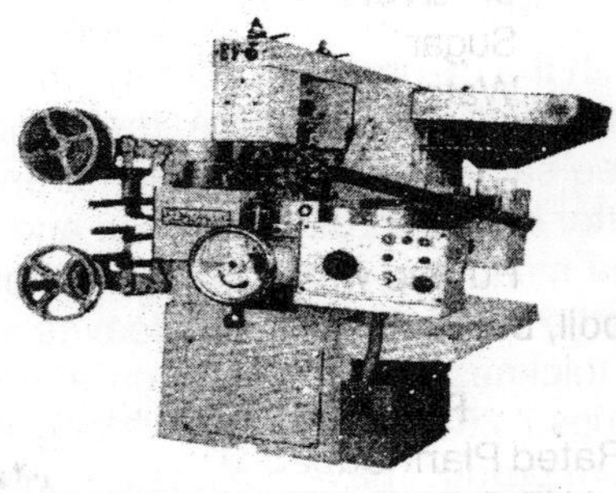

CANDY WRAPPING MACHINE
CAPACITY 250 - 350 PCS / MIN

VACCUM BATCH COOKER
BATCH SIZE - 50 KGS.

2. Run Butter Toffee (wrapped)

Condensed Whole milk (40% sugar)	40 lb
Corn Syrup	30 lb
Nulomoline	10 lb
Grandwas molasses	5 lb
Fine Granulated Sugar	30 lb
Hard coconut Butter - No. 90 -	15 lb
Salt	503

Rum & Butter Flavour

Place the condensed milk, corn syrup, Nulomoline, molasses and land coconut butter in a caramed cooking kettle equipped with double action mixers. Turn the heat on partly & mix the batch until the batch is completely melted. Then add the granulated sugar mix well. Turn the steam on full & boil the batch as rapidly as possible to a medium firm ball. Turn off the heat. Add the salt and the rum- butter flavour, and mix thoroughly spread the batch and to cool. Then cut into the desired size & wrap.

3. Everton Toffee

Sugar	4 lb
Water	3 lb
Cream of Tartar	1/2 tsp
Butter	203

Put the water, sugar, and cream of tartar into a pan and stir until they boil, but no layer. Add the butter but do not stir it.

PLANT ECONOMICS OF CONFECTIONERY INDUSTRY

Rated Plant Capacity	=	1400.00 KGS/Day
LAND & BUILDING (Land 750 sq.mt.)	=	Rented

PLANT & MACHINERY

1. Homogeniser
2. Steam and Vacuum Pans
3. Drop cutting machines
4. Pulling machines
5. Toffee cutting machines
6. Revolving comfits pans
7. Tableting machines

8. Wrapping and packing machines
9. Kneading machines
10. Boiler
11. Pumps,Valves,fittings & other equipments
12. Laboratory testing equipment
13. Moulds, dies and other tools, jigs, fixtures
14. CHEWING GUM/BUBBLE GUM PLANT: Dry solid blender
15. High intensity mixer
16. Intermediate intensity mixer
17. Dough mixing machine
18. Cooling bath
19. Crimpel machine
20. Storage tank
21. Miscellaneous plant equipments

FIXED CAPITAL

1.	Plant & Machiner	Rs.	17,10,000.00
2.	Other Fixed Assets	Rs.	4,25,000.00
	TOTAL	Rs.	21,35,000.00

RAW MATERIALS

1. Sugar
2. Milk
3. Corn syrup
4. Invert sugar
5. Flavours
6. Colours
7. Butter
8. Miscellaeous chemicals
9. Wrapping paper
10. Synthetic gum
11. Ester gum
12. Polyvinyl acetate
13. Cocoa butter

14. Glyceryl monosterate
15. Calcium carbonate
16. TiO
17. Flavour
18. Corn Syrup
19. Saccharin acid
20. Sugar
21. Dextrose
22. Peppermint oil
23. Lecithen

TOTAL WORKING CAPITAL/MONTH

1. Raw Material	Rs.	7,80,287.00
2. Salary & Wages	Rs.	93,280.00
3. Utilities & Overheads	Rs.	1,56,600.00
TOTAL	Rs.	10,30,167.00

TOTAL CAPITAL INVESTMENT

Total Fixed Capital	Rs.	21,35,000.00
Total Working Capital for 1 month	Rs.	10,30,167.00
TOTAL	Rs.	31,65,167.00

TURN OVER/ANNUM

1. By selling 300 tonnes of Candy & Toffee
2. By selling 120 MT Chewing gum

TOTAL	Rs.	1,85,40,000.00

PROFIT SALES RATIO = Profit / Sales x 100 = 28.89 %
RATE OF RETURN = Operating profit / T.C.I x 100 = 169.21 %
BREAK EVEN POINT (B.E.P) = 27.40 %

Chapter - 16

Corrugated Sheet Board and Boxes

Corrugated cartons were firstly developed by the Thomsan and Norris Company in 1980, and the first regular slotted style containers were the products of the Robert Gair Company. The first use of corrugated cartons in freight shipments was for lamp and chimneys.

Corrugated board is used for making corrugated boxes which find applications in packing of a wide variety of consumer products like:-

1. Cosmetics
2. Drugs
3. Food products
4. Household goods
5. Electrical and Electronic goods
6. Cigarettes
7. Textiles
8. Beverages
9. Chemicals
10. Hardware
11. Tea and Coffee

TYPES OF CORRUGATION

FLUTE	NO. OF CORRUGATIONS per meter	HEIGHT OF CORRUGATIONS (mm)
A BOARD	105-125	4.5 - 4.7
B NARROW	150-185	2.1 - 2.9
C MEDIUM	120-145	3.5 - 3.7
D MICRO	290-220	1.1 - 1.5

REQUIREMENTS FOR SOLID FIBREBOARD BOXES

Weight of contents Max.	Combined International dimensions (L+W+H) Max.	Thickness of Board Min.	Substance of board Min.	Bursting strength Min.	Puncture resistance Min.
1	2	3	4	5	6
KG	MM	MM	g/m²	kg/cm²	cm-kg.
10	1000	1.10	800	8	39
20	1500	1.80	1.350	14	63
30	2000	2.25	1.700	18	90
40	2250	2.50	1.950	21	102

* Glossary of terms relating to paper and pulp based packing material.

Glossary of terms relating to paper and flexible Packing

MANUFACTURING PROCESS

Machine which usually takes container board from three rolls and combines it into a corrugated board consisting of two outer facings and an intermediate fluted members. The corrugator forms the intermediate sheet into a series of a riched trusses and attaches the facings to them with adhesive applied at the tips of flutes. The resulting sheet is called single wall corrugated fibre board by taking container board from five rolls, it also produce a corrugated board, commonly known as double wall consisting of three facings and two corrugated mediums .

By adding another corrugated sheet and facing, triple corrugated sheet and facing, wall corrugated board is produced. The machine also scores the fibre board in one direction and outs it to size to firm boxes blanks or cartons.

One essential components of corrugated board is a sheet known as 'corrugating medium 0.009 thick (9 caliper) or 0.23 mm, has been given a wary shape by passing it through the rolls of a corrugating machine. Jute and kraft liner board, or any other board is attached to this sheet on one or both sides with starch and silicate of soda adhesive.

When only one liner is used the product is known as 'Single face'. This is flexible in one direction, when the corrugated element is combined on both side with other boards, it is known as 'Double face' corrugated board or corrugated shipping container board.

There are three standards sizes of corrugations, called 'A' flute 'B' and 'C' flute. In 'A' flute there are about 36 corrugations to the liners foot and the thickness of the combined board is about 0.205". In 'B' flute there are about 52 corrugations per liner foot with the board thickness being about 0.125". While in 'C' flute here are about 42 corrugations per liner foot with the board thickness being about 0.125", while in 'C' flute here are about 42 corrugations per liner foot with the board thickness being about 0.125". While in 'C' flute here are about 0.165". The usual basic weight of the corrugating medium is about 125 gms.

Corrugated board is fabricated on a machine known as corrugating machine which consists in its simplest form a set of corrugating rolls, glue applicator rolls and a shot plate section. Before entering the corrugation rolls, the corrugating medium is pre conditioned by steaming and is then further heated at the steam heated corrugated rolls.

Heat is very important in the corrugating operations. As mentioned, heat supplied by steaming is necessary to control the plastic properties of the corrugated medium at the time of corrugating. The liners are generally preheated also by passing over steam heated preheater rolls, about 36" in diameter where the heating is determined by the amount of wrap of paper around the roll. The direction of the wrap of paper around the rolls is important, and sherman recommends with liners upto 90% moisture content the heat

PAPER CORRUGATED BOARD & BOX MAKING MACHINERY

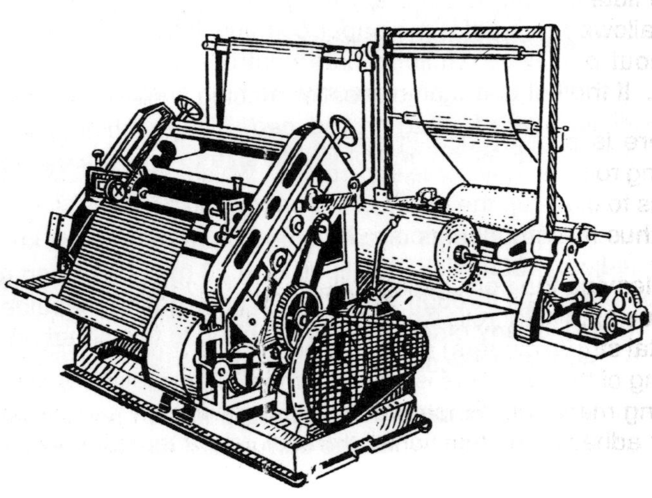

applied to the outside to drive the moisture to the inside where the glue is to be applied.

The corrugated rolls are heated also using steam of about 30 to 175 psi to produce a surface temperature of about 320 to 341°F.

The treatment of the corrugating medium with moist heat make the paper soft and pliable so that also prevents a sticking of the paper of the corrugating rolls.

The number of corrugations per foot of board and the height of the corrugations are standarised as follows although there is a considerable variation from standard.

Type of Flute	Height of Flutes/in.	No. of flute/ft.
A		36
B	48	51
C	5132	41

'A' flute is used where high top to bottom compression and where maximum cushioning is desired e.g. for board used in the packaging of paper cartons and glass fars.

'B' flute is used where high end-to- end compression is desired. It is used for the packing of canned goods and where the box is stitched instead of being taped.

The flute contour is generally fairly sharp. Clearance between teeth must be allowed to so that the paper can flow into the nip to produce the flute without pinching. Uniform flute controns with no highs or lows is essential. If the flutes are uneven only the high flutes will receive glue.

There is a difference in speed between the tip and the valley of corrugating rolls as they come into contact, which produces a sliding action. This tends to close up the pores of the paper and "Burnish" the corrugating medium thus making gluing difficult.

On leaving the corrugating rolls, the corrugating medium fluffs out to meet a glue applicator rolls which applied adhesive to one side of the paper. Long metal strips (gingers) are set to control the amount of this fluffing out, and setting of these fingers is ce of the most important parts of operation of corrugating machine. Since the improper setting causes damaged flutes and poor adhesive applications. Immediately after the application of the glue, the first liner is brought into contact with the glued sieve of the corrugating medium, and then (non pressure type machines) high pressure is applied for a fraction of second to set the adhesive.

The resulting board is known as single face. If double face board is to be made, the single faced moves up an elevator to a bridge where it collects in folds to provide a continuous feed for the double backer glue station. As the double back glue station adhesive is applied to the flutes on the other side of the corrugating medium and a second liner applied about 5-30 second later.

Adhesive consumption figures are generally reported in pounds/ thousand sq.ft. or board. Because consumption depends upon the type of flute and number of sheet elements it is customary to use 'A' flute double face board as to the basis for reporting. Factors are used to convert other type of board to this basis. One set factor in use is:

A flute, double face	1.0
A flute, single face	0.3
B flute, double face	1.3
B flute, single face	0.4
A flute, double wall	2.6
A flute double wall	2.6

After leaving the double back glue station, the combined board enters the hot plate section where the board is held against plates by means of heavy belts. Setting of the adhesive on the double back side takes places at this board. At the end of the machine the board is slit and flap scored. The blanks are then taken off the machine piled in such a way as to minimize wraping and sweating of the board. There are many operating variables to watch at the single face stage to prevent defects in the final board. The importance of the proper settings of the fingers has already been mentioned some corrugating media are very springy and it is extremely important that the fingers are adjusted close to the large corrugating the teeth before it reaches the relief or fluff out position. The setting of the transfer roll is very important. The setting depends upon the type of adhesive, pear, speed and other factors. The pressure at the double backer glue station must not be excessive because of to danger of crushing the corrugations. However, slight flattenings of the tips of the flutes, is desirable when starch adhesive is used to increase the glue line area of contact build shoulders into the board.

There are many operating variables to watch at the single face stage to prevent defects in the final board. The importance of the proper setting of the figures has already been mentioned some corrugating media are very springy and it is extremely important that the fingers are adjusted close to the large corrugating rolls so that the paper will not spring out of the teeth before it reaches the relief or fluff out position. The setting of the transfer roll in relation to both the glue roll and the corrugating roll is very important. The setting depends upon the types of adhesive, paper speed and other factors. The pressure at the double backer glue station must not be excessive because of the danger of crushing the corrugations. However, slight flattenings of the tips of the flutes, is desirable when starch adhesive is used to increase the glue line area of contact and build shoulders into the board.

The applicators roll has a slightly rough surface for picking up the glue. The speed of this roll in relation to speed of the paper is very important general practice is to run the glue rolls at a surface speed less than paper board speed. This produces a wiping action of the front side of the flute which applies a 'Bead of glue' in about the same quantity as applied action. The most desirable speed is about 95% of the paper board speed at the single face and about 80% at the double backer much better board is obtained under these conditions than can be obtained when running the glue rollat 100% of paper board speed.

Speed in excess of 100% of paper cause 'throwing' of the adhesive. The speed can be adjusted to obtain a greater wiping action at low machine speeds and the little or no wiping action at high machine speeds so as to control the amount of adhesive applied. The overall operating and mechanical feature of the corrugating machine which need checking included heating system, corrugating roll system, finger bar, machine live up from roll stands through hot plate section to keep paper centered, belting, and glue roll speed. The major sources of trouble are as listed below:-

1. Paper components too wet or too dry.
2. Improper heat balance on the machine.
3. This alingment, cross pull, or other mechanical stresses which prevent firm and continuous contact with the adhesive.
4. Moisture saturated or imprevious belts.
5. Dirty glue rolls.
6. Improperly prepared adhesive.

The wet glue bond must be fairly strong as the board comes off the machine to withstand and hand ling at this point. Later the adhesive sets to produce the final dry bond. This bond makes an important contribution to the overall strength of the finished board, affecting such properties a bending moment, compression tensile strength, puncture resistance, and water resistance. Improperly applied adhesive resulting in starved or flooded joints and poorly made corrugations, maked flutes and deep fingers lines reduce the strength of the board.

Moisture content of the glued board is important because it affects the ink recaptivity. Moisture can be preheating the paper liner before corrugating. (2) Controlling the amount of adhesive applied on the corrugating machine. However, in spite of the best attempts to control moisture, it varies with the machine speed. Speeds in corrugating have been increased steadily over the past few years, and today speed up to 500 to 600 f.p.m. are common. Well formed board has been made at speeds upto 1150 f.p.m. on an experimental machine, although satisfactory gluing has not been obtained at this speed. As speeds have increased and with a trend toward more frequent order changes on the corrugator a need has developed for reducing waste during change overs. This is achieved by the running double facer feature, on automatic device for changing ordered while the corrugator is still running. The rotary out off slitters and scores are present when the previous order is finished the change over is made automatically in about 25 seconds.

PLANT ECONOMICS OF CORRUGATED BOARD & BOXES

Rated Plant Capacity	=	2650.00 Kgs./Day
Land & Building (Land Area 750 sq.mts.)	=	Rented

PLANT & MACHINERY

1. Corrugated Sheet Making Unit
2. Board Cutters
3. One reel Stand, Light model
5. One sheet pressing machine,
6. One eccentric slotter
7. One 4-Bar Rotary cutting & Creasing machine
8. Stitching machine
9. One Partition slotter
10. One slotting machine
11. One vertical Bending machine
12. Corner cutting machine
13. Two colour Board Printer
14. Laminating M/c.
15. Miscellaneous charges as Packing, forwarding, excise duty and all applicable taxes etc.
16. D.G. set

Corrugated Sheet Board and Boxes

FIXED CAPITAL

1. Plant & Machinery	Rs.	13,59,000.00
2. Other Fixed Assets	Rs.	4,85,000.00
TOTAL	Rs.	18,44,000.00

RAW MATERIALS

1. Kraft Paper in Rolls
2. Glue (Starch)
3. Stitching wire
4. Printing ink
5. Polyethylene film

TOTAL WORKING CAPITAL/MONTH

1. Raw Material	Rs.	23,36,375.00
2. Salary & Wages	Rs.	1,26,390.00
3. Utilities & Overheads	Rs	1,27,950.00
TOTAL	Rs.	25,90,715.00

TOTAL CAPITAL INVESTMENT

Total Fixed Capital	Rs	18,44,000.00
Total Working Capital for 1 Month	Rs.	25,90,715.00
TOTAL	Rs.	44,34,715.00

TURN OVER/ANNUM

By sale of 7,95,000 kgs. of Corrugated Board & Boxes	Rs.	3,81,60,000.00

PROFIT SALES RATIO = Profit / Sales x 100 = 16.22 %
RATE OF RETURN = Operating profit / T.C.I x 100 = 139.57 %
BREAK EVEN POINT (B.E.P) = 25.36 %

Chapter - 17

Coolant (Engine)

The coolant used in this cooling system must fulfill the requirement of the engine, which is basically the removal of one third of heat produced during combustion of fuel.

An antifreeze is a substance that is added to a liquid usually water-to lower its freezing point. The applications of coolant are different from Antifreezer. The main uses is to protect internal combustion engines against freezing and the resultant damage to the engine water jacket and the radiator.

Two general types of cooling systems are used in the engines, liquid and air. All current domestic passenger cars, heavy vehicles, use a liquid cooling system. In this system the liquid or coolant constantly circulates throughout the engine, absorbing heat from the engine.

For a given volume, water has the ability to absorb more heat from engine parts than any other type of liquid coolant used in vehicles. However, water presents some problems when used as a primary engine coolant. First, metal components exposed to water will corrode and rust creat contaminants that will close the water jackets and radiator passages. The second one is that water has a boiling and freezing temperature limit.

Almost all the antifreeze used in the market, as a engine coolants, comprrises essentially ethylene glycol. Water was selected early as the coolant, because of its universal availability, low cost, and good heat-transfer properties. Despite its valuable characteristics, water has serious disadvantages.

1) It corrodes the metal found in cooling system.

2) It has a relatively high freezing point, and when it freezer, its volume expands by about 9%, which raptures the radiator or even an engine block.

3) Due to its low Boiling point, as the heat output of engines has increased, pressure must be used to increase the boiling point.

The use of glycol's as antifreeze also elevates the coolant's boiling point.

Other antifreeze successfully used are methanol, denatural ethanol, glycerol, and calcium chloride or salt brines. Kerosene or lubricating oils mixed with water may employed as coolants eliminating the use of antifreezer.

The principal antifreeze materials during the period 1930 -40 were ethanol, synthetic methanol, and ethylene glycol. The glycerol, isopropyl alcohol, and methanol was also in use.

Now a days, the use of methanol has decreased. The use of propylene - glycol is increasing as the heat transfer fluid in solar energy systems and is used as a coolant.

1-Methoxy - 2 - propanol is used were ebullient cooling required and for heavy duty diesels. Since metoxypropanol forms azeotropes with water, it provides freeze protection in the vapor phase as well as the liquid phase in ebullient cooling. Heavy duty diesels often have wet liners that permit seepage into the crank case. The high vapor pressures of methyoxypropanol permits it to evaporte with the water rather than remaining to form a sludge or varnish as would glycols. A recent study reported that lower metal tempeatures are maintained when methoxyporpanol, rather than glycol solution is used as a coolant in rotary engines.

Unless water-type coolant contains a corrosion inhibitor or antifreeze with the inhibitor in it, it will tend to corrode cooling system, metals, which results in many types of damages. To counteract the temperature limits of water as a primary engine coolant, it is recommended the use of an ethylene glycol-based antifreeze and water mixture, in different proportion, for the engine's coolant. This type of antifreeze is known as a permanent type.

MANUFACTURING PROCESS

The main component of the coolant is ethyl glycol, which makes the body of the coolant it is taken about 70% by weight. Ethylene glycol is a clear, colorless, hygroscopic liquid, having sweat taste. Ethylene glycol is derived by heating ethylene chlorohydrin with oxidation of ethylene with air, folowed by hydration of ethylene oxide formed.

It is highly toxic by ingestion lethal dose in 100 cc.

The other basic component is anti corrosion elements or substances, which eliminate or minimize corrosive attack. These include organic, inorganic compounds and silicons. Some of which are listed below.

A. ORGANIC COMPOUNDS

1. Mineral or Vegetable Oils
2. Sulfonated Mineral/Vegetable Oils
3. Amides, Amines.
4. Benzoates.
5. Mercaptaus.

B. INORGANIC COMPOUNDS

1. Borates
2. Nitrates.
3. Nitrides
4. Phosphates.
5. Molybdates
6. Silicates
7. Carbonates

C. SILICONS

Most coolant formulations contain various combinations of two or more anticorrosion compounds; because no single compound is complete corrosion protection to all metals under all conditions.

The choice of individual components and their proportions affect the quality of the coolant. Some materials pan through a concentration of maximum effectiveness and may become more aggresive toward some of the metals at higher concentrations. The anticorrosive agents are dissolved in such a proportion that after dilution of coolant it is in enough proportion.

There are various formulation of coolants, most of them are patented or kept as a trade secret. One formalation having a good performance is as given below :-

Ethylene Glycol	70%
Propylene Glycol	20%
Sodium Benzoate	2.5-5%
Organic Pigments	0.5-1%
Sodium Silicate	1-2%
Sulfonated Lard Oil	2-4%

The formulation given above is very effective coolant with anticorrosive properties.

All the ingredients are mixed in a mixer/blender hairing an impeller. Impellers may either radial flow or axial flow. The flat blade turbine is normally placed 0.5-1 impeller diameter off bottom and has a coverage of 1-2 impeller diameters. The spacing between multiple impellers is somewhere between I.5 & 3 impeller diameters.

Radial flow turbines are preferred for mixing of ingredient of this formulation. The fluid force acting in a radial direction on the impeller tendes to deflect the shaft. Mixer shaft has natural vibrational frequency; when it is rotated at that speed shaft deflectioin becomes infinite, resonance occurs, and it may be destroyed . Thus mixer shaft must be operated at a speed below its critical speed. The power drawn by an impeller at a given speed and diameter is independent of process performance.

Ethylene glycol is heated continuously during uniform stirring. Stirring must not be vigorous. The heating kettel contains thermostat at which is so adjusted that it maintains the temperature of fluid between 70° to 80°C.

Other anticorrosive agents are added slowly one by one with continuous and homogenous stirring. When mixing/blending is complete and a homogenous fluid is obtained this is then transferred to another cooling kettle in which it is cooled down.

This cooled fluid is ready for packaging in bulk containers or in pouches of 1 Kg as desired.

It is desired to fill in pouches of 1 kg. It is fed to the automatic pouch filling and sealing machine. The pouches are printed with the product name, manufacturers address and other essential information which is necessary for customers; such as use method, dilution needed, possible hazard, other safety informations about the product with the date of manufacture and batch no.

Formulation--

Ethylene glycol	-----	93.00 Parts
Water	-----	3.15 Parts
Sodium Silicate	-----	1.00 Parts
Sodium Mercapto Benzothiazole	-----	0.60 Parts
Mineral oil	-----	1.00 Parts
Trisodium Phosphate	-----	2.15 Parts
Dimethyl Silicone	-----	0.10 Parts

Manufacturing Process

First of all, take suitable grade of proper chemicals and separate out organic and inorganic chemicals.

Then take proper weight for proper amount finished product. The Inorganic additives are mixed with water and homogenized in ribbon blender. Similarly take the organic additive and mix with mineral oil and homogenize properly. Now take ethylene glycol in jacketed vessel where the temperature is maintained in the range of 70 to 80°C, by passing the steam through jacket of vessel. Then slowly the organic and inorganic mixtures are added in the not ethylene glycol and stir slowly with an-stirrer fitted in the jacketed vessel. After 30-40 minutes the operation will be completed. Then the product is strained or filtered to separate out the suspended particles and its quality is tested.

As the Quality Standard is coming in the range, then product is packed in the glass or plastic printed bottles and send for marketing.

PLANT ECONOMICS OF COOLANT (ENGINE)

Rated Plant Capacity = 500.00 LIT/Day

LAND & BUILDING(Land area required 500 sq. mtrs.) = Rented

PLANT & MACHINERY

1. Stainless steel Jacketed Vessel oil heated with Stirrer with 1/2 HP motor
2. Small Stainer to strain the coolant
3. Steel tank
4. Laboratory testing equipment.
5. Weighing balance, weights and other miscellaneous.
6. Pipes fittings, motors pumps.

FIXED CAPITAL

1.	Plant & Machiner	Rs.	3,65,000.00
2.	Other Fixed Assets	Rs.	1,11,000.00
	TOTAL	Rs.	4,76,000.00

RAW MATERIALS

1. Ethylene glycol
2. Propylene glycol
3. Sodium Benzoate
4. Sodium Silicate
5. Sulfonated Lard oil
6. Organic Dye
7. Packaging material Tin container

Coolant (Engine)

TOTAL WORKING CAPITAL/MONTH

1. Raw Material		Rs.	5,70,375.00
2. Salary & Wages		Rs.	16,875.00
3. Utilities & Overheads		Rs.	49,175.00
	TOTAL	Rs.	6,36,425.00

TOTAL CAPITAL INVESTMENT

Total Fixed Capital		Rs.	4,76,000.00
Total Working Capital for 1 Month		Rs.	6,36,425.00
	TOTAL	Rs.	11,12,425.00

TURN OVER/ANNUM

By selling of Coolant Engine 1,50,000 litre Coolant.	Rs.	90,00,000.00

PROFIT SALES RATIO = Profit / Sales x 100 = 12.26 %

RATE OF RETURN = Operating profit / T.C.I x 100 = 99.22 %

BREAK EVEN POINT (B.E.P) = 34.30 %

Chapter - 18

Cleaning Powder (Vim Type)

The powder commonly employed for the cleaning of household utensils is known as utensils cleaning powder. It is available in the market in various trade names such as "Vim" "NIP" and many others.

The cleaning powder for utensils is of universal type and can be employed for cleaning of aluminium, Brass & Stainless Steel utensils, crockery, sanitaries etc. The product is a very common known in every houses from lowest to highest class.

Among all brands, cleaning powder VIM has captured a good market because people do not respond the products which have recently been introduced in the market, but VIM is most popularized for more than last two decades.

MANUFACTURING PROCESS

The manufacture of Utensils cleaning powder is very simple and involves only mixing in proper proportions according to the selected formulations. During the compounding of product, it should be strictily noticed that what qualities are alkalinity or PH, values, capability of cleaning, water, conditioning effect, capability of cleaning, water, conditioning effect, capability to convert the oil or oilyness into emulsion foamness etc.

There are different compound procedures, for the manufacture of utensils cleaning powder and the proper method should be adopted depending upon the formula used to obtained good quality product. All procedures are described below :

If the soap Powder has to be incorporated in the formula, it is better to add in a little wet conditions though soap powder can also be added in dry form. If it is mixed in wet from the water is prinkled on the soap powder and the quantity of water should be so adjusted that the mixture is obtained in crystalline hydrated form. In this soap powder mixture, other ingredients, mixed together as per formula.

Cleaning Powder (Vim Type)

In the dry mixing of ingredients, the care should be taken that no lumps or cakes are formed. The reason for forming of lumps is presence of eater soluble contents in the mixture. Inspite of complete, absorption of moisture in the mass, a thin layer, or moisture is formed in the materials which mix with whole of mass and as a result the mixture may become wet and form lumps.

For example, caustic soda which produces moisture and trisodium crystals which become effloresence with the effect of moisture, when mixed becomes, gummy and lumpy. Therefore such chemicals should be selected in the formula which produces moisture or effected to moisture. For instance, trisodium should not be used where caustic soda has been in use and when caustic soda in use no effloresent chemical should be used.

The above details have been given for the quality control point of view.

Now, the cleaning powder is prepared in the powder mixer. Here, all the ingredients are fed one by one in the mixer which is

kept on. When in the ingredients, are added, it is stopped for few minutes and after adding whole quantity of the ingredients, it is again started. Finally, when all the ingredients, have been added the mixer is again started for about one hour.

The ribbon blender type mixer is used for blending or compounding of the ingredients.

This mixer uses helical ribbons to move and mix the materials can be fed to one end of the mixer and removed from the other end.

Ribbon cross section and pitch, clearance between outer ribbon and shell, and number of spirals, on the ribbon are some features which can be varied to accommodate materials, rapidly to fibrous sticky materials that require positive discharge aid. Twin shell blenders is a popular mixer for blending solid. The units rotates, there by continually dividing and remixing the batch of solids to be blended. The materials to be blended is loaded into the unit through the two batches, at the top of each shell. After mixing, the material is discharged through the value attached to the flange at the bottom.

Tip speed of ribbon mix is about 90 meter/minutes and twin sheel tumbler is 500 to 1000 m/minutes.

After thorough mixing of the ingredients, the powder is now screened to 200 mesh screen and packed in 1 kg, 2-1/2 kg and 4 kgs containers as per requirements of the customers.

For packing of the materials, there is an electric operated packing machine driven with 2 HP motor.

The product after packing is marketed.

FORMULATIONS

NO.1 :	PARTS
Sodium Carbonate	50
Soda Ash	200
Sodium Metasilicate	50
Tetra Sodium Phosphate	50
French Chalk	35
Fine Ash (of Burnt Wood's Chemical)	600
Basic Violet Colour	10
Basic Methyl Blue Colour	05
	1000

NO.2 :	
Trisodium Phosphate	10
Sodium Carbonate	20
Sodium Metasilicate Pentahydrate	15
Sodium Tripolyphosphate	25
Sodium Dodecyl Benzene Suffonate (Solid)	5
Telcom Powder	25

PLANT ECONOMICS OF CLEANING POWDER (VIM TYPE)

Rated Plant Capacity = 800.00 Bags/Day

LAND & BUILDING (Land 500 Sq.mt.) = Rented

PLANT & MACHINERY

1. Grinder machine with motors
2. Mixer equipped with motors
3. Spray Drier
4. Polythene bags sealing machines

FIXED CAPITAL

1. Plant & Machinery	Rs.	2,00,500.00
2. Other Fixed Assets	Rs.	55,000.00
TOTAL	Rs.	2,55,500.00

Cleaning Powder (Vim Type)

RAW MATERIALS

1. Soda Ash
2. Soda Metasilicate
3. Tetra Sodium Phosphate
4. French Chalk
5. Fine screened & grinded burnt wood charcoal Ash
6. Violet color
7. Baric Methylene blue colours

TOTAL WORKING CAPITAL/MONTH

1. Raw Material	Rs.	1,02,272.00
2. Salary & Wages	Rs	36,661.00
3. Utilities & Overheads	Rs.	68,000.00
TOTAL	Rs.	2,06,933.00

TOTAL CAPITAL INVESTMENT

Total Fixed Capital	Rs.	2,55,500.00
Total Working Capital for 1 Month	Rs.	2,06,933.00
TOTAL	Rs.	4,62,433.00

TURN OVER/ANNUM

By sales of 240000 bags of 2.5 kg. each	Rs.	28,80,000.00

PROFIT SALES RATIO = Profit / Sales x 100 = 9.94 %

RATE OF RETURN = Operating profit / T.C.I x 100 = 61.89 %

BREAK EVEN POINT (B.E.P)= 68.17 %

Chapter - 19

Cosmetics Industry (Modern)

Shampoos:-

Soaps usually contain too much alkali which is bad for hair and scalp. Shampoos are safer-they are designed to clean the hair and scalp without seriously reducing natural, oiliness, so that the hair is left with a natural gloss and in a soft and managable condition. In selecting a proper detergent for the shampoo it is necessary to know the effect of detergent on the surface, its stability and efficiency at an economic concentration.

Modern shampoos are based on sulphated fatty alcolhols and sulphonated fatty alcohol ethers. Triethanolamine lauryl sulphte is a brown transparent viscous liquid and is the most widely accepted cleaning agent used in shampoos. Sodium lauryl sulphate is powder highly soluble in water and is a good emulsifier, it may also be obtained as a paste. Mono ethanolamine laurly sulphate is similar to triethanolamine laryl sulphate and its viscosity can be increased by adding sodium chloride. Turky red oil or sulphated castor oil is a viscous water-miscible liquid having good detergent and emulsifying properties.

AUTOMATIC FFS BM 240 L

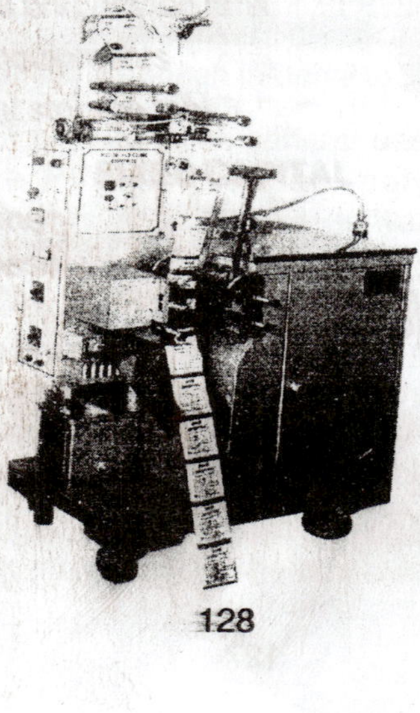

To get a good shampoo it is necessary to add certain additives to basic detergents to impart certain good properties. These additives are described here. Opacifiers like spermaceti, common salt, magnesium stearate and magnesium silicate etc. are used. Some people prefer clear shampoos and for this clarifiers like butyl alcohol, isopropyl alcohol, ethyl alcohol, terpinol, pine oil, diethylene glycol, STPP and TSP are used. Lanolin and its derivatives, isopropyl myristate, and CMC are good finishing agents; they give shine to the hair. Glycerol, propylene glycol, sorbitol and urea help retain moisture thus keeping the hair soft thus conditioning the hair.

Thickening agents increase the visosity of the shampoo thus increasing the consumer appeal who thinks that more viscous shampoo means more powerful product. CMC, tragacanth and acacia gums, methyl cellulose, PVA and PVP are good thickeners but tend to leave a film on the hair. Newer thickners are diethanolamides of lauric acid and the glycol or glycerol stearates. They do not leave any films. Foam builder are also incorporated in shampoos to give better and stable foam, preservatives are added to shampoos to protect them from deterioration by bacterial or mould action. Formaldehyde, methyl-and prophyl-hydroxybenzoate are the usual preservatives. Newer preservatives used are chloro salicylanilides and thiuram disulphides. To finish the bacteria of the scalp certain antibacterials like chlorosalicylanilide, thymol, bacitracin and hexachlorophene are added. In some cases antidandruff compounds are also incorporated.

TALCUM POWDER

Talcum powder is used after bath to absorb moisture and perspiration. It works as a lubricant and reduces irritation caused by rubbing of two body parts. A good talcum powder should be white, should posses good 'slip' and should be lustrous without being gittery.

Talcum powder should contain a metallic stearate preferably zinc stearate to give extra lubrication. Zinc stearate being mildly antiseptic is considered to be better than magnesium stearate. The amount of these stearates use is from 4% to 10%. Boric acid is used sometimes for its antiseptic action. Light calcium carbonate or light magnesium carbonate is used to increase fluffyness. They are absorbant carriers of the perfumes used for powders.

HAIR REMOVERS

Various methods are in use since a long time for the removal of hair for various purposes. Hair is removed of hair by plucking, electrolysis, X-Ray etc; and the term depilation is used when chemical degradation of human hair is carried out by locally applying various preparations, containing sulphides. Apart from all these saving with razor is also down, but this procedure is considered to be tedious and hazardous due to cuts and scratches. Electrolysis is very costly and while shaving all the areas can not be seen; so much so pulling out with tweezers is painful and dangerous. This two methods consisting of depilatory creams and use of epilating waxes or other adhesives compositions are in use.

PERFUME SPRAY

Every aerosol consists of a gas tight container, a valve closure, an actuator button and a protective cap; in a majority of packs dip tubes are present. The operation an aerosol is based on the discharge of its contents by the pressure of a compressed gas or the vapour phase generated by a propellent presant in the container as a liquid. The container may be constructed of metal, glass or plastic. The most extensively used materials being tin plate and aluminium. The design of the actuator button attached to the valve particularly the shape and size of the orifice, largely determines how the product is dispensed. When the valve is actuated, the pressure inside the container forces the liquid concentrate through the dip tube, pass the value, into the actuator button and then out into the atmosphere in the form of a stream, must, spray or foam.

The perfume compounds used in aerosol containers contain mostly essential chemicals. Essential oils are obtained from plants, flowers etc. Commonly used essential oils are rose, bay, theyme, patchoulli, lavender, orange blossam, caraway almond, sandalwood, cedar, cinmammon, cascarilla, lemon & nutmeg oils. Musk, Civet, ambergus etc. are the commoly used perfumery materials from animal sources. Natural perfumery materials are quite expensure and thus synthetic materials are now-a-days being increasingly used.

FORMULATIONS

1. SHAMPOOS:-	percent
Sodium Lauryl Sulphate 30%	20
Coconut diethanolamide	5
Glycol Stearate	1.0
Preservative:	
Methyl p-hydraoxybenzoate	0.1
Formaldehyde	0.1
Sodium benzoate	0.1
Phosphoric acid to pH 7.5 - 80	q.s

Sodium Chloride	0.25
Yellow dye	q.s
Perfume	q.s
Egg (Powdered or whole)	2.0
Water	To 100

2. Coconut oil Shampoo:	Percent
Coconut oil	7
Potassium hydroxide 85%	1.1
Water	68.7
Perfume	1.0
Olive Oil	9.9
Sodium Hydroxide 95%	4.4
Ethyl alcohol	2.8
Palm oil	5.1

MANUFACTURING PROCESS (SHAMPOO)

The formulation being dealt with is as described below :

1) Sodium lauryl sulphate 30%	20
2) Coconut diethanolemide	5
3) Glycol Stearate	1.0
4) Preservative	
Methyl p-hydroxy benzoate	0.1
5) Formaldehyde	0.1
6) Sodium benzoate	0.1
7) Phosphoric acid to PH 7.5 to 8.0	q.s
8) Sodium chloride	0.25
9) Yellow Dye	q.s
10) Perfume	q.s
11) Egg (Powder or whole)	2.0
12) Bithionol	0.1
13) Selenium sulfide	0.1
14) Water	to make 100

The detergent is sodium lauryl sulphate. Coconut diethanol amide which is used acts as a foam stabiliser. Glycol stearate acts as an opacifier and pearlescent agent. Coconut diethanolamide is dissolved with about half the total amount of detergent untill a solution is effected. The remaining quantity of detergent is then added. Gradually the perfume is dissolved in the cold concentrated detergent. The yellow or any other dyes is dissolved in adequate amount of water and added to the mix. The remaining water is finally added with gentle stirring to avoid incorporating air bubbles and the formation of an excessive amount of broth. The preservative included in the formulation should be added in the form of solution of formaldehyde, as per the stoicometric requirements of the formulation. Perfumes are used in shampoos at concentrations of 0.3 to 1.0 per cent and 0.5% being generally accepted level. It is also used to add a suitable water soluble dyestuff and other ingredients of suitable proposition.

Coconut fatty acid diethanolamide is a yellow viscous liquid which finds application as foam booster in the manufacture of detergents and shampoos and also as an emulsifier and solubilishing and foam boosting properties to the liquid detergents. The coconut diethanol amides are good cleansing agents of the non-ionic type but the solubility involves a certain proportion of free diehanolamine in the product to make it completely soluble and useful. These ester amides of the dispersible type are extremely useful finishing agents and impart softness. Its composition is usually 60-70% amide, 1% water and 7% ester. PH of 1% solution of this compound is 8 to 9. Reactor is charged with 60 Kgs. coconut fatty acid and 63 kgs. diethanolamine. Heaters are switched an stirrer is given maximum speed. When the temperature reaches 130°C nitrogen is passed in the reaction mixture. Temperature is maintained at 165°C. As the reaction progresses the acid value of the product falls down which is determined at every 30 minutes. The raection is stopped when the acid values falls to 5 PH.

Lauric acid diethanolamide is a white waxy material having the composition - amide 90% water 0.5% ester 5-6% and free amine 1.2 to 3 %. It is used as foam stabilizer, as a surfactant and thickening agent in the manufacture of shampoos and detergents and as a perfume fortifier in soaps. The reactor is charged with 60 kgs. of lauric acid and 63 kgs, diethnolamine. Heaters are switched on an when the temperature reaches 50°C nitrogen is passed in the reaction is carried out at 170° till the acid value drops to 5.

Oleic acid mono-etha-molamide is an amber coloured viscous liquid soluble in naptha and kerosine. Its composition is 85% amide 1% water and 7-8% ester. It is used as a foam stabiliser and as a surfacing and thickness agent for shampoos and detergents. The reactor is charged with 84 kgs. of double distilled oleic acid and 18 kgs. of monoethamolamine. Heaters and stirrer are switched on. Nitrogen is passed at 120°C and temperature is mainted at 170°C. Acid value is checked every half hour till it drops to 5.

It may be noted that any of the above three chemicals may be used as a foam stabilizer in the formulation.

FORMULATIONS AND MANUFACTURING PROCESS

Talcum Powder

1.

	Parts
Talc	95
Light Magnesium Carbonate	5

Perfume is added magnesium carbonate and allowed to stand for some time. The remaining powders are then added and sieved. A concentration of 0.5 % of perfume is generally adequate.

2.

	Parts
Zinc stearate	5
Light Calcium Carbonate	25
Talc	70

3.

	Percent
Zinc Stearate	5
Zinc oxide	5
Light magnesium Carbonate	15
Talc	75

Zinc oxide is a mild astrigent for the skin and is also soothing and has some healing effect to skin chafing or minor abrasion. It also helps in releving the prickling and irritation associated with prickly heat.

Hair Remover

		Parts
1.	- Calcium Thioglycolate Trihydrate	60
	- Calcium Carbonate	200
	- Titanium Dioxide	20
	- Cetyl alcohol	50
	- Sodium Lauryl Sulphate (Powder or needles)	5
	- Water (softened or distilled)	615
		1000

Perfume	0.2 %
Calcium Hydroxide sufficient to adjust pH value.	

2.

	Parts
Calcium Thioglycollate trihydrate	60
Calcium Carbonate	175
Mineral oil (Cosmetic grade)	50
Cetyl Alcohol	50
Sodium lawryl sulphate	5
Glycoine	35
Water	625
	1000

NAIL LACQUER/ NAIL POLISH

			%
(A)	Nitrocellulose RS ½ Sec. Dry	-	15
	Santolite	-	7.50
	Dibutyl phthalate	-	3.75
	Butyl Acetate	-	29.35
	Ethyl Alcohol (From Nitrocellulose)	-	6.40
	Butyl Alcohol	-	1.10
	Toluene	-	36.90
(B)	Pigments	-	3%
	Pearl essence	-	2%

Pigments Organic Type

Lithols (D & C Reds Nos. 10, 11, 12 and 13).

Lithol rubines (D & C Red No. 7)

ToB-BoN Marron (D & C Red No. 34)

D & C Yellow No. 5 Lake

D & C Red No. 2 Lake.

Inorganic Type (Cosmetic Grade)

Titanium Dioxide

Yellow and red iron oxides.

NAIL BLEACH

Formulation - I

Orange flower water	-	95
Citric Acid or Lemon Juice	-	5

Method

Mix all the ingredients together.

Formulation - II

Glycerine	-	10
Rose Water	-	40
Hydrogen Peroxide (5 Vol.)	-	50

Method

Mix all the ingredients together.

NAIL VARNISH REMOVER

Acetone	-	98
Glycerine	-	2
Perfume -		1-3 drops.

Method: Mix all the ingredients together.

NAIL LACQUER

Cellulose nitrate	3.2
Denatured alcohol	1.4
Butyl acetate	19.3
Ethyl alcohol	19.3
Toluene	19.3
Propyl methacrylate resin	15.0
Plasticizer (D.B.P)	3.2

2. An example of nail lacquer is given below which can be modified according to need. It may be pigmented by adding a sufficient quantity of a concentrated dispersion of colour to bring the pigment upto 3.5% of the total. This higher pigment content improves wear resistance of the enamel.

	Percentage
Nitrocellulose (R. S. 1/2 sec dry)	15.0
Santolite (Antiscaling agent)	7.5
Dibutyl phthalate	3.8
Butyl acetate	29.3
Ethyl alcohol (associated with ethanol)	6.4
Butyl alcohol	1.1
Toluene	36.9

Process

Nitrocellulose is dissolved in solvent and then plasticizer and resin are added with thorough stirring. Agitation is continued for several hours or unitl solution of all ingredients are complete pigment dispersions are then added.

After Shave Lotions	**Percentage**
Ethyl Alcohol Specially denatured	60
Prinylene glycol	3
Water demineralised	36
Perfume	1

Process

Dissolve the perfume and propylene glycol in the alcohol and add the water slowly, stirring well to avoid locally high concentrations of water precipitating. The less soluble components of the perfume. Allow the solution to stand for several hours at about 4°C. Then filter.

LIPSTICKS

Formulae		Gms.
1.	Castor oil	60.0
	Lanolin, anhydrous	12.0
	Candellila wax	9.0
	Isopropyl myristate	8.0
	White beeswax	5.0
	Carnauba wax	3.0
	Ozokerite	3.0
	Flavour (usually rose)	one drop
	Eosin	one microspatula-full
	Colours	one to fifteen micro-spatula-full.
	Perfume	one drop
	Preservative (Nipagin M) or (0.25 g Nipasol M + 0.02 g Progallin)	one microspatula-full

Method : Weight the ingredients very carefully. Then take a clean beaker and melt all the oils and waxes together with eosin and preservative. Add perfume and flavouring. This base is sufficient for making about 18-24 lipsticks. If more than one colour is desired, about ¼ of the base is taken and mixed together with the required colour. This is then melted down and poured into a mould and allowed to set. Each stick is then removed and passed through a bunsen flame quickly to give gloss. If muted colours are required, the colours are mixed with titanium dioxide to the required shade.

Note: The eosin in the lipstick can be left out if anyone is allergic to this.

2.

White beeswax	17.0
Ceresin wax	33.5
Lanolin	5.5
White petroleum jelly	27.0
Cetyl alcohol	6.0
Olive oil	11.0
Eosin	one microspatula-full
colours	one microspatula-full
Flavour	one drop
Perfume	one drop
Preservative (Nipagin M) or (0.25 g NIpasol M + 0.02 g Progallin)	one microspatula-full

Method : As above

3.

White beeswax	36.0
Lanolin	8.0
White petroleum jelly	36.0
Cetyl alconol	6.0
Castor oil	8.0
Carnauba wax	5.0
Colours	one to fifteen micro-spatula-full
Flavour	one drop
Perfume	one drop
Preservative (Nipagin M) or (0.25 g Nipasol M + 0.20 g Progallin)	one microspatula-full

Method: As above.

4.

Castor oil	60.0
Candellila wax	8.0
Isopropyl myristate	7.5
Lanolin	10.0
Beeswax	4.5
Carnauba wax	2.5
Ozokerite	2.5
Colours	5.0
Flavour	one drop
Perfume	one drop
Preservative (Nipagin M) or (0.25 g Nipasol M + 0.02 g Progallin)	one microspatula-full.

Method: As above

Chapter - 20

Dry Cleaning

Laundry workshops work on job work basis. This industry can be set up at any scale of production without a disadvantage. The scope of industry is directly linked with the population growth.

On an average 300 kgs per Capita fabric cleaning in India leads to a demand of 225 million tonnes of laundry load. This demand is yet to rise with the rising awareness towards laundry washed clothings.

The number of laundries have certainly increased in last few decades, but still, the demand is not fully met. Many more new laundry workshops need to be established in every part of the country.

LAUNDERING PROCESS

SORTING

The sorting process is for the purpose of grouping articles according to their use and subsequent washing, consideration being paid to fabric and colour.

INSPECTION AND MENDING

Articles are looked over so that attention may be given to those that need mending, or any other special attention. For example, pockets should be brushed out, and any pins or metal buttons likely to rust should be removed.

STAIN REMOVAL

1. Try to ascertain nature of stain.
2. Remove immediately, or as soon as possible.
3. Note the material to be treated.
4. Try simplest methods first, i.e. washing land open-air bleaching.
5. Treat area covering stain rather than the whole article.
6. Repeated applications are better than one strong one.
7. Test use of any strong agent on corner of article before use.

8. Neutralize acidic substance after use, and rinse in four changes of water.
9. Wash and boil article, if possible, after use of chemicals.
10 If nature of stain is uncertain, treat in the following way until it is removed: (a) with cold water; (b) with warm water; (c) with open-air bleach if necessary; (d) in an alkaline solution, and rinse; (e) in an acidic solution, and rinse; (f) bleach by artificial means; (g) repeat processes as above; (h) try solvents, on dry material.

STEEPING

This process is of great importance, and its value is often underestimated. Soft water is essential to obtain maximum results, and enough time (as fabric permits) must be allowed.

PURPOSE OF STEEPING

1. To wet the article, the necessary preliminary to washing.
2. To dissolve soluble matter, with the result that it is removed, held by the water in solution.
3. To loosen and remove insoluble matter by means of the "Brownian movements" of the molecules of which the water is composed, so that it is held by the water in suspension.
4. To emulsify grease.
5. To break down the resistance of complex stains.

WASHING

Soiling matter which has been loosened in the steep is absorbed by the washing solution and held in suspension, and grease still in the fabric is emulsified. A synthetic detergent solution emulsified more effectively than soap, but is likely to be less capable of holding matter in suspension. When the use of a synthetic detergent is desirable, the fact that it is less cleansing than soap can be overcome, when washing very soiled articles, by steeping in synthetic detergent solution, and washing with soap first, and then synthetic detergent. Particularly soiled parts can be treated by applying the synthetic detergent, in powder or concentrated liquid form, to the damp fabric and applying friction suitable to the fabric.

RINSING

Rinsing carries away the washing water, and with it the soiling matter removed from the fabrics. After washing with soap, hot rinsing waters are used until the soap is clear, followed by cold rinse.

WRINGING

This process is carried out by hand or by means of a machine wringer, worked by hand or electricity. Both methods are suitable for cotton and linen. Delicate cotton, woolen, silk and rayon fabrics are squeezed by hand, in place of wringing, followed by squeezing or machine wringing in a towel to absorb the water.

BLUEING AND STARCHING

Blueing is a method of treating white articles to obtain an apparent improvement of colour, the blue counteracting yellow discoloration from soap.

DRYING

The purpose of drying is to evaporate moisture, and, whenever possible, to bleach at the same time by carrying out the process in the open air.

DAMPING AND FINISHING

Damping gives back to the dried fabric sufficient moisture for good finishing.

PLANT ECONOMICS DRY CLEANING

Rated Plant Capacity = 400.00 Kgs. Garments/Day

LAND & BUILDING (Land 300 sq.mt) = Rented

PLANT & MACHINERY

1. Cleaning machines
2. Steam press
3. Hydro-Extractor Machine
4. Drying Tumbler
5. Boiler

FIXED CAPITAL

1. Plant & Machinery	Rs.	1,84,000.00
2. Other Fixed Assets	Rs.	20,000.00
Total	Rs.	2,04,000.00

RAW MATERIALS

1. Benzene petroleum
2. Scented Solvents
3. Soap of Benzine
4. Benzol
5. Turpentine

TOTAL WORKING CAPITAL/MONTH

1. Raw Material	Rs.	39,100.00
2. Salary & Wages	Rs.	59,437.00
3. Utilities & Overheads	Rs.	22,500.00
TOTAL	Rs.	1,21,037.00

TOTAL CAPITAL INVESTMENT

Total Fixed Capital	Rs.	2,04,000.00
Total Working Capital for 1 Months	Rs.	1,21,037.00
TOTAL	Rs.	3,25,037.00

TURN OVER/ANNUM

Receipt by charging 1,20,000 kg cloth (dry cleaned) per year	Rs.	26,40,000.00

PROFIT SALES RATIO = Profit / Sales x 100 = 41.61 %

RATE OF RETURN = Operating profit / T.C.I x 100 = 337.97 %

BREAK EVEN POINT (B.E.P) = 30.51 %

Chapter - 21

Distilled Water

Distilled water is a special type of water is used extensively in laboratories, pharmaceuticals storage batteries etc. The impurities contained in natural water may be small in amount but their effect is cumulative. Natural waters vary considerably from one point to the other and at one fine of the year too another. Rain water is the purest form of natural occuring water. The water vapours thus rising from the surface are drifted by the winds onwards. They rise to high altitudes, where the condense in the form of small droplets. These droplets move in the sky in the form of clouds and go on aggregating continuously till they become heavy enough unable to support their weight when they fall down in the form of rain. Rain water in considered to be very pure, being produced by a kind of distillation and is used as distilled water in laboratories. The rainfall is however, during monson season lasting generally from July to September and a shoot spell during winter. Therefore this water is not sufficient, and hence the need for distilling water arise. Moreover this type of water collected in rainy season can be used in laboratories and storage batteries but for pathological purpose and pharmaceutical purpose, this type of water should not be used because while coming to earth, it is certain that some impurities get mixed which are wanted in distilled water used for above said purpose.

Water for injection must be distilled and sterlized with in 24 hours. This time elapsing between distillation and use of water in reparing injection should not be over twenty four hours. Unused portions should be discarded or resterilized unless following sterlization; the container is kept closed at all times and nothing enters except the filtered air needed for replacement as the water for injection is drown off.

RAW MATERIAL

The distilled water can be manufactured from potable water, from tubewell water, from well water, water from pond, and well etc. Sometimes sea water distilled out and salt is separated out etc.

PROCESS OF MANUFACTURE

Process of manufacture of distilled water is very simple and automatic. The raw water is heated in the evaporator and once the gases are removed the vapour is made to pass through a specially designed baffle to allow only pure dry steam to the condenser. The horizontally mounted inclived condenser with detachable and covers for cleaning has an outlet at the extreme end to allow volatile substance. Only pure distilled water passes out. The raw cool water is first made to pass around the tubes in the condenser where it reaches nearly to the boilling point thus economising the heating energy. This heated water passes to the evaporator through a water level maintaining pipe. Excess water is let out through the drain.

The evaporator is made of heavy gauge stainless steel plate wi detachable top cover and drain cock at the bottoms. The condenser and other parts coming is to contact with the distillate evaporator and the haffle are made completely of stainless steel.

If still is provided with a water level gauge glass inlet & outlet connectors. A aqua clear feeder unit is provided at the water inlet pipe end for the prevention of hard scale forming.

PLANT ECONOMICS OF DISTILLED WATER

Rated Plant Capacity	= 6,00,000 No/Year
Land & Building (Land Area 300 Sq.mts.)	= Rented

PLANT & MACHINERY

1. Distilled water still
2. Distilled water storage tank
3. Aqua clear feeder unit
4. Bio - filler
5. Miscellaneous, pipe fitting testing equipment etc.
6. Bottle filling & sealing machine.

FIXED CAPITAL

1. Plant & Machinery		Rs.	4,55,000.00
2. Other Fixed Assets		Rs.	90,000.00
	TOTAL	Rs.	5,45,000.00

RAW MATERIALS

1. Water
2. Packaging material (P.V.C. Bottle ml.)
3. Miscellaneous.

TOTAL WORKING CAPITAL/MONTH

1. Raw Material	Rs.	2,00,900.00
2. Salary & Wages	Rs.	25,250.00
Total	Rs.	2,26,150.00

TOTAL CAPITAL INVESTMENT

Total Fixed Capital	Rs.	5,45,000.00
Total Working Capital for 1 Months	Rs.	2,26,150.00
TOTAL	Rs.	7,71,150.00

TURN OVER/ANNUM

By sale of 600 in Bottle of cap. 1000 ml. each. (6,00,000 Nos.)	Rs.	48,00,000.00

PROFIT SALES RATIO = Profit / Sales x 100 = 39.16 %
RATE OF RETURN = Operating profit / T.C.I x 100 = 243.78 %
BREAK EVEN POINT (B.E.P) = 14.84 %

Chapter - 22

Detergent Powder

Synthetic detergents occupy a vital place in the present age particularly when the modern society is constantly looking for quick, effective and economic cleaning agents. Synthetic detergents emerged as a regular industry after second world war only. The development of this industry is closely linked with Petro-chemical industry which forms the basic for its raw materials.

Detergents when dissolved in water, acquire better cleaning properties and hence facilitates easy removal of dirt & dust and grease etc.

Apart from their use in clothes washing detergents also have applications in the following industries.

1. In industry, in laundry and dry cleaning.
2. In textile processing, grain milling, metel plating and foods canning.
3. In dairy foods and beverages processing and in restaurants.
4. In plant maintenance and industrial house-keeping.

Today, synthetic detergents are developed and developing countries account for the bulk of the washing product market.

The principal types of synthetic detergents are an ionic, non-ionic and employtics. Sodium dodecyle benzene sulphonate is an example of the ionic type while nylon phenol, nylone oxide obtained from ethylene oxide is the non-ionic type. The amploytic detergents like the alkyl amino propionates behave as cations in acidic solutions and like anions in alkaline solution.

The present project profile envisage the manufacture of Nirma Type detergent.

PROCESS OF MANUFACTURE

Detergent powder is made from acid slurry by incorporating into it various additives and builders and spray drying the product so formed. On a cottage scale, the ingredients are mixed in open air. The following ingredients are used in detergents :-

1. Acid slurry
2. C.M.C. (Carboxy Methyl Cellulose)
3. Trisodium polyphosphate
4. Trisodium Phosphate
5. Sodium Perborate
6. Optical whitening agent
7. Foam booster
8. Sodium silicate
9. Sodium carbonate
10. Sodium sulphate
11. Perfume

The composition of a good quality detergent can be written as under:-

Acid slurry	13%
C.M.C	1.0%
Trisodium phosphate	25.0%
Optical whitening agent	0.2%
Sodium perborate	1.0%
Trisodium polyphosphate	10.0%
Foam booster	1.0%
Sodium silicate	10.0%
Sodium carbonate	6.0%
Sodium sulphate	26%
Perfume	0.05%
Colour	0.05%
Moisture	7.7%

There are three processes which can be used for manufacture of detergent powder.

a) Pulverisation	By blending all components in a pulveriser.
b) Cold spray process	By crystallisation of a cold spray mix in a current of cold air.
c) Hot spray process	By rapid drying of cold spray mix in a current of hot air.

Process (a) gives a dense, heavy and dusty product and may form lumps in water. Process (b) and (c) require a spray tower and give product of better grade and lower density. This is particularly the case with hot spray process at a high temperature, which produce free flowing non dusting in the form of tiny hollow heads.

AUTOMATIC FFS BM 240 A (With Auger Filler)

In the hot spray process, optical whitner is dissolved in hot water and the desired colour is then dissoved in this solution. The blender is charged with the acid slurry (dodecyl benzene sulphonic acid). The above solution is then added followed by addition of solid ingredients like phosphates, carboxy methly cellulose, soda ash, foam booster, sodium silicate solution is added in the last. The order of addition of ingredients, pH and the temperature at each stage of addition determine the quality of the detergent powder. The stirring efficiency of the blender has important bearing on the production of a workable detergent powder.

The following formulations are applicable manufacture to the detergent powder:

FORMULATION

Ingredients	Parts/Wt.
1. Sodium dodecyl benzene sulphonate	10-30
2. Mixed phosphate	15-40
3. Sodium silicate	3-15
4. Carboxy methyl cellulose	1-12
5. Optical brightening agent	0.2-0.4
6. Sodium carbonate	0-20

7. Sodium sulphate 0-20
8. Foam booster 3-5
9. Perfume 0-2

PLANT ECONOMICS OF DETERGENT POWDER NIRMA TYPE

Rated Plant Capacity = 500.00 Kgs./Day

Land & Building (land requirement 200 sq.mt) = Rented

PLANT & MACHINERY

1. Mixer/Blender (hand operated)
2. Trays/Pan made of stainless steel
3. Grinding Machine
4. Weighing Machine
5. Weighing balance for packing
6. Miscellaneous

FIXED CAPITAL

1.	Plant & Machinery	Rs.	65,000.00
2.	Other Fixed Assets	Rs.	52,500.00
	TOTAL	Rs.	1,17,500.00

RAW MATERIALS

1. Soda ash
2. Acid slurry
3. T.S.P.
4. Sodium silicate
5. Sodium sulfate
6. Urea
7. Ethanolamine
8. Trialkylamine
9. Sodium perporate

TOTAL WORKING CAPITAL/MONTH

1.	Raw Material	Rs	72,765.00
2.	Salary & Wages	Rs.	23,250.00
3.	Utilities & Overheads	Rs.	38,750.00
	TOTAL	Rs.	1,34,765.00

TOTAL CAPITAL INVESTMENT

Total Fixed Capital	Rs.	1,17,500.00
Total Working Capital for 1 Month	Rs.	1,34,765.00
TOTAL	Rs.	2,52,265.00

TURN OVER/ANNUM

By sale of 1,50,000 kg Washing Powder	Rs.	22,50,000.00

PROFIT SALES RATIO = Profit / Sales x 100 = 25.61 %

RATE OF RETURN = Operating profit / T.C.I x 100 = 228.45 %

BREAK EVEN POINT (B.E.P) = 38.06 %

Chapter - 23

Dhoop Batti Sticks

The scope of dhoop sticks is not only in India, they have good export potential too. Every day, dhoop costing lakhs of rupees are exported to various countries particularly to Sri Lanka, Burma, Africa, Malaysia and Britain.

This industry is very simple and even a layman can start it with little investment. It also does not require full time job and some people in India are manufacturing it in part time and earning a lot.

The principal form in which incense is burnt in this country is as sticks. These are particularly made of sandal wood dust, but the incense burned in the western countries is mainly made of olibanum, some specimens contain a little charcoal, benzoin and storax. Of the incense sticks available in the market Mysore variety is the most popular and is sold in large quantity during religious ceremonies.

In manufacturing incense sticks, powdered woods and pieces are used but where possible they are replaced by essential oils and charcoal.

This industry can be started with an investment below ten thousand rupees and can provide good bread to family members if they are all prepared to do labour work.

Dhoop Batti, is a well known product amongest every children, men and women.

Dhoop Batti reminds an Indian mind of a temple, a shrine, its sacred perfume and the holy atmosphere of the places of worship. The perfume spread by dhoop sticks while it burns makes it more sacred to religious mind. Scientifically, the smoke which carries with it the volatile oils of incense is known to destroy air born material, deodorise the atmosphere and render the surroundings less congenial to communicable diseases. The qualities of dhoop sticks generally depends on the type and quality of the perfumes and chemicals used.

Dhoop Batti Sticks

PROCESS OF MANUFACTURE

The important raw material is maida lakri available with big grocery houses. The other raw material used is wood charcoal. These are got powdered with pulveriser. Thin bamboo sticks called tilli or seenk.

The details of the ingredients used in manufacturing dhoop sticks are given below:-

Woods-Agar, Sandal

Roots-Vetiver, Camphor Chips etc.

Barks-Cassia, Cinnamon

Leaves-Devdar leaves, Pacholi, Marjoran

Flower-Rose, Cloves and Champak

Seeds-Cardamon, Mace

Gums and Resins-Lohan Shilajeet etc.

	Part
Finely ground maida lakri	1/2
Finely ground wood Charcoal	1

This is made into a dough with the requisite quantity of water. The dough is kept on a table tapering towards the worker. A handful of bamboo sticks are held in the left hand at one end spread over the dough like Japanese fan, with the right hand these are rubbed over the dough which spreads over and covers the bamboo sticks very easily. About 2 inch length of sticks is left uncovered.

The above is a commercial process used by dhoop sticks maker and can be learned in a day. This produces ordinary stuff. For a better quality product processed as below :

	Part
Sandalwood flour	1
Raal	1
Wood charcoal	1
Googal	1

First of all, googal is kept in a mortar and rubbed with a sufficient quantity of water so that it becomes like sticky paste. The other ingredients already finelly ground and sifted, are incorporated in it and a dough is made. Rest of the procedure is the same as outlined before.

For deluxe quality product, about 10-15 grammes musk crystals per mound in the above dough are mixed. This will give very fine aroma whils burning the incense sticks.

Other Formulation with Process

	Percentage
Sandal	30
Black Agar	20
Vetiver	5
Kapur Kachri	5
Flowers and Leaves	10
Myrrh	20
Wood Coal and Other Material	10

Mix all the ingredients and stir to make homogenous mixture. Sift the mixture through 200 sieve mesh and little water to make the pasty form. This paste is spread on the wood sticks leaving about 2-3 space.

PLANT ECONOMICS OF DHOOP BATTI

Rated Plant Capacity = 200.00 Kgs/Day

LAND & BUILDING (Total Land 200 Sq. Mt.) = Rented

PLANT & MACHINERY

1. Pulverizer
2. Mixing Cum-Kneader
3. Weighing Machine
4. Wooden Tables
5. Rolling Machine
6. Other Miscellaneous

FIXED CAPITAL

1. Plant & Machinery		Rs. 45,000.00
2. Other Fixed Assets		Rs. 9,000.00
	TOTAL	Rs 54,000.00

RAW MATERIALS

1. Wood Coal
2. Ground Rel
3. Sandal Flour
4. Gel (Ground Wood)
5. Sticks
6. Plastic Containers

Dhoop Batti Sticks

TOTAL WORKING CAPITAL/MONTH

1. Raw Material		Rs	80,633.00
2. Salary & Wages		Rs.	28,750.00
3. Utilities & Overheads		Rs.	53,900.00
	TOTAL	Rs.	1,63,283.00

TOTAL CAPITAL INVESTMENT

Total Fixed Capital		Rs.	54,000.00
Total Working Capital for 1 Month		Rs.	1,63,283.00
	TOTAL	Rs.	2,17,283.00

TURN OVER/ANNUM

By Sale of 60 M.T. Dhoop Batti

Sticks in Plastic Packs of 10 Stick Rs. 45,00,000.00

PROFIT SALES RATIO = Profit / Sales x 100 = 55.63 %

RATE OF RETURN = Operating profit / T.C.I x 100 = 1,152.08 %

BREAK EVEN POINT (B.E.P) = 14.78 %

Chapter - 24

Dal Moth, Chanachur & Bhujia (Namkeen Industry)

Dal Moth, Chanachur & Bhujia are the important names enhancing the flavour and taste as processed foods. These are food products having no historical background and becomes in market and in social and cultural synonym as the society became more advanced.

Initially in long-long ago, people did not heard the name of Dal moth, Chana-Chur or Bhujia like food products. But now a days it is well known not only in India but world wide. These are mainly consumed during breakfast period and are very much during social & cultural periods. These are used as tasty & flavored food as well as in medicinal way, however, a little it may be, (according to ayurveda) because of their carminative stimulative digestive properties. India produces almost all these types of salty processed food products of grains all these types of salty processed food products of grains like Grams, Pulses etc.

It aid in digestion and adsorption of food possesses anthelmintic and anticeptic properties.

The main raw materials for these products are gram, pulses & spices. The various food additives & colours may be used to provide sophistications in the products. The raw materials are frequently available in India.

MANUFACTURING PROCESS

The manufacturing process of these food products are nearly same with a little difference. The various food products is i.e Dal Moth, Chanachur & Bhujia, manufacturing processes are given below individually :-

Dalmoth:

The process comprises soaking of pulses (Arhar, Moong, or whatever it may be) in water and washing in a washing tanks. It is adaptable or batch or continuous processing or a combination of these processes. The outer skin is then peeling off in a skin peeling barrel drum. The peeling may also be done by sharp bamboo stick. The skin peeling is necessary to facilitate removal of moisture.

The pulses are then dried. The drying may be done in sun but sundry takes a long time for which an electrically drier is best suited. The drier may also be corn Gined with steam heating arrangement. Generally, the pulses are loaded in a trolley fitted with suitable trays & fed to the drier. The drying temperature is around 50-60°C.

After drying, whole of the pulses are fried in deep edible hydrogenated oil at 100-180°C for about 60-90 seconds. Excess oil is drained from the pulses. These are mixed with common salt, powder and spices mix. These are then packed in polythene bags. Storage can be prolonged by preventing rancidity, adding antioxidant and a synergost to the frying oil.

Chanachur:

The processing's of chanachur differ from Dalmoth upto frying & mixing with spices.

Initially the required amount of chana is soaked in water in washing tanks and then it is beaten by light hammer it can be done manually but manual beating will take more time and will not be economical. Machine hammering is to be preferred for this purpose. When all came in flattered round shape then it is sent to frying section where these are fired with in edible hydrogenated oil. Then these are mixed with common salt powder & other spices mix. These are then sent to packing section where these are packed in polythene bags, Before packing addition of antioxidant and synergies can be done.

Bhujia:

Both yellow and white varieties of maize can be used for preparation of Bhujia, but the bhujia made from yellow maize will yield dense colour. Wheat & Gram can also be used to prepare bhujia. The gram or maize seeds are cleared and sintered and then these are polished, so that any foreign material deposited on its upper surface are removed. Then seeds are sent to pulverizer. The ground flours coming from pulverizer, which pass through sieve of mesh no. 1, are good for the purpose.

Then, dough is made from flour and other spices ingredients etc. i.e. floured spices and ingredients are mixed with water herewith in this stage. When a thin dough has been formed then it is fried on a deep edible oil contained in a pan heated with a local furnace or electrically or automatic furnace. The thin dough is passed through a siever having temperature. The aperture should be selected as per requirement. The frying is done around temp. 100 - 180°C. Then the fried material (Bhujia) is placed into a shape & size maker where required size can be get through it. Ultimately it should be sent to packing section where these all have been packed in polythene bags.

Dal Moth

Roasted or fried pulse	-	50 Parts
Black Pepper	-	2 Parts
Fumygreek	-	1 ,,
Cumin powder white	-	1 ,,
Cumin powder, black	-	1 ,,
Turmeric	-	1 ,,
Salt	-	3 ,,
Vinegar of mustard oil	-	2 ,,
Chilli	-	1 ,,

Chanachur

Channa (Gram)	-	20 Parts
Salt	-	2 ,,
Black Pepper	-	1 ,,
Mustard Rye	-	1 ,,
Cumin black	-	1 ,,
Lemon Oil (Terpeneless)	-	1 ,,
Chilli	-	1 ,,

Bhujia

Flour	-	50 Parts
Salt	-	4 Parts
Lemon Oil (Terpeneless)	-	2 ,,
Black Pepper	-	2 ,,
Cumin	-	1 ,,
Chilli	-	1 Parts

FLAVOUR & ESSENCES

The following flavour & essences may be used to provide flavour and aroma to the final product:-

Lemon Flavour Essence

Lemon Oil	-	28 Oz.
Orange Oil	-	8 Oz.
Amyl acetate	-	6 Oz.
Amyl butyrate	-	16 Oz.
Ethyl acetate	-	40 Oz.
Alcohol	-	16 Oz.

Orange Flavour Oil

Lemon Oil	-	4 Oz.
Amyl acetate	-	4 ,,
Ethyl acetate	-	2 ,,
Sweet Orange Oil	-	12 ,,
Amyl Butyrate	-	12 ,,
Alcohol	-	16 ,,

Universal Flavour Essence

Amyl butyrate	-	4 Oz.
Ethyl formate	-	12 Oz.
Amyl acetate	-	12 Oz.
Ethyl acetate	-	20 Oz.

PLANT ECONOMICS OF NAMKEEN

Rated Plant Capacity	=	60,000 Packs/Annum
Land & Building (Land Area 200 sq.m.)	=	Rented

PLANT & MACHINERY

1 Pulveriser
2. Disintegrator
3. Drying oven
4. Sewing Machine
5. Skin peeling barrel drum
6. Filling and Sealing Machine
7. Weighing Machine

FIXED CAPITAL

1. Pland & Machinery		Rs.	1,12,000.00
2. Other Fixed Assets		Rs.	55,000.00
	TOTAL	Rs.	1,67,000.00

RAW MATERIALS

1. Grains (Pulses & Gram)
2. Other ingredients
   (Like spices, chemicals etc.)
3. Oil (ediable oil as groundnut oil, sunflower oil) etc.
4. Packing Materials

TOTAL WORKING CAPITAL/MONTH

1. Raw Material		Rs.	59,500.00
2. Salary & Wages		Rs.	31,875.00
3. Utilities & Overheads		Rs.	20,400.00
	TOTAL	Rs.	1,11,775.00

TOTAL CAPITAL INVESTMENT

Total Fixed Capital		Rs.	1,67,000.00
Total Working Capital for 1 Month		Rs.	1,11,775.00
	TOTAL	Rs.	2,78,775.00

TURN OVER/ANNUM

Receipt by sale of 1/2 kg. Packs

(30000 kgs.x 2 = 60,000 Packs) Rs. 18,00,000.00

PROFIT SALES RATIO = Profit / Sales x 100 = 21.90 %
RATE OF RETURN = Operating profit / T.C.I x 100 = 141.42 %
BREAK EVEN POINT (B.E.P) = 44.44 %

Chapter - 25

Dairy Farm

The domesticated water buffallo is one of the gentiest of all farm animals. Despite an intimidating appearance it is more like a house hold pat-sociable, gentle and serve. In rural area the care of buffaloes is after turned over to small boys & girls aged about 4 to 9.

Another belief is that the buffallo is exclusively a tropical animal. River type buffalloes, However. have been used to pull snow plows during Bulgarian winter.

Breeds: The major genetic division of the buffalo are the swamp Buffalo of the eastern half of the Asia, which has swept back horns and the river buffalo of the western half of Asia which usually has the curled horns. There is also the mediterranean buffalo, which is of the river type but has been isolated for so long that it has developed some unique characteristics.

Although there is only one breed of swamp buffalo, certain sub-groups seem to have specific inherited characteristics. Swamp buffaloes range from 250 kg for some small animals in China, 200-300 kg in Berma and 500-600 kgs in Laos. Only in India and Pakistan are there well defined breeds with standard qualities. There are eighteen (18) river buffalo breeds in south asia which are further classified as the Murrah, Gujarat, Uttar Pradesh, Central Indian & South Indian breeds. These are the five groups and main breeds :-

Groups	**Breeds**
Murrah	Murrah,Nili/Ravi, Kundi
Gujarat	Surti, Mehsana, Jafarabadi,
Uttar Pradesh`	Bhadawari, Tarai,
Central Indian	Nagpuri, Manda, Pandharpuri,
	Sambal pur, Jerangi, Kala Handi,
South Indian	Toda, South Kanara,

The best known breeds are Murrah Nili/Ravi, Surti, Jafarabadi, Mehsana & Nagpuri.

Genetics:- The swamp buffalo has forty eight chromosomes, the river buffalo fifty similar in the two types and they cross breeds to produce fertile hy-brid progeny. Cattle however, have sixty (60) chromosomes and although mating between cattle & buffaloes is common, hybrids from the union are unlikely to occur.

Individual buffaloes show large variation in milk yield, conformation, horn shape, colour, meal production, temperament, growth rate & other characteristics.

The large bulls that would be best for breeding purposes are often being selected as draft animals and castrated, or sent to slaughter or shot by hunters.

YIELDS : In countries like India & Egypt, the milk yield of buffaloes is generally higher (680-800kg) than for local cattle (360-500 kg). However since selection for exceptional, large variations in yield occur between individual animals and milk production of dairy buffaloes falls short of its potential. Indian Government forms, average yields for milking buffaloes range from 4-7 kg per day in lactations averaging 285 days, Daily yields of 12 kg have been reported for some Bulgarian buffalo cows and a daily production of over 20 kg has been reported for some remarkable animals in India. A peak milk yield of 31.5 kg/day has been recorded from a champion Murrah buffalo in the All India Milk yield competition conducted by Govt. of India.

COMPOSITION OF CATTLE FEED

There is no definite composition to Buffalo feed compound but in general practice the following composition is followed :-

Ground nut Cake	25%
Wheat bran	27%
Grain Husk	15%
Maize	30%
Mineral	1%
Salt	2%

Some more formulations are as follows :-

A.

1. Wheat or rice bran	55%
2. Soyabean or ground nut cake	35%
3. Molasses	8%
4. Mineral supplement	2%

B.

Wheat or rice bran	26%
Coconut cake	64%
Molasses	8%
Mineral supplement	2%

C.

Citrus pulp	27%
Coconut cake	63%
Molasses	8%
Mineral supplement	2%

COMPOSITION OF MILK

Buffalo milk contains less water, more fat, slightly more lactose, and more protein than cow's milk. It seems thicker than cow's milk because it generally contains more than16 percent total solid compared with 12-14 percent for cow's milk. Although the butterfat content is usually 6-8 percent, it can go much higher in the milk of some well fed dairy buffaloes and in the milk of Swamp buffaloes (which are not normally used for milking). Cow's milk butterfat content is usually between 3 and 5 percent.

Because of its high butterfat content, buffalo milk has considerably higher energy value than cow's milk. Phospholipids are lower but cholesterol and saturated fatty acids are higher in buffalo milk. Studies have shown that digestibility is not adversely affected by this. Because of the high fat content, the buffalo's total fat yield per lactation compares favourably with that of improved breeds of dairy cattle, it is much higher than that of indigenous cows.

Normally the protein in buffalo milk contains more casein and slightly more albumin and globulin than cow's milk. Several researchers have claimed that the biological value of buffalo milk protein is higher than that of cow's milk, but this has not yet been proved conclusively.

MANUFACTURING PROCESS

The manufacturing process for dairy milk is started with the milking buffaloes by hand (at small scale) & milking buffaloes by machine (at large scale).

The detailed process is given here with :-

MILKING BUFFALOES BY HAND

The profitable operation of a dairy herd depends in a large part upon how well you milk your buffaloes. You can do everything else carefully and well, but if you do not milk your buffaloes properly, you can never be successful in dairying. Poor milking habits cause low production, mastitis, and poor quality milk. An important part of milking buffaloes is to produce the cleanest possible milk. Milk must be low in sediment.

Although machine milking is rapidly replacing hand milking, many dairymen still use the latter. In milking by hand, buffaloes must be carefully prepared to produce high quality milk.

PLANT ECONOMICS OF DAIRY FARMING (BUFFALOES)

Rated Plant Capacity = 300.00 Litres/Day

LAND & BUILDING (Owned land) = Rented

PLANT & MACHINERY

1. Milk reception tanks
2. Milk cans
3. Buffaloes
4. Misc. other equipment such as laboratory and testing equipments
5. Tubewell and Misc. etc. machines

FIXED CAPITAL

1. Plant & Machinery	Rs.	6,55,000.00
2. Other Fixed Assets	Rs.	8,000.00
TOTAL	Rs.	6,63,000.00

RAW MATERIALS

1. Raw Material for Buffaloes feed green fodder/Cattle feed
2. Health expenses (medicines) etc.

TOTAL WORKING CAPITAL/MONTH

1. Raw Material	Rs.	48,000.00
2. Salary & Wages	Rs.	12,320.00
3. Utilities & Overheads	Rs.	2,625.00
TOTAL	Rs.	62,945.00

TOTAL CAPITAL INVESTMENT

Total Fixed Capital	Rs.	6,63,000.00
Total Working Capital For 1 Month	Rs.	62,945.00
TOTAL	Rs.	7,25,945.00

TURN OVER/ANNUM

By sale of 108000 litres of Milk	Rs.	12,96,000.00

PROFIT SALES RATIO = Profit / Sales x 100 = 27.29 %

RATE OF RETURN = Operating profit / T.C.I x 100 = 48.72 %

BREAK EVEN POINT (B.E.P) = 42.24 %

Chapter - 26

Food Supply/Catering Business

Out Door Catering Business is the mobile Kitchen of modern vogue which caters to the taste of the modern man. It serves Veg./Non Veg. foods of different varieties including (Veg. Food, Chinese, South Indian and non-vegetarian foods).

In this business, one must have full-furnished kitchen comprising cooking system, ingredients for various foods, utensils, plates, sauces, spoon, forks, knives, etc. The cooking system comprises LPG-gas stove, gas cylinder and gas lighter. The counter of the van serves the purpose of serving the dishes to the customers where upon they put (if they like) their eatables for eating.

As people are becoming more modernized and meticulous about taste and they want ready-made instant food which there out door catering serve there to fulfill their desire at nominal cost.

CLASSIFICATION OF FOODS

VEGETARIAN FOOD

Chapati, Rice, Various veg. dishes etc.

CHINESE FOODS

Vegetable Chowmein.

Egg Chowmein.

SOUTH INDIAN FOODS

Idli, Dosa(Masala,Plain, Paper, Onion, Rava, Uthappam,etc.), Vada, Upma.

METHOD OF PREPARATION OF DIFFERENT ITEMS

IDLI

Ingredients

1 Cup rice.

½ Cup urad dal.

1 Teaspoon salt.

Method

1. Put mixture into oiled idli containers and steam in pressure cooker 5 minutes without the pressure cooker weight; or steam 15 to 20 minutes in a pan.

2. Serve with Sambhar and Chutney.

Chicken Stock

Ingredients

1 Carcass of chicken, with neck and wing sections.

1 Small onion cut into half.

1 Small carrot.

1 Tea spoon salt. .PA

Method

1. Add 4 cups water, onion, carrot and salt to chicken and pressure-cook 20 minutes.

2. If not using pressure cooker, add 6 cups water to chicken and cook,covered on slow fire almost 1 hour.

3. Strain.

4. Remove chicken flesh and add to soup when serving, if desired.

Masala Dosa

Ingredients

1 cup rice

½ cup urad dal

1 tea spoon salt.

Vegetable oil or ghee for flying.

For filling

½ teaspoon mustard seeds

1 large clove garlic, finely chopped

1 medium onion, finely sliced

1 green chilli, finely chopped

½ tea spoon turmeric powder

6 curry patta

3/4 teaspoon salt.

1 tea spoon vegetable oil or ghee.

Method

1. Soak rice and dal separately in water for 12 hours.

2. Blend 10 minutes or longer in electric blender, with required amount of water, till mixture is almost smooth.(It will remain, slightly gritty.) Mixture should be as smooth as possible and consistency of thick pancake batter.

3. Keep, covered 12 hours or longer till mixture has doubled in bulk and is frothy.

4. Add salt and stir.

5. Heat a tava or heavy dosa griddle and grease its surface with 1 or 2 teaspoons oil. Heat oil to medium hot (a few drops water sprinkled on it should splutter immediately) and pour about ¼ cup mixture onto middle of griddle, with the back of ball-shaped spoon, and starting from the centre, spread and mixture out thinly and evenly till you have a dosa about 15 cm (6 inches) in diameter.

6. Pour 1 teaspoon oil around outer edge of dosa, and allow to cook till golden on the under-side. Then turn over and cook other side for 1 or 2 minutes.

7. Remove onto a plate, place some potato filling onto half of dosa and turn the other half over the filling. Serve with Sambhar and Chutney.

For Potato Filling:

1. Boil potatoes, then peel and cut them into very small pieces.

2. Heat oil and fry mustard seeds. When they stop spluttering, add garlic and onions and cook 5 minutes.

3. Add chilli, turmeric powder and curry patta, and cook till onions are soft.

4. Add potatoes and salt and blend well. Add 2 to 3 tablespoons water and cook 2 minutes.

Hamburgers

Ingredients

½ kg(1 lb) minced beef
1 large onion, sliced into thin rounds
1 large tomato, sliced into rings
8 hamburger buns
Prepared mustard as needed
2 Tablespoon vegetable oil or ghee

Mix together

1 tsp salad oil

1½ tsp tomato ketchup

1 tsp Worcestershire sauce

1 tsp freshly ground black pepper

1 tsp salt

1 egg

Method

1. Mix salad oil mixture into minced beef.

2. Divide mixture into 8 equal portions. Flatten out each portion into a round 8 cm (3 inches) in diameter and keep 1 hour.

3. Heat oil in large frying pan, tilting pan so that entire surface is coated. Fry hamburgers 4 at a time cooking each side for 5 minutes. Remove and fry remaining hamburgers in the same way.

4. Slit buns horizontally in half and heat in oven. Spread bottom round of each bun with mustard, place one hamburger on it, pour some meat juice from frying pan over it, and top with onion and tomato rings. Put a dollop of mustard on hamburger and cover with top portion of bun. Prepare the remaining hamburgers the same way.

PLANT ECONOMICS OF FOOD SUPPLY/CATERING BUSINESS

Rated Plant Capacity	=	500.00 Nos/Day
LAND & BUILDING (Land Area 300 sq.mt.)	=	RENTED

PLANT & MACHINERY

1. LPG Stove
2. Gas Cylinders
3. Utensils
4. Electric Generater Set
5. Mixer
6. Deep fat freezer
7. Van & Its Body Fabrication

FIXED CAPITAL

1. Plant & Machinery		Rs	4,99,500.00
2. Other Fixed Assets		Rs.	43,500.00
	TOTAL	Rs.	5,43,000.00

RAW MATERIALS

Vegetables
(Potato, Peas, Cabbage etc)
Flour,
Pulses (All Types),
Onion,
Vinegar,
Salt,
Spices etc.

TOTAL WORKING CAPITAL/MONTH

1. Raw Material	Rs.	75,000.00
2. Salary & Wages	Rs	25,300.00
3. Utilities & Overheads	Rs.	18,750.00
TOTAL	Rs.	1,19,050.00

TOTAL CAPITAL INVESTMENT

Total Fixed Capital	Rs.	5,43,000.00
Total Working Capital For1 Month	Rs	1,19,050.00
TOTAL	Rs.	6,62,050.00

TURN OVER/ANNUM

By Serving Lunch Packs (Veg. & Non Veg.) to 150000	Rs. 30,00,000.00

PROFIT SALES RATIO = Profit / Sales x 100 = 47.13 %

RATE OF RETURN = Operating profit / T.C.I x 100 = 213.58 %

BREAK EVEN POINT (B.E.P) = 20.69 %

Chapter - 27

Gem Clips, Paper Pins & Staples

Paper pins are known to most of the people as these are used widely for pinning paper sheets in offices schools etc. The paper pin is made of mild steel wire of 20-22 SWG with a pointed end at one side and a well formed head on the other end. The pins are plated so as to make them resistant to rusting and corrosion, immediately after mechanical forming.

In the growing economy like ours, where establishments (both in public and private sectors) are growing in up by leaps and bounds to cope with development programmes, stationery articles like gem clips and paper pins stapples, being an intimate of parts office stationery, will have a bright future.

Gem clips and paper pins are used to hold two or more papers together, in every office. There are so many papers in an office related to correspondence, typed in loose pages, that they may get mixed up leading to confusions, so to keep them togeather some device was needed to hold them together. This job is done by paper pin and stapples etc. Gem clip present a number of advantages over the allpins. Gemclip does not damage the paper. It just holds the papers with spring effect, while pins make holes in the paper. But, paper pins provide a greater reliability in withholding papers together and just by removing the pin paper can be freed easily when so required.

Gem clip is made of nickel polished steel wire.

All pins, Gem clips and Staples Pins are used to hold two or more papers together. The only difference being that an all pin and gem clip can be removed easily when papers are needed to be separated, while a staple pins, if needed to be removed, is destroyed and can not be reused while an all pin can be removed and used again & again. An all pin is a straight pin with flattened head which never deserts papers tied with it unless & until some outer force is applied from the pointed size to push it headward.

PROCESS OF MANUFACTURE:-

Pin Manufacture: All pins are made on semi-automatic machine. These machines differ greatly in size and in design, but the principle of operation is much the same in all of them. Pins are made in a machine by five distinct operations :

Namely:

1) Forming the head.
2) Feeding the wire.
3) Pinching the wire.
4) Cutting the wire and forming the point.
5) Expelling the pin.

The head is formed by compressing and flattening against a die. The portion of the wire which project beyond this die remains after the precisely formed pin has been cut from the wire. This compressing and flattening is done by a hammer which is attached to a receprocating member, called a hammer stock, which in turn is actuated usually by a crank pin. The amount of wire which projects beyond the die, governs the size and thickness of the head and is regulated by adjusting the cutting knives to the proper distance form two dies.

Feeding the wire:

Wire coil hangs on the decoiler stand. Its one free end is fed into the machine where the pin-head forms. After the head is formed, the hammer moves away from the die, and the die opens up and allows the feed mechanism to push the wire with a nail-head. At the end, the correct distance is adjusted through the die, to give a nail of the required length. The feeding mechanism is driven by an adjustable crank on the flywheel of the machine and by adjusting this crank various lengths can be obtained. The feed mechanism also pulls the wire through a series of staggered rolls to straighten it.

Pinching:-

When the hammer has reached the end of the stroke, the wire has been fed the correct amount for the pin required and the die closes to pinch the wire. This thin action is motivated by crank at the crank shot.

Cutting Length:

Immediately after the wire is pinched, two knives each attached to a lever come together and cut the wire. These cutting knives are ground to form the point of the pin. At the same time, that the cut is made, this point is formed by pressing the wire into the shape required and in doing so, some of the metal is squeezed out or protrudes between the knives and is cut off by the machine. These cut-offs are called whiskers.

Ejection of ready pin :

Sometimes, because of dull knives or in sufficiently close adjustments, the pin will still adhere to the wire, when the cutting knives open up. The cutting knives opening the return stroke of the hammer and in order to remove this adhering nail, an expeller comes into action, knocking the pin downward out of the die cavity, or else, the next stroke of the hammer will break it.

Nickel Polishing:

After all mechanical operations, nickel polish is done as the ciips and pins polish done in Barrel type set-up.

Bright Nickel plating, which deserves the name, have been employed for barrel plating. Electrolytes are available which can be used with the same efficiency in open-ended and immersed barrels as the modern plating solutions employed in still baths.

The composition of solution used in barrel plating are similar to those used for still plating, although earlier solutions used to have much lower metal concentrations. Concentrations of 100 gms/ litre nickel sulphate used to be regarded as high and 150 gms/litre nickel sulphate as very high. Apart from nickel sulphate, earlier solutions also contained ammonium chloride, sodium sulphate, magnesium sulphate, magnesium chloride and sodium chloride etc.

Addition Agents:

The type of organic addition agents used in modern barrel plating solutions is less well known than the addition agents used in still baths.

Normally primary brightener i.e. a so called carrier brightener, such as benzoic acid sulphmide, sulphonamides or acryl sulphonic acid is employed. Other addition agents, such as, caramel sugar, have also been used.

In addition, a small amount of wetting agent is normally added in consideration the choice of wetting agent. Care must be taken to ensure that it does not give size to excessive foaming in the barrel are of the advantages of the use of melting agents is that they reduce the risk of staining an flat parts which tend to adhere to the barrel walls.

Typical brighteners for barrel nickel plating solution are:

1. Acetylene derivatives
2. Derivatives of oxypyrinidine
3. Quaternary ammonium compounds.

4. Amines.

5. Pyridine derivatives.

6. Dye stuffs eg.

The pH of barrel nickel plating solutions used to be maintained is below.

Barrel nickel plating solutions operate at room temperatures between 40 and 60°C.

Current densities of between 1 & 1.5 A/dm^2 or more in some cases may be considered.

The deposition rate of nickel in a barrel plating bath is normally higher in an immerged barrel unit than in an open ended barrel.

Plating Solutions:

The main characteristic of bright nickel plating solution is that it contains special addition agents which effect the deposits agents which effect the deposition of bright nickel. Bright nickel plating solution bath containe cobalt sulphate, nickel formate and formaldehyde as addition agents and is used cut with following camposition

	gms/litre
Nickel Sulphate	240
Nickel Chloride	30
Boric Acid	30
Nickel Format	45
Cobalt Sulphate	2.6
Formaldehyde	2.5
Ammonium Sulphate	0.8

The pH of the solutions is maintained at 5.5 to 4.5 and the temp. is 60°C.

The manufacturing process of staples is completely semi-automatic. The wire of required thickness is purchased from outside and is fed into the machine. The wire is cut and bent at 90°C on two points and come out. The pins are then packed manually and despatched.

PLANT ECONOMICS OF GEM CLIPS, PAPER PINS & STAPLE PINS

Rated Plant Capacity = 60.00 Kgs/Day
Land & Building (Land Area required 150 sq.mts.) = Rented

PLANT & MACHINERY

1. Gem clips & paper pins producing machine semi-automatic with dies and accessories
2. Wire stand & wire straightener with tensioning system
3. Automatic stapler pin making machine with all accessories
4. Electroplating unit with all the standard accessories.
5. Testing & Inspection Equipments Working tools, fixtures, weighing and counting m/c (electronic) etc.

FIXED CAPITAL

1. Pland & Machinery		Rs.	5,35,000.00
2. Other Fixed Assets		Rs.	1,00,000.00
	TOTAL	Rs.	6,35,000.00

RAW MATERIALS

1. M.S. wire (20 & 22 swg sizes) for Gem clips & Allpins (Paper pins)
2. Electroplating Chemicals and additives, Pickling Chemicals, etc.
3. Staple pin wires (as per specifications)
4. Packaging materials (ie. different sizes of printed card board/paper boxes) etc.
5. Miscellaneous stores

TOTAL WORKING CAPITAL/MONTH

1. Raw Material		Rs	1,24,500.00
2. Salary and Wages		Rs.	49,795.00
3. Utilities & Overheads		Rs.	52,700.00
	TOTAL	Rs.	2,26,995.00

TOTAL CAPITAL INVESTMENT

Total Fixed Capital	Rs.	6,35,000.00
Total Working Capital for 1 Month	Rs.	2,26,995.00
TOTAL	Rs.	8,61,995.00

TURN OVER/ANNUM

1. By selling 15000 Kgs.(3.0 crores) Gem Clips
2. By selling 15000 Kgs. (2.4 crores) Paper Pins
3. By sales of 4 lakh packets of Staple Pins of all sizes

TOTAL Rs. 34,05,000.00

PROFIT SALES RATIO = Profit / Sales x 100 = 12.92 %

RATE OF RETURN = Operating profit / T.C.I x 100 = 51.03 %

BREAK EVEN POINT (B.E.P) = 62.50 %

Chapter - 28

Herbal Cosmetics

Hair Dye Powder

The colouring of hair is one of the most important acts of adornment among those made by human since the origin of man. The guest for a change of external appearance has for expression in various ways in all civilization. This desire from being a secondary activity, as it is some times considered today can be linked to a whole series of fundamental attributes in the life of the individual and can even be linked to the several interact of the species and thus reflect its presence.

Heaving on one side the most ancient attempts and the imperial formula used, the matter has now entered the phase of a major industrial development, in that since world war -II there has been a great advance in the discovery and utilization of a series of now synthetic colorants for hair. Indeed it is established today due to 30 - 40 % of men & women uses its for this good appearance.

The usual reason for colouring the hair are the following to change the external colour of hair such as while to black or red. Because colour of hairs changes according to age.

The shade of the human hair results mainly from two pigments and cumelanin which is brown or black and phacomalanin, which is yellow or reddish. Eumelanin is formed from the amino acid tyrosine by oxidation with the enzyme tyrosinase. Tyrosine is also the precursas of phaeomalanin, but it seems that the presence of an O - eminophenol derived from tryptophane is also necessary.

Shampoo

It is used to wash and clean hair. During old days very rough soaps and other materials were used to wash hair. The rough type of soaps contained major preparation of caustic soda among their constituents. No doubt these soaps had good cleaning powder due to caustic content in the shape of saponific materials yet they spoil the human skin by their drastic action. This actually produced irritation and in some it ended in the production of some skin disease like irritation, skin iteping and also in some cases gave rise to demodetic scabies.

With the introduction of shampoos all the above muskscance was removed as they replaced the soaps at a very high speed. These shampoos are available as solid, paste liquid varieties.

Powder owing to the abundance of soft lather produced and it is possible that the use of liquid shampoos does not entail so much trouble. Liquid shampoos are virtually solution of soft soap in water with just sufficient spirit to aid through saponification. At one time more spirit was used to prevent a slight gelatation, the popular demand in bulk shampoos being for those with high viscosity, this can be obtained by leaving the shampoo exposed to air for a week or a fornight at the most. Emulsified coconut shampoos popularised the liquid variety but the demand for coconut preparation is probably not so great as it was the reason are the difficult in covering the odour of the oil and to fact that some coconut shampoos have the hair in a slightly greasy condition.

Creams

The word creams is in such common use that definition is almost superfluous. Indeed "Creamy" is often used to describe the texture or appearance of objects or products that cannot themselves claim to be creams.

In the content of cosmetics, the term "cream" usually signifies a solid or semi-solid emulsion, although it may be equally well be applied to non-aqueous products such as wax-solvent based mascras, liquid cycshadoures and ointments. Such are the number and variety of raw materials that are available to the cosmetic scientist for the formulation of skin creams and lotions, that no general text book could spare the space needed to list them all. The good, stable formulae to which these ingredients can give rise are too numerous for a complete catalogue even to be contemplated. Further, new materials emulsidhers, emolliens, moisturisers, heating materials are being produced and made available by suppliers continuously be out of date even before it was printed.

Hair Tonic

Hair tonic oil have a popular appeal for men and women through out the world. Today they are used in the most exclusive beauty saloons and by the primitive friber of Africa. The tonks of egyption king dating as for back as 3500 B.C. contain evidence of perfumed hair oils and it is known as the Indian, greeks and spomans made extensive use of available job and oils for personal grooming most of the products formerly used are were home made, being desired from special or sieset recipes although during the last few countries many shops and stores sold their own brands.

The need for hair oil appears to be constantly increasing. Hair not only oily acts as a protective covering for the head but is also an attractive features of men and women. Both of these factors protection and attraction are best accomplised by healthy hair and the beauty of hair is a measure of its health and of the efficiency with which it accomplis it task. The scalp normally sceretes more oils than do other skin surfaces. This oil coats the hair fibres and prevents loss of moistures. It keeps the hair in place and provides some easter.

Conditioner Shampoo

It is known as conditioning shampoo or shampoo conditioner. They are similar in application. However the former are intended primarily to cleanse and secondarily to improve manageability and promote desired feel and appearance. The latter are mainly designed to enhance untangle of wet hair and improve manageability of both wet and dry hair. The development of shampoo conditioners is mainly the result of the benefits and optimizing the properties of synthetic cationic polymers of which the efficacy is linked to the characteristics and amount of film deposited on the hair.

The ways in which conditioners act as well as the affects obtained, are various, it should always be borne in mind that they involve a number of extremely complete intractions, both among the compainds themselves which in most cases are statistical mixtures and with the hair. As a consequence, adjustment and the control of these affects stiffening, softening, untangling, compability, body , springback, antistacle, etc require a careful and skilled development according to the type of hair concerned and the surfactant system used.

Moisturizing

Of all the beneficial properties claimed for cosmetic creams, moisturizing is possibly the most widely used. The term stems from the discovery that water is the only material which will plasticize the order dead layers of the epidermos to give the much desired attribute we call "soft" smooth skin. Only the oil alone will not restore the flexibility.

To this end, many occlusive, non-water- permeable substances can be used, among them mineral and vegetable oils, lanolsis and silicones. These simple materials have occasionally been augmented by the use of mixtures of lipids and other fatty chemicals which have been designed to imitate the composition of the skin's natural oily secretions. The use of such artificial skin lipid has not been a noted commercial or even scientific success, largely because they are difficult to formulate into an emulsion that can be preserved microbiologically, and because they have not been shown to be air improvement ever simples, less expensive and readily available oils.

MANUFACTURE OF DYE POWDER

We heat D.A.P.P. emolient ester and stearyl alcohol also heat proplylene glycol and acetic acid in the separate tank at 80°C with the help of boiler.

In a big mixing tank disperse sulphur of black colour in the heated propylene glycol and acetic acid in 68% water and add D.A.P.P. emolliens ester it S.A. with the help of agitators slowly. Slowly when the fine mixing takes place then cool it until cream begins to get heavy and smooth sludge then add very slowly lead acetate and water into it, also use agitator for mixing upto the temperature of 35°C.

Now we use a drier to make the powder of it. The temperatures of drier is 90 - 100°C to form powder. After the collection of powder from drier we pack it in the glass bottles and polythenes bags for the market.

For the purpose of cooling we uses water for cooling with the help of cooling system.

Herbal Black Hair Dye Powder

Formulation

		Wt. %
1.	Powdered mehandi leaves (Henna)	60
2.	Powdered caanill flowers	10
3.	Walnut bark	12
4.	Kohl Powder	12
5.	Indigo leaves	6
	Total	100 %

Method of Manufacture of Dye Powder

In a grinder or pulveriser, add all the ingredients viz. mehandi leaves, comomile flowers, walnut bark, kohl powder, Indigo leaves in requisite proportionates and are well ground to fine powder which is packed in bottles or pouches (as desired)

HERBAL CREAM (COMFREY CREAM)

Melt the oils and waxes together over a water bath, cool and store in a refrigerator. Take a couple of teaspoons of this cream, melt it and add a teaspoon of any herb lotion or infusion of your choice.

Comfrey is a healing herb which is ideal if your skin is sensitive or has any irritation or spots. Take a handful of comfrey, liquidize it, then strain it and use. The comfrey residue should not be thrown away. Add a teaspoon of honey to a tablespoon or residue and use it as a face mask.

MANUFACTURING PROCESS

Manufacturing process of it is very simple. Only very less numbers of equipments required to make it. We should maintain the temperature of it at 40°C in starting.

We take a huge stainless steel tank with the jackets and agitator and connected with high speed motor. Then pour the isopropyl linoleate, glycerylstearate, di-sopropyl adipate, myslityl mysistate, PEG - 40 stearate, cetyl alcohol, ceteareth -20, quaternium-22 and propylene glycol. First mix these uniformly with the help of agitator and heat at 80°C with the help of steam. Steam is manufactured by baby boiler. After the homogeneous mixture we cool it upto 40°C and then add hydroxy ethyl cellulose (2% aqueous) then add water 59% slowly into it. Again agitate it for 1 hour. Now add preservative and perfume for the effersence. Now the moisture is ready to pack. Pack it in the glass bottle of 10 ml - 200 ml and more.

Formulation of Moisturizer

1	Isopropyl livioleate	2.0
2.	Glyceryl stearate	3.0
3.	Di-sopropyl adipate	2.0
4.	Myrestyl myristate	1.0
5.	PEG -40 stearate	1.0
6.	Cetyl alcohol	1.5
7.	Ceteareth -20	0.5
8.	Quaterinium -22	2.0
9.	Hydroxy ethylcellulose (2% aqueous)	25.0
10.	Propylene glycol	3.0
11.	Water	59.0
12.	Perfume, preservative	9.5

Herbal Anti-Dandruff Shampoo

Formulation No.2

Ingredients	Parts	% of by wt.
1. Lanolin	2.0	6.779
2. Castor oil	3.0	10.169
3. Coconut oil	0.5	1.695
4. Vegetable card	1.0	3.390
5. Vinegar	5.0	16.949
6. Glycerine	1.0	3.390
7. Liquid soap	1.0	3.390

8.	Lemon juice	2.0	6.780
9.	Eggs	2.0	6.780
10.	Perfume	2.0	6.780
11.	Water	10.0	33.898
		29.5	100.000

Manufacturing Method of Herbal Anti-Dandruff Shampoo

In a steam-jacketed reaction vessel (S.S) fitted with agitator introduce the requisite quantities of lanolin, castor oil, coconut oil, vegetable lard, vinegar, glycerine, liquid soap. Lemon juice & eggs gradually pass steam into the jacket to provide heat to the ingredients so that the solid over will start melting. Then pass more steam so as to heat the contents and meanwhile, start mixing. The contents by means of agitator and heat the mixture to about 55-60°C.

In a separate vessel, heat the requisite quantity of water to about 65 - 70°C by mean of passing steam the jacket of the vessel. Then pour the hot water into the first reaction vessel, agitating the mixture all and continue heating till all the ingredient are thoroughly mixed.

A viscous mass of the anti-dandruff shampoo will be produced. Which is filled in bottles or pouches and sent for marketing.

MANUFACTURING PROCESS FOR HAIR TONIC

The process of manufacture of all the hair oil is mostly the same the process can be briefly stated like this. Mixing the oil with colour & perfume and then filtering and packing in bottles.

Here we will discuss about the manufacturing process of scented coconut hair oil.

40 Kgs of refined coconut oil taken in a mixing tank equipped with stirrer. To this 40 grams of benzoic acid and about 40 grams of oil soluble red dye or orange dye as the case may be added to the coconut oil. This oil and other ingredients should be stirred well for some time. After this required amount of scent or perfume about 40°C should also be added and mixed thoroughly. Then the oil will be filtered through a filter.

After filteration the oil has to be filled in bottles and the bottles have to be scaled with a Cap sealing machine. Labels have to be affixed and then the bottles will be packed and despatched.

PLANT ECONOMICS OF HERBAL COSMETIC

Rated Plant Capacity	=	1.83 Ton/Day
LAND & BUILDING (Land area 700 sq.mts.)	=	Rented

PLANT & MACHINERY

1. Baby boiler
2. Mixer
3. Storage tank
4. Reaction vessel
5. Dryer
6. Jacketed mixer
7. Packing machine

FIXED CAPITAL

1. Plant & Machinery	Rs.	10,25,000.00
2. Other Fixed Assets	Rs.	1,83,000.00
TOTAL	Rs.	12,08,000.00

RAW MATERIALS

1. Hair tonic
2. Moisturizer
3. Skin cream tonic
4. Conditioning shampoo
5. Herbal cream
6. Antidandruff
7. Hair dye powder

TOTAL WORKING CAPITAL/MONTH

1. Raw Material	Rs	1,89,325.00
2. Salary & Wages	Rs.	58,500.00
3. Utilities & Overheads	Rs.	58,500.00
TOTAL	Rs.	3,06,325.00

TOTAL CAPITAL INVESTMENT

Total Fixed Capital	Rs.	12,08,000.00
Total Working Capital for1 Month	Rs.	3,06,325.00
TOTAL	Rs.	15,14,325.00

TURN OVER/ANNUM

1. Hair tonic (5 Ton) 5000 Kg.
2. Moisturizer (5 Tons)
3. Skin cream tonic
4. Conditioning shampoo 5000 Kg.
5. Herbal cream 5000 Kgs.
6. Antidandruff shampoo 5000 kgs.
7. Hair dye powder 5000 Kg.

TOTAL Rs. 61,10,000.00

PROFIT SALES RATIO = Profit / Sales x 100 = 32.57 %

RATE OF RETURN = Operating profit / T.C.I x 100 = 131.42 %

BREAK EVEN POINT (B.E.P) = 33.57 %

Chapter - 29

Ice Cream & Ice-Candy

Ice - Cream is a frozen dairy food made by freezing a pasteurized mix with agitation to incorporate air & insure uniformity of consistency. The mix is composed of a combination of milk products, sugar, dextrose corn syrup in dry or liquid form, water or other optional ingredients, with or without eggs or eggs products with harmless flavoring and with or without added stabilizer or emulsifier and all of wholesome edible material.

Ice - candy is the hardened ice cream without emulsifier. In ancient times, sugar must have been a highly valued consumption item. Therefore, there was no candy that used sugar as liberally as we do in the present age. But a complete change occurred in the picture. Anyone can now enjoy the sweet taste of candy. Today, there is a great varieties of candies, which meet the desires of children.

FORMULATION

CANDY PRODUCTS AND CONFECTIONERY CHOCOLATE PEANUT BARS

Sugar	3 Lb
Corn Syrup	3 Lb
Water	1 Pt.

Cook to 240°F. Then cold and pour of washed peanuts and cook for 10 minutes. Remove from fire and add chocolate.

Fruit Jelly Candies

Fruit Juice	2 qt.
Sugar	3 Lbs.
Corn Syrup or Invert Syrup	3 Lb.
Commercial Pectin Syrup	1 qt.

Mix fruit juice and pectin syrup. Add the sugar and corn, or invert, syrup. Boil to 222-223°F Remove from fire. Pour into starch molds or oiled pans, about 1/2 inch deep. Allow to burden 24 hours. Remove from molds and dust with powdered sugar or dip in chocolate.

Sugar Coating for Candy

Cocoa Butter Substitute	35 lb.
Powdered Skim milk	15 lb.
Powdered Sugar	50 lb.
Salt	2 oz.
Vanillin	1/2 oz.

This may be coloured and flavored with oil soluble colours. After melting the cocoa butter substitute, add the other materials gradually in a dough mixer and finally run over finishing rolls at a temperature of 110°F. In using, run an enrober at 104°F.

French Chewing Candy

Mixture No. I

Corn Syrup	25 lb.
Albumen - Dissolved in	3 lb.
Nulomoline	25 lb.
Water	6 lb

Boil the corn syrup to 245°F. Add the Nulomoline and stir until it is melted. Place the batch into a heater. Start the beater. Then gradually add the aqueous albumen solution and heat until light.

Mixture No. 2

Sugar	30 lb.
Cream (20% butter fat)	10 lb.
Numbomoline	5 lb.
Coconut Oil (76°F m.p.)	7 lb.
Corn Syrup	25 lb.

Ice-Cream Preparation

Albumen	10 oz.
Sugar	80 oz.
Whole dried milk	10 oz.
Indian Gum	5 oz.
Vanillin	1.5 oz.

Or

Dried Milk	50 oz.
Sugar	50 oz.
Cream of Tartar	4.4 oz.
Sodium	2 oz.
Vanillin	0.06 oz.

Chocolate Ice Cream

Milk	32 oz.
Sugar	16 oz.
Flour	2 oz.
Salt	1/8 oz.
Eggs	4 oz.
Cream	32 oz.
Vanillin	1/4 oz.
Unsweetened	5 oz.

MANUFACTURING PROCESS

PREPARATION OF THE MIX

A very important process involved in the manufacture of ice cream is preparing the mix. Preparing the mix involves, assembling the ingredients from storage area to the preparation zone, weighing or metering and mixing ingredients and the pasteurization, homogenization, cooling and storage of the mix.

According to the recent studies on ice cream manufacturing plant methods, equipment, and layout it is found that four methods are involved for processing mix.

1) The bulk ingredients and continuous high temperature short time pasteurization.
2) Ingredients in cans and high temperature short time pasteurization
3) Bulk ingredients and batch pasteurization.
4) Ingredients in cans and batch pasteurization

The lowest cost method for preparing mix is the can and batch pasteurization method due to the low cost of requirement involved.

ORDER OF ADDING INGREDIENTS

All liquid ingredients (cream, milk, condensed milk, syrup etc) are placed in the vat and the agitation and heating shorted at once. The dry ingredients including MSNF, dried eggs, cocoa, sugar, and stabilizer are added while the liquid material is agitated and before the temp. reaches 120°F. It gelatin is the stabilizer used, it is best to and it after it is thoroughly mixed with an equal volume of sugar and before the liquid reaches 120°F. When butter plastic cream, frozen cream are added they should be cut into fairly small pieces and added in time to allow complete melting before the pasteurizing temp. is reached.

PLANT ECONOMICS OF ICE CREAM & ICE - CANDY

Rated Plant Capacity = 500.00 Lit./Day
LAND & BUILDING (Land Area 400 sq.mt.) = Rented

PLANT & MACHINERY

1. Milk Storage Tank
2. Freon compressor
3. Brine tanks (Freezers)
4. Homogenizer (Churner)
5. Blending tank
6. Lab. Equipment
7. Baby Boiler
8. Mis. Equipments & Accessories

FIXED CAPITAL

1. Plant & Machinery		Rs.	2,24,500.00
	TOTAL	Rs.	2,24,500.00

RAW MATERIALS

1. Fresh Milk
2. Fat Cream
3. Sugar
4. Stabilizer, colour essences, Chemicals dry fruits
5. CONTAINERS
   Big Cup
6. Small Cup
7. Stocks for bar
8. Ice blocks for trolleys

TOTAL WORKING CAPITAL/MONTH

1. Raw Material		Rs.	3,05,625.00
2. Salary & Wages		Rs.	26,040.00
3. Utilities & Overheads		Rs.	45,000.00
	TOTAL	Rs.	3,76,665.00

TOTAL CAPITAL INVESTMENT

Total Fixed Capital	Rs.	2,24,500.00
Total Working Capital for 1 Month	Rs.	3,76,665.00
TOTAL	Rs.	6,01,165.00

TURN OVER/ANNUM

1. By sale of Big cup	Rs.	6,00,000
2. Small Cup	Rs.	9,00,000
3. Ice Cream bars	Rs.	4,50,000
4. Ice Candy bar	Rs.	4,50,000
TOTAL	Rs.	74,25,000.00

PROFIT SALES RATIO = Profit / Sales x 100 = 37.40 %

RATE OF RETURN = Operating profit / T.C.I x 100 = 461.90 %

BREAK EVEN POINT (B.E.P) = 14.46 %

Chapter - 30

Jam, Jellies, Pickles and Squashes

Among preserved fruits, Jams, Jellies, Marmalades, Pickles, squashes forms an important class of products. during world war II, fairly large quantities of these were imported to into India from the U.S.A. the U.K. and Australia. Now a days, such products are being manufactured extensively in several factories in this country, as by products or joint products in fruits. They are also made in many of the homes all over the country. Their production and demand can be increased manifold by making better use of fruit that is being wasted at present.

A Jam differs from a preserve in that it does not contain pieces of the whole fruit as in the case with a preserve. In preparing the jam, the fruit is crushed or otherwise finely cut, so that when cooked, the mass is fairly uniform throughout. It is rich in flavour, because the ripe fruit, which have developed full flavour, are used in its preparation.

Chutneys, pickles of various kinds are prepared in Indian homes and also on a commercial scales. They find a ready market in many countries. Standard recipes have been modified to suit local taste in the country and consumer acceptability in other parts of the world. Fruits such as apple, peach, plum, apricot and mango and vegetables like turnip, cauli flower, carrot etc. are the basic raw materials. Onion, garlic, spices, herbs etc. are added for flavour. Vinegar, common salt and sugar are also used to make the products more palatable. The method of preparation is similar to that adopted in the case of jams except that spices and vinegar are added.

Pickles of various kinds are known throughout India and many parts of the world. The process of preservation of food in common salt or in vinegar is called pickling. Spices and edible oil also may be added to the product. Some of typical Indian pickles made from mango, lime, turnip, cabbage, cauliflower etc. have become popular in several countries. There is a good export market for these products which are associated with the well known Indian condiments. Pickles are good appetizers and add to the palatability of a meal. They aid digestion by stimulating the flow of gasteric juice. Very little scientific data is, however, available regarding their nutritive value. Different kinds of pickles contain varying amount of nutrients depending upon the raw material taken and the method of preparation followed.

The other products has also very good market in our country as well as in foreign countries.

AUTOMATIC LIQUID-FILL & SEAL MACHINE

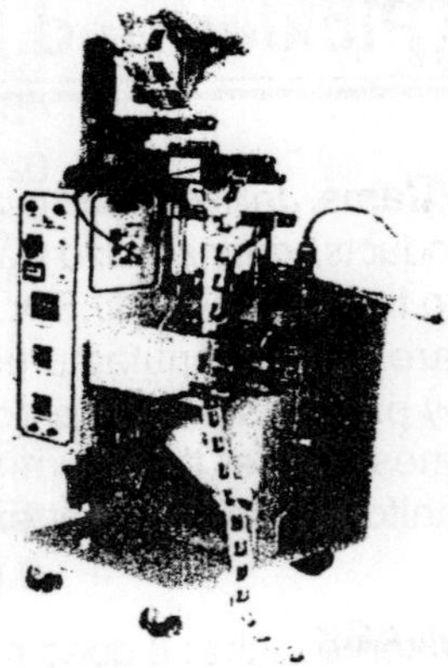

MANUFACTURING PROCESS FOR SQUASHES

1. ORANGE SQUASH :

First of all oranges are peeled and rags sticking to the the segments is removed. Now the juice from segments is extract by using screw type juice extractor and juice is collected and sieved to remove coarse seeds etc. and if necessary heated and packed in bottles.

The formulation is given below:-

Orange juice 10° Brix	45 Kgs.
0.8% acidity	45 Kgs.
Sugar	74 Kgs.
Citric Acid	2.33 Kgs.
Essence of orange	1.125 Kgs.
Water	57 Litres.
orange colour	qs
Potassium metabisulphite	110 gms.

From the above formula, the squash obtained will have the following specification :

Juice	25%
Brix	45°
Acidity	1.5%

2. FORMULATION FOR OTHER SQUASHES:

In all types of squashes the method is same that is extraction of juice and addition of ingredients. Therefore, it is needless to repeat the process but to be familiar with formulations is essential.

(a) MANGO SQUASH:

Mango Pulp 18°	45 Kgs.
Brix 0.5% acidity sugar	62.6 Kgs.
Citric acid	1.2 Kgs.
Water	71.8 lit.
Preservative	110 gms.

SPECIFICATIONS:

Juice	25%
Brix	45°
Acidity	0.8%

(b) PINEAPPLE SQUASH

Pineapple juices 80° Brix	
0.5 acidity	45 kgs.
Sugar	74.8 Kgs.
Citric Acid	2.475 kgs.
Pineapple flavour	1.125 Kgs.
Water	56.5 Kgs.
Yellow colour	qs
Preservative	110 gms.

SPECIFICATIONS:

Juice	25%
Brix	45°
Acidity	1.5%

(c) LEMON SQUASH:

Juice 10° 5% acidity	45 Kgs.
Sugar	76 Kgs.
Citric Acid	460 gms.
Water	57.5 lit.
Essence of lemon	1.125 Kgs.
Preservative	110 gms.

SPECIFICATIONS

Juice	25%
Brix	45°
Acidity	1.5%

The equipments required for squashes are as under:-

1. Conveyor type juice extractor 1 No.
2. Mixer with heating arrangement 1 No.
3. Sealing Machine 1 No.
4. buckets etc.

MANUFACTURING PROCESS FOR SAUCES & KETCHUP

Sauce of any fruit can be prepared but the most popular sauce. It is also used as chutney. Manufacturing process of all varieties of fruits sauces is almost similar.

First, the fruits are peeled, sliced, and ground. The spices, and other additives are added. Thickening agents also are added to prevent or retard sedimentation of the solid particles in suspension. In India, apple pulp is often used for this purpose. Sometimes, the fruit, which is used for making sauce, is boiled pulped as a filler. The starches of maize potato, arrowroot, sago and rye also are used as thickening agents. The use of Indian gum locust, kernel gum tragacanth, karaya gum, gelatin, irish moss, pectin and other similar substances is also advised. These are however, as good as the starches.

Formula for tomato sauce:

Tomato pulp (6% soluble solids)	29.250 Kgs.
Cardamom, pepper and cumin in equal quantities	8.5 gms.
Cinnamon, broken	10 gms.
Cloves, headless	8.5 gms.
Mace	5.7 gms.
Salt	5.7 gms.
Onions, chopped	154 gms.
Garlic ground	18 gms.
Sugar	2.140 Kgs.
White vinegar 100 grain	580 c.c.
Red chilli powder	15 gms.

It is cooked to about half its volume i.e. about 28% solids. It is filled into plain cans and processed for 45 min in boiling water.

CHILLI SAUCE

To 22.4 kgs. of peeled tomatoes, add 1 kg. of sugar 10 gm. of red chillies 0.9 Kg. of washed, peeled finely chopped onions, and the following spices tied loosely in a cloth bag.

Mace	7 gms.
Cinnamon broken	18 gms.
Cumin cardamom and black pepper in equal quantities	22.5 gms.
Ground white pepper	10 gms.
Ground ginger	10 gms.

Cook the whole mass in steam :- jacketed kettle to about 25.2 Kgs. crushing tomatoes with a ladle, if necessary. Add 2.14 Kgs. of sugar and 0.675 Kg of salt and 1.57 Kgs (100 grain) vinegar. Continue the cooking of the mass further for about 5-10 minutes after which pack immediately in plain cans seal and sterilize for half an hour in boiling water.

JAMS AND JELLIES

Jam is a product prepared from fruits. Jams should have 45% minimum of fruit in final product based on fresh fruit but in case of respberry and strawberry, minimum percentage of fruit is be 25% minimum percentage of soluble solids in the final product is 68% and the finished product shall have a heavy consistency.

MANUFACTURE OF JAMS

They are generally prepared from almost all the fruits and from some vegetables. First, fruits are boiled in small quantity of water and thus pulp is made. Now the sugar is added to the pulp. The proportion of sugar to fruit varies with the variety of the fruit its ripeness, and the effect desired, although usually the amount of sugar used in equal to the amount of fruit in case of berries, plums, apricots, pineapple and other fruits. Sweet prunes require lesser sugar and in some cases even one fourth the amount of fruit is sufficient.

In manufacturing jams, boiling is essential so that fruit pulp and sugar are mixed ultimately. Jams are concentrated to a boiling point of 102-105°C, and point varying with fruit variety, proportion of sugar and other factors. A jelly thermometer may be used with advantages to determine the end point of the boiling processes. The usual finishing point is 65 to 68% soluble solids as determined by refractometer.

At this stage, jams are packed in cans or tins but sometimes, glass bottles of wide mouth may also be used. If the product contains a very high concentration of sugar (70% or above), it will not spoil in most climates. Most commercially prepared jams are not concentrated to this high density, however, and should be pasteurized at 80°C for 30 mins. or packed at 90 to 95°C in preheated glass containers, in order to prevent moulding or fermentation.

JELLY

In manufacturing unit, the essential substances are pectin, acid and sugar, of these pectin is most important. To obtain good quality jelly, proper proportions of substances may be used. Pectin and acid are added to those fruit juices which are deficient in these substances. Citric, tartaric or suitable acid are added to make up the deficiency of acidity in fruit juice.

MANUFACTURING PROCESS

Jellies are prepared from aqueous fruit extracts fruits are cut into slices so that pectin and acid may be extracted easily. Only a minimum quantity of water would be added to the fruit for a simple extraction of pectin. If necessary, a second or even a their extraction may also be taken and mixed with the first extract. If large quantities of water are used, jelly will be weak, and if too little water is used, the extract will be difficult to clarify. The length of boiling will vary according to the variety of and texture of the fruit. Apples normally require only 20 minutes or less and oranges from 30 to 60 min. The fruit should be heated only long enough to soften it sufficiently to permit through extraction of the juice by pressing and long enough to render it mushy.

In jelling making process, boiling is most important step because it dissolves the sugar and cause union of the sugar, acid and pectin to form jelly. Its principal purpose is to increase the concentration of the sugar too the point where jelling will occur. Prolonged boiling results in loss of flavour, injury to colour, and hydrolysis of the pectin consequently it is a frequent cause of jelly failure. The boiling is continued until on cooling the product will form a jelly of the desired consistency. The concentration of the mixture, when this point is reached will depend upon several factors viz, the concentration of pectin concentration of acid, ratio of sugar to pectin and acid and texture desired.

Finally, jelly is packed in cans or bottles near boiling point or nearly 95°C and sealed hot. Such procedure sterilizes the jelly glass and lid, and as the package is hermetically sealed, the product does not mould or ferment. It has been noted that at 0.05% acidity (as citric) 75 gms. of sugar per 100 gms of jelly was necessary to form jelly, while at 1.05% acidity jelly formed when the finished product contained only 53.5 gms of sugar per 100 gms of jelly.

PLANT ECONOMICS OF JAMS, JELLIES, PICKLES, SQUASH ETC.

Rated Plant Capacity = 416.66 Bottles/Day

LAND & BUILDING (Land area 1000 sq.mt) = Rented

PLANT & MACHINERY

1. Screw type juice extractor
2. Vacuum filling machine
3. Pulveriser/Grinder
4. Pulper
5. Steam Jacketed Kettle
6. Fruit Mill
7. Storage tank and mixing tanks
8. Drying/Heating/Dehydrator
9. Vacuum Tester
10. Working table stainless steel top
11. Boiler (steam)
12. Aluminium trays & trollies
13. Crown corking heavy duty
14. Bottle washing
15. Peeling knives made of stainless steel.
16. Fruit cutting knives
17. Fruit Cutting knives
18. Stainless steel knives
19. Sterilization tank
20. Miscellaneous other equipments

FIXED CAPITAL

1. Plant & Machinery		Rs.	4,01,760.00
2. Other Fixed Assets		Rs.	1,25,000.00
	TOTAL	Rs.	5,26,760.00

RAW MATERIALS

1. Pine Apple ripe (fresh)
2. Mango
3.. Bamboo Shoot
4. Citric Acid
5. Lemon fully pipe
6. Sugar
7. Pectin
8. Common salt

9. Spices
10. Chemical preservatives potassium metabisulfite sodium Benzoate etc.
11. Packaging materials Glass Bottle etc.

TOTAL WORKING CAPITAL/MONTH

1. Raw Material	Rs.	1,24,353.00
2. Salary & Wages	Rs.	49,750.00
3. Utilities & Overheads	Rs.	33,250.00
TOTAL	Rs.	2,07,353.00

TOTAL CAPITAL INVESTMENT

Total Fixed Capital	Rs.	5,26,760.00
Total Working Capital for1 Month	Rs.	2,07,353.00
TOTAL	Rs.	7,34,113.00

TURN OVER/ANNUM

1. By sale of 10,500 Bottle of 450 gm. Mixed Jam & Jellies
2. By sale of 21000 (250 gm) Bottle of Mixed Jam & Jellies
3. By sale of 10,500 (500 gm) Bottles Mango pickles
4. By sale 21000 Bottles 250 gm) of Mango pickles
5. By sale of 9000 Bottles (500 gm) of Mixed pickles
6. By sales of 18000 Bottles (250 gm) of Mixed pickles.
7. By sales of 9000 Bottles (500 gm) Bamboo shoot pickles
8. By sales of Tomato Products (Ketchup, Sauces Etc.) 9000 Bottles
9. By sale of Squashes (Full range) 17077 Bottles of 650 ml each.

TOTAL Rs. 34,28,195.00

PROFIT SALES RATIO = Profit / Sales x 100 = 21.69 %

RATE OF RETURN = Operating profit / T.C.I x 100 = 101.27 %

BREAK EVEN POINT (B.E.P) = 44.45 %

Chapter - 31

Tissue Paper/Toilet Roll Paper

Face fresher tissue paper, when applied on the face, it removes the dirts, soils from face skin and freshen the face and keep it moist. The skin becomes glossy and fresh appearance.

In a modern age, people are more prone to sophisticate modes of maintaining health and hygienic conditions of their body through the contingencies of cosmetics and other allied measures which promote these functions effectively. This is elegantly achieved by the application of wet face freshner tissue. This is very economical item and portable. It can be easily carried out in pocket while going in a car, flight, train etc.

This is a product of recent times as a nice out come of innovation in cosmetology. After the use of this item one feel very much fresh, comfortable, cosy. Now a days, it is even a part of fashion to use such a handy item in the upper stetra of society. Where grace is often exhibited. By using this item people feel highly dignified while attending seminar, meetings conferences, symposium, congregations, debates, gettogether marriage parties and other parties, social function etc. Even it is very much acceptable item by the modern working lady, models, filmstars, air hostess, college girls, opera dancers, business executives, corporate executives etc.

The technology involved in the production of this item is very simple and the inventory as well as plant & machinery are indigenously available.

By virtue of its innovative nature its demand is increasing by leaps and bounds in almost every sphere of human activity.

MANUFACTURING PROCESS

For the preparation of tissue paper, the tissue paper in the form of big rolls is purchased from the market and cut by means of slitting machine roll to roll slitting into desired size tissues and subjected to folding operation and in cardbox into packets (100 Nos. per packet)

Subsequently, these paper tissues are packed and sealed into cardboard boxes by means of cardboard sealing machine (manual) and despatched for marketing.

In the case of toilet paper, the paper purchased from the market is cut by slitting machine into small toilet rolls and packed in desired manner in cardboard boxes and subsequently despatched for marketing.

PROCESS FLOW DIAGRAM FOR TISSUE PAPER & TOILET PAPER

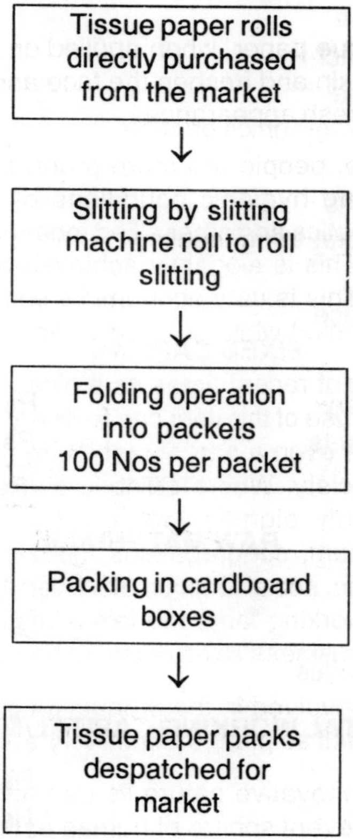

PLANT ECONOMICS OF PAPER NAPKINS BY TISSUE PAPER CUTTING

Rated Plant Capacity	=	200.00 Kgs./Day
Land & Building (Land area 500 sq.mts.)	=	Rented

PLANT & MACHINERY

1. Roll unwinding machinery
2. Calendering machine
3. Slitting machine
4. Roll winding machine
5. Cutting machine
6. Two colour flexographics printing machine
7. Embossing units
8. Automatic packet filling, sealing machine
9. Weighing balance

FIXED CAPITAL

1. Plant & Machinery	Rs.	6,75,000.00
2. Other Fixed Assets	Rs.	1,35,000.00
TOTAL	Rs.	8,10,000.00

RAW MATERIALS

1. Tissue paper
2. Printing inks
3. Packaging materials

TOTAL WORKING CAPITAL/MONTH

1. Raw Material	Rs.	3,88,500.00
2. Salary & Wages	Rs.	25,802.00
3. Utilities & Overheads	Rs.	61,300.00
TOTAL	Rs.	4,75,602.00

Tissue Paper / Toiler Roll Paper

TOTAL CAPITAL INVESTMENT

Total Fixed Capital	Rs.	8,10,000.00
Total Working Capital For 1 Month	Rs.	4,75,602.00
TOTAL	Rs.	12,85,602.00

TURN OVER/ANNUM

1. By sale of 60,000 kgs of Paper-napkins
2. By sale of waste paper 600 kgs.

TOTAL Rs. 66,03,000.00

PROFIT SALES RATIO = Profit / Sales x 100 = 8.61 %

RATE OF RETURN = Operating profit / T.C.I x 100 = 44.24 %

BREAK EVEN POINT (B.E.P) = 56.71 %

Chapter - 32

Leather Garments

The Indian leather garments are by and large manufactured from sheep (lamb) leather. The few factories that have come up in this line are indeed of excellent quality. About 50% of the leather garments exported all over the world are manufactured in Bangalore and it has fast developed as an important source for leather garments. Chennai, Delhi and Mumbai have very good units for manufacture of leather garments. All these factories are equipped with latest equipment and machines.

In manufacture of leather garments, India is guided by foreign buyers for styles and designs, However, over a period of time Indian manufacturers hope to develop their own designs suited to the foreign markets. The Indian leather garments have found excellent market in West Germany. The prices quoted by exporters are competitive and they are willing to undertake orders of smaller size in a number of styles and designs.

The Indian exporters have now a fairly good idea of what the western market needs. A number of existing units have suitably equipped themselves. Their production capacity has also increased, New entrepreneurs are coming into this field, It is believed that the Indian leather garment industry will have a significant share in the world market for leather garments in the near future.

PROCESS OF MANUFACTURE

Process of manufacture of leather garments starts with the pattern procurement. Patterns are made either with in the units or general patterns are purchased and then modified according to the size, shape, demand of the garments etc.

Now working with a leather which has a grain which runs lengthwise along the backbone of the animal from head to tail. Pattern pieces should be placed of the hide so that they run with the grain. This insures a proper drape to the eventual garment. Never place the pattern across the grain or from side to side. It makes no difference which end of the hide the pattern pieces face as long as they run with the grain. For example, if you're working with a dress pattern, you would place the neck of the pattern lengthwise along the hide. This is also true of garments with sleeves; the length of these sleeves should with the grain, as well as all other pattern pieces.

Always place the pattern on the flesh side of the hide-tis minimizes damage to the exposed surface. Check to see that there are no thin sports or imperfections falling within the pattern pieces.

There are many ways to attach the pattern to the hide. You can use making tape, mending tape scotch tape, or even the new spray material which, when applied to the back of the pattern, will make it pressure sensitive. Your can also use paper clips if you're careful not to mark the leather. And then it's also possible to use pins, as long the pins fall within the seam allowances and don't poke holes in any exposed area of the leather. Once the pattern is attached to the hide, you can trace around it with chalk, a pencil, or a felt-tip pen for additional placement insurance. A good rule to follow throughout the construction is to protect the leather from pin holes, and scrapes, leather is not a weave fabric. If it's marked, especially on smooth grains, the mark will show. You don't have to be quite as fussy with suedes and splits, but it still helps to keep this rule in mind.

If the pattern requires two of any single pattern piece, and one pattern piece is included in the package, as for example with sleeves, be sure to make an extra sleeve out of brown paper and place it on the hide along with all other pieces. When laying these duplicate pattern pieces on the hide. Be sure to reverse the second, or duplicate, pattern piece, This reversing of the pattern pieces will insure that you don't end up with two right sleeves, or two right front garment panels.

Leather pattern pieces aren't cut on the fold (by folding the material in half as with other fabrics). On some pattern pieces, you may find markings on the pattern requiring that certain pieces be cut on the fold. To cut on the fold means to fold the material, Do not follow this procedure on leather. When encountering these fold marking, simply cut another duplicate pattern piece out of brown papers tape it to the original pattern piece along the edge that had the fold marking, and then lay it out on the hide along with the rest of the pattern. Before you begin cutting anything, all garment pieces must be accounted for, laid out on the flat of the material and then attached to the hide.

When laying out the pattern on the leather, you may run into weak or thin spots in the hide. Many crafts men reinforce these weak or thin sports by simply using a standard iron-on tape pressed to the flash side of the leather over the thin spot before cutting out the pattern. In ironing this tape to the leather, follow the usual ironing procedure for leather-use no steam, and press over brown paper a pressing cloth.

Lining are another important thing to consider when constructing leather garments. Leather against bars skin, or even against other material, has a tendency to cling. Because of this, linings are an important part of many leather garments, especially jackets, trousers and coats, As for leather skirts, a lining can be omitted by wearing a half-slip, or by stitching a half-slip permanently in place at the skirt waist. Lining fabrics recommended for leather should be colorfast, such as satin, taffeta, and rayon twill. These are the lining fabrics normally used in any garment or construction; lining leather is the same as lining any other kind of fabric.

If you want less leather waste, you can always increase the number of seams on the garment in order to make smaller pieces. This should only be done, however, after you've gained some experience and confidence, for example, it's possible to seam a vest up the centre of the back even though the pattern may call for a single piece across the back. The pieces instead of one would give you more area on the hide to work with.

Leather can also be combined with other garment materials such as wools, knits and other equally heavy fabrics, if you plan to make combinations, I suggest you to it sparingly and in gold taste so as not to clutter a garment with all manner of complex construction. One can either trim other garment with other fabrics. For example, collars, cuffs, buttons, and some times even front panels can be tastefully interchanged either as a complementary fabric on leather or by using leather as the trim fabric.

PROCESS FLOW CHART

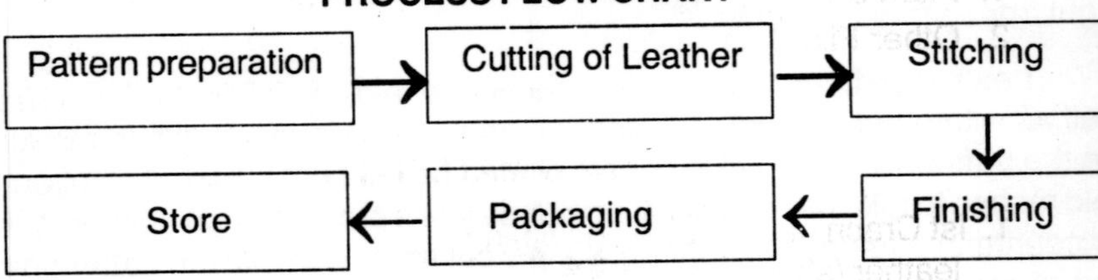

PLANT ECONOMICS OF LEATHER GARMENTS

Rated Plant Capacity	=	300.00 Nos/Day
Land & Building (Land area 750 sq.mt)	=	Rented

PLANT & MACHINERY

1. Single needle lock stitch flat bed sewing machine
2. High speed single needleflat bed lo ck stitch industrial sewing machine
3. Flat bed single needle sewing machine
4. Flat bed single needle sewing machine
5. Heavy duty cylinder bed sewing machine
6. Zig zag flat bed sewing machine
7. Button Stitch sewing machine
8. Button hole making rule
9. Sole edge manual trimming model machine
10. Upper folding machine (complete)
11. Upper & lining stamping machine
12. Upper skiving machine
13. Packing & sealing machine

FIXED CAPITAL

1. Plant & Machinery		Rs.	3,63,500.00
2. Other Fixed Assets		Rs.	1,80,000.00
	TOTAL	Rs.	5,43,500.00

RAW MATERIALS

1. Ist Crach napper/swede clothing leather (sheep/goat/cow)
2. Silk lining
3. Zip buttons thread rubber solutions bucrum etc.
4. Packing Material

TOTAL WORKING CAPITAL/MONTH

1. Raw Material		Rs.	27,75,625.00
2. Salary & Wages		Rs.	66,125.00
3. Utilities & Overheads		Rs.	79,500.00
	TOTAL	Rs.	29,21,250.00

TOTAL CAPITAL INVESTMENT

Total Fixed Capital	Rs.	5,43,500.00
Total Working Capital for 1 Month	Rs.	29,21,250.00
TOTAL	Rs.	34,64,750.00

TURN OVER/ANNUM

1. By sale of 30000 Pants
2. By sale of 30000 pieces of Jackets
3. By sale of 30000 pieces of Skirts

TOTAL Rs. 4,50,00,000.00

PROFIT SALES RATIO = Profit / Sales x 100 = 20.95 %

RATE OF RETURN = Operating profit / T.C.I x 100 = 272.12 %

BREAK EVEN POINT (B.E.P) = 11.42 %

Chapter - 33

Liquid Toilet Cleaner (Harpic Type)

Liquid toilet cleaner is becoming very popular now-a-days owing to the sense of awareness of maintaining hygienic sanitary conditions in toilets, bathrooms, etc.

Harpic liquid toilet cleaner is gaining immense eminence owing to its exquisiteness.

Such a cleaner kills germs due to its germicidal action, removes tough stains as well as deodorizes the toilet system. Overall aseptic and hygienic conditions are well maintained.

The popularity of Harpic liquid toilet cleaner owes to the unique efficaciousness and handy applicability of the product, resulting in clean and odour free toilet system.

It is very powerful in action, removing even the most stubborn stains, dirt, etc. imparting a shining surface.

By its action, the disease causing bacteria are killed, and a very agreeable and hygenic clean conditions are established.

FORMULATION OF LIQUID TOILET CLEANER (HARPIC TYPE)

FORMULATION NO. 1 :

Linear alkyl benzene sulphonic acid :

1	Alkyl Benzene Sulphonate	40%
2.	Sodium Bi-Sulphate ($NaHSO_4$) (Nitra Cake)	5%
3.	Foaming agent (Foam Booster)	0.5%
4.	Blue Dye (Phthalocyanine Blue) (Chemically (Acid/Alkali) Stable)	Q.S.
5.	Captan* (Vancide TBS) (Germicide/Bacteriostatic)	0.5%
6.	Preservative viz. Benzakonium Chloride	3%
7.	Water	51%

* Captan=N-(Trichloromethylmercapto)-4-Cyclohexene-1.2-Dicarboximide.

PROCESS OF MANUFACTURE OF LIQUID TOILET CLEANER (HARPIC TYPE)

For the manufacture of Liquid Toilet Cleaner (Harpic Type), in a reaction vessel M.S. (epoxy-lined), requisite quantities of Linear Alkyl Benzene Sulphonic Acid) Alkyl Benzene Sulphonate, Sodium Bisulphate ($NaHSO_4$) (Nitre Cake) dissolved in water (whose aqueous solution is acidic) and water are introduced and stirred. Into this is gradually added solution of Veegum (Magnesium Silicate Aluminate) in water, in small amounts, agitating continuously until smooth, and a tentative check up of the solution being carried out for desired viscosity. The solution is acidic medium.

The contents are heated together at 50 - 60°C. The stirring of the solution is continued for 1-2 hours. After the completion of the reaction, this detergent concentrate is cooled, and checked for desired viscosity (which, if required, may be adjusted by veegum solution/water).

Then, in another reaction vessel MS (epoxy-lined) fitted with an agitator, the above resulting solution is introduced and heated to 50-60°C with constant slow speed stirring till all the ingredients are well mixed together.

Now, into this solution, introduce as per the formulation, requisite quantities of Blue Dye (Q.S), Foaming agent captan/vancide TBS (Germicide/ Bacteriostatic), and Benzakonium Chloride (Preservative) and the ingredients are mixed together in a homogenious manner till a uniform product is obtained.

The product is then subjected to quality control test.

After it confirms to the desired quality, it is packed in air-tight plastic containers and further packed in cartons and despatched for marketing.

PROCESS FLOW DIAGRAM FOR THE MANUFACTURE OF LIQUID TOILET CLEANER (HARPIC TYPE)

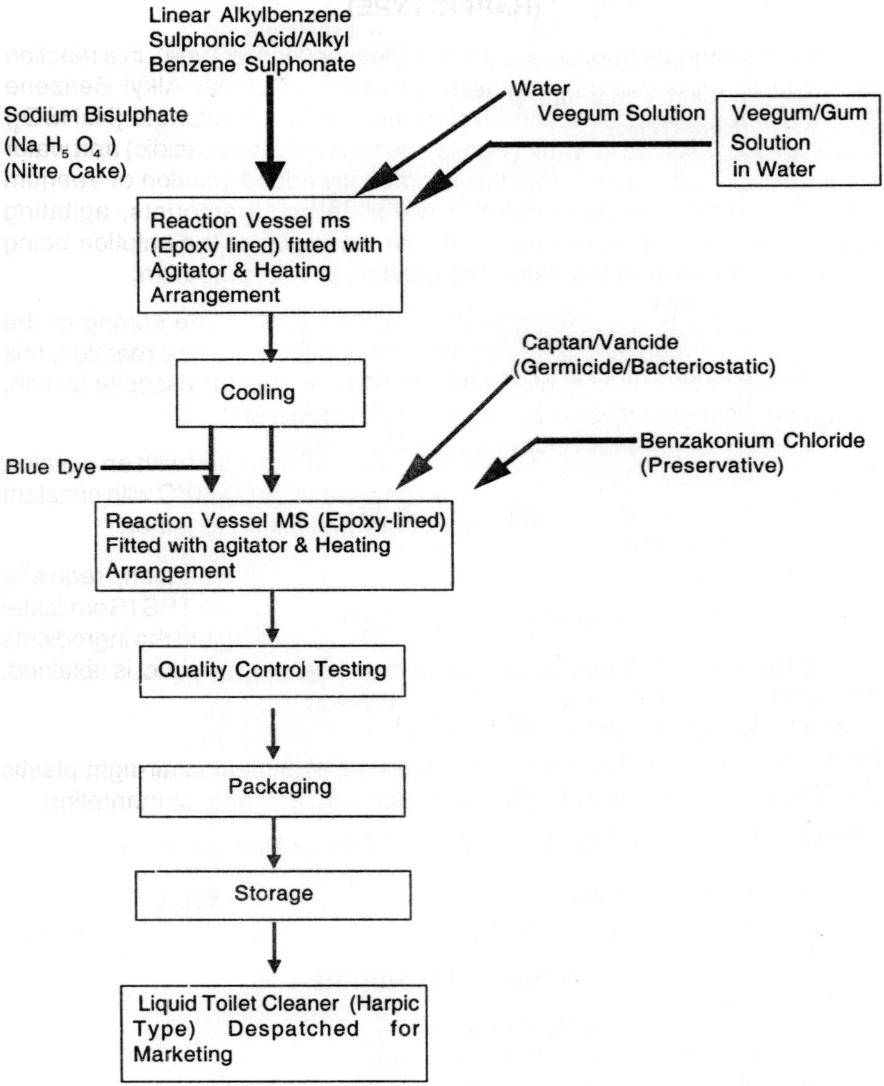

FORMULATION OF LIQUID TOILET CLEANER (HARPIC TYPE)

FORMULATION NO. 2 :

1.	Linear Alkyl Benzene Sulphonic Acid/Alkyl Benzene Sulphonate	:	40%
2.	Sodium Bisulphate (NaH_5O_4) (Nitre Cake)	:	5%
3.	Darvan No. 7/Anionic Surfactant	:	2%
4.	Triton X-102 Alkylphenol Ethoxylate)/ (Surfactant)	:	5%
5.	Foaming Agent (Foam Booster)	:	0.5%
6.	Blue Dye (Phthalocyanine Blue) (Chemically (Acid) Alkali Stable)	:	q.s.
7.	Captan*/rancide TBS (Germicide/ Bacteriostatic)	:	0.5%
8.	Veegum (Magnesium Silicate Aluminate) (Viscosity Improver)	:	q.s.
9.	Preservative Benzakonium Chloride (Preservative)	:	3%
10.	Water	:	44%

* Captan=N-(Trichloromethylmercapto)-4-Cyclohexene-1,2-Dicarboximide.

Process : Process is similar to that mentioned earlier, with the difference that in the beginning alongwith linear alkyl benzene sulphonic acid, Alkyl Benzene Sulphonate, requisite quantities of Darvan No. 7/Anionic Surfactant & Triton X-102 (Alkylphenol Ethoxylate)/Surfactant are introduced into the reaction vessel M.S. (epoxy-lined).

PLANT ECONOMICS OF LIQUID TOILET CLEANER (HARPIC TYPE)

Rated Plant Capacity	=	500.00 Litres/Day
Land & Building (Land 600 sq.mtrs.)	=	Rented

PLANT & MACHINERY

1. Reaction vessel (MS)(epoxy lined) (Jacketed vessel) with accessories.
2. PVC (Syntex Type) water storage tank.
3. Baby Boiler.
4. Manual weighing, Filling & Sealing Machine.
5. Weighing Balance (Platform Type) (Electronic Digital balance)

6. Carton Sealing machine
7. Lab. Testing Equipments.
8. Pipes,Pumps,Valves, Tanks & Miscellaneous items.
9. D.G. Set
10. Miscellaneous

FIXED CAPITAL

1. Plant & Machinery	Rs.	11,98,000.00
2. Other Fixed Assets	Rs.	4,30,000.00
TOTAL	Rs.	16,28,000.00

RAW MATERIALS

1. Sodium Linear Alkyl Benzene Sulphon ate (Soft acid slurry)
2. Alpha Olefin Sulphonate.
3. Blue Dye (Phthalocyanine Blue) (QS)
4. Benzalkonium Chloride.
5. Plastic Containers
6. Cartons
7. Veegum

TOTAL WORKING CAPITAL/MONTH

1. Raw Material	Rs.	3,73,050.00
2. Salary & Wages	Rs.	29,925.00
3. Utilities & Overheads	Rs.	85,000.00
TOTAL	Rs.	4,87,975.00

TOTAL CAPITAL INVESTMENT

Total Fixed Capital	Rs.	16,28,000.00
Total Working Capital for 1 Month	Rs.	4,87,975.00
TOTAL	Rs.	21,15,975.00

TURN OVER/ANNUM

By sale of 300000 Nos. containers of Liquid Toilet Cleaner (Harpic Type) of 500 ml cap	Rs.	78,00,000.00

PROFIT SALES RATIO = Profit / Sales x 100 = 17.70 %

RATE OF RETURN = Operating profit / T.C.I x 100 = 65.26 %

BREAK EVEN POINT (B.E.P) = 44.67 %

Chapter - 34

Masala (Spices)

Pulveriser machine which is used for grinding spices . It is a versatile grinding unit of heavy and rugged construction; and built for continuous operation day after day. This unit is designed especially for the medium fine and fine grinding.

Size :- 6" Impact Pulveriser

Power capacity : 1/4 H.P. motor used.

Outstanding Features

(i) Combines raggedness, dependability high efficiency and automatic operation.

(ii) Dust free, completely integrated system for grinding and classifying.

(iii) Assures low cost production with consistent uniform product.

(iv) Operates at peak efficiency and highest tonnage per H.P.

(v) Flexible control over product.

(vi) Requires minimum attention other than ordinary maintenance.

MINI PULVERIZER

PRODUCTION PROCESS:

Processing of condiments requires machines :

1. Pulveriser (Grinder)
2. Sealing machine (Centre sealing)
3. Cutting and bottom sealing machine.

PROCESSING PROCEDURE

The process of preparation of any masala involves the following steps in general.

1. Purchasing of Raw materials
2. Cleaning
3. Drying in sun
4. Grinding
5. Mixing
6. Packing.

All the operations are so simple that they need no explanation except that the constituents are to be mentioned. Once again we are to mention that it would not be possible to give constituents of all possible masalas. However, the same is given to suit large No. of masalas is given the followings.

DRYING

All the spices are dried in sun in consideration with the cost factor. This operation would be carried out at a place from which dust & dirt is away.

GRINDING

The spices are ground. We must have a cooling arrangement for grinder. It is because sufficient amount of heat is produced during grinding operation. The grinding is done on Impact Pulverizer.

Principles of Operations:

The standard pulveriser of an encased main rotor carrying swing hammers, fineners regulator and exhaust fan. Raw materials from the feed hopper enters the roll feeder and, as the feeder pockets rotate, spills into the grinding chamber to be reduced by impact with rotating hammers and sides of the chamber. The air steam flowing through the pulveriser carries the ground material towards the outlet, the oversize particles being rejected by the fineness regulators and returned for further grinding. Classified material is then conveyed through the fan and into the cyclone for separation from the air system. Clean air is returned to the inlet of the pulveriser for recirculation. The small quantity of air entering the feeder with the raw material is usually exhausted directly to a dust collector with an almost negligible quantity of dust.

The impact pulveriser has a cast iron beater chamber, fan chamber and regulator chamber fitted with adjustable whizzers for varying the fineness of the ground products, the whole being mounted on a cast iron bedplate.

Renewable pulverizing hammers are mounted on the main shaft of shock resisting steel which is supported in two dust-tight housing fitted with heavy duty rolled bearing. The beater chamber is fitted with renewable liners.

The roll feeder is super imposed on the pulveriser and is operated by means of a rocket and pawl mechanism driven through a reduction gear from the main beater shaft.

In the beater chamber a pocket is arranged for the purpose of removing foreign material such as tramp iron which might be unintentionally introduced with the feed into the pulveriser.

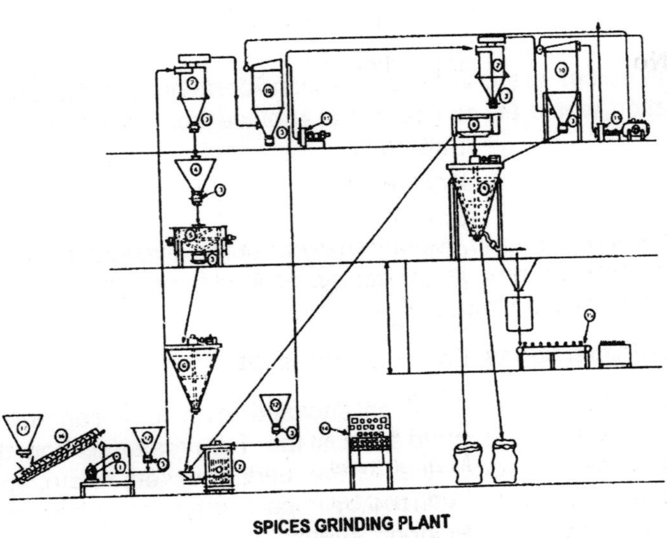

SPICES GRINDING PLANT

MIXING

After the process of grinding of different spices is done, the different spices are mixed together in the requisite quantities to from the required masala. For the manufacture of different masalas, the spices are mixed in different quantities as given.

Pouching : Pouches are made at sealing and cutting machine. Raw material for pouches is procured from vendors. Pouches of 100 g and 250 g are to be made.

PACKING

After the masalas are manufactured, they are packed in pouches of requisite quantity. The pouches are then packed in card-board boxes, which are then covered by polythene covering and then sent to the market.

PRODUCTION PROGRAMME : Time required to make one unit of 100 g is 24 second and 60 second for 250 g

. ONE DAY (8 HOUR) - 120 kgs.
. ONE WEEK (6 DAYS) - 720 Kgs.
. ONE MONTH (25 DAYS) - 300 Kgs.
. ONE YEAR (300 DAYS) - 36000 Kgs.

CHAT MASALA

S.No	Ingredients	Quantity (by Weight kg)
1.	Salt White	3
2.	Dry Mango	2
3.	Salt Black	1
4.	Cumin	2
5.	Black Pepper	1
6.	Chillies	1
7.	Pomegradate seeds	1
8.	Musk melon	1
9.	Coriander	1
10.	Mini Leaves	1
11.	Long pepper	1
12.	Bishop's seeds	1/2
13.	Asafoetida	1/2

JAL JIRA

S.No.	Ingredients	Quantity (by weight kg)
1.	Salt White	1
2.	Salt Black	1
3.	Dry Mango	1
4.	Citric	1/2
5.	Chillies	1
6.	Dry ginger	1
7.	Sal amoniac	
8.	Long Pepper	1
9.	Asafoetida	1/2
10.	Caraway	1
11.	Clove	1/2

SAMBHAR

S.No.	Ingredients	Quantity (Weight Kg)
1.	Coriander	1
2.	Pulse Arhar	7.5
3.	Cumin	1.1
4	Turmeric	1/2
5.	Fenugreek Seeds	1
6.	Chillies	1
7.	Rai	1/2
8.	Black pepper	1/2
9.	Poppy seeds	1/2
10.	Mustard	1/2
11.	Cloves	1/4
12.	Nutmeg	1/4
13.	Mace	1/4
14.	Caraway	1/4
15.	Asafoetida	1/4
16.	Salt	1

MEAT MASALA

S.No.	Ingredients	Quantity (Weight)
1.	Coriander	.40
2.	Chillies	.84
3.	Turmeric	1.02
4.	Cumin	1.25
5.	Pulse	4.1
6.	Black pepper	1.2
7.	Fenugreek	0.4
8.	Cardamom seeds	0.6
9.	Dry ginger	0.7
10.	Poppy seeds	0.2
11.	Mustard	0.8
12.	Cassia	0.6
13.	Nutmeg	1.1
14.	Garlic powder	1.7
15.	Asafoetida	6
16.	Salt white	2

PUNJABI CHOLA KA MASALA

S.No.	Ingredients	Quantity (Weight Kg)
1.	Coriander	1.2
2.	Dry Mango	1
3.	Pomegranate seeds	0.4
4.	Salt White	2
5.	Chillies	1
6	Cumin	0.8
7.	Fenugreek	0.6
8.	Carsia	0.4
9.	Black pepper	0.8
10.	Dry ginger	0.8
11.	Cardamomseed	0.6
12.	Mini Leaves	1
13.	Mustard	0.8
14.	Nutmeg	0.6
15.	Mace	0.4
16.	Cloves	0.6
17.	Chinnamon	0.5
18.	Caraway	0.5

PLANT ECONOMICS OF SPICES/MASALA

Rated Plant Capacity = 120.00 Kgs./Day
LAND & BUILDING [Rented (on lease)] = Rented (Area 100 sq. mt)

PLANT & MACHINERY

1. Grinder
2. Weighing balance
3. Sealing Machine
4. Stainless Steel vessel
5. Cutting & Bottom Sealing

FIXED CAPITAL

1. Plant and Machinery	Rs.	1,39,485.00
2. Other Fixed Assets	Rs.	35,000.00
TOTAL	Rs.	1,74,485.00

RAW MATERIALS

1. Spices
2. Pouches
3. Cardboard Box

TOTAL WORKING CAPITAL/MONTH

1. Raw Material	Rs.	2,19,665.00
2. Salary & Wages	Rs.	21,125.00
3. Utilities & Overheads	Rs.	84,615.00
TOTAL	Rs.	3,25,405.00

TOTAL CAPITAL INVESTMENT

Total Fixed Capital	Rs.	1,74,485.00
Total Working Capital for 1 Month	Rs.	3,25,405.00
TOTAL	Rs.	4,99,890.00

TURN OVER/ANNUM

By sale of 36,000 Kgs of Masala	Rs.	43,20,000.00

PROFIT SALES RATIO = Profit / Sales x 100 = 7.69 %
RATE OF RETURN = Operating profit / T.C.I x 100 = 66.46 %
BREAK EVEN POINT (B.E.P) = 19.97 %

Chapter - 35

Mustard Oil (Edible Oil)

Oil seeds and oil seed products have also proved to be a valuable foreign exchange earned for the country. Yet, with the envisaged expansion in the out put of oil seeds in the comping years, their importance in the Indian economy is anticipated to increase further.

These mustards are grown in various parts of the world, including India, China, Europe and the United States. The composition and characteristics of the oils of white mustard and black mustard fall in or near the same range as those of rapeseed oil. As in the case of rape seed oil, the older ideas of the fatty acid composition must be revised on the basis of the most recent work to include a much large proportion of linolenic acid than previously formed and a significant proportion of eicosenoic acid.

Another mustard is Bjuncea brown mustard or Indian mustard, native to South, Central and East Asia. This species has many varieties and is growth some times for its edible herbage and sometimes for the essential oil or the fatty oil in its seed. The Indian mustard raiorrayo usually is B. Juncea but seed sold under these names may be mixtures or may come from other species.

PROPERTIES

Density, viscosity, and milling behavior are the physical properties of oils that are most general interest to processors and users. Free fatty acids constitute the most important class of minor components in vegetable oils and normally must be removed in order to make the oil acceptable to edible purposes. The phosphatide one important components because their value in the form of led them and its derivatives as well as their effects on oil processing. Some of the datas available on mustard oil are tabulated below:

Fatty acid content	-	About 50%
Oil content of oil bearing material	-	Between 40.5%
Phosphatide content	-	0.1%

Total unsaponifiable matter	-	0.6-1.2%
Sterals	-	0.35 - 0.84%
To Cophrals ppm	-	500 - 700 ppm.

The colour of the oil is due to the presence of carofenoids and chlorophyle and its derivatives. The carofenoid content will be less than 50 ppm. There will be about 50 ppm sulphur in the mustard oil sometimes and it must be removed in order to avoid subsequent processing difficulties.

MANUFACTURING PROCESS

The mustard are first graded, during which the foreign materials and the husk is removed by the use of sieves and an air blower the oil seeds should posses the main acceptable level of moisture.

Percentage of oil in seed depends on the type and variety, the soil type level of fertility, and elimatic conditions prevailing during growth rapeseed variety usually, contains not less than 40% oil. The seed is usually pressed to an oil content of 12-15% in the pre oil crushers known as "Ghani" in our local terms. This is mechanized crusher and the oil taken out from its obtained from ghanis is now fed to the expeller units in this unit the oil cakes hard coming out of the expeller. The oil obtained is now filtered in the filter press of frame type stored in the storage tanks, the oil is further refined for making it free of insoluble micro impurities, gums, etc. for this the steam is termed on in the closed and it is placed in the oil storage tanks. A little alum solution can also be added for facilitating. The oil is continuously stirred at high speed. The charge is heated to a max 1/2 hour stirrer running at high speed. The charge is then rested for 1 hour and the coagulated gums and condensed water drained off. At degumming stage canemute be taken not to heat the charge above 05-90°C or else the gums have a tendency to re-dissolve now the refined oil is stored in the storage tanks from where it is packed in 16 kgs oil containers by exact weighing on the weighing balance of platform type. The filled containers are then sealed and stored in the store for marketing. Thus refined oil of edible grade is produced from mustard oil seeds.

Mustard Oil (Edible Oil)

PROCESS FLOW CHART - MUSTARD OIL - EXPELLER PROCESS

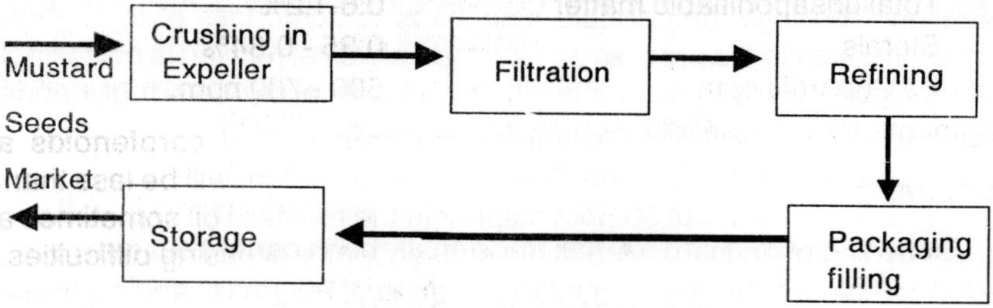

REFINING

The need to remove waxes (qu) applies only to a few oils, the outstanding example being sunflower oil. Dewaxing may be carried out the miscella from a seed extraction plant or in combination with neutralization, but the traditional method of dewaxing as applied to the refined oil is similar to fractional crystallization (withinzation), Prior removal of phosphatides leads to significantly higher rates of filter ration of the suspension of wax particles apparently because larger crystals form in the absence of the phosphatides. Filtration is normally carried out in the presence of a filter acid.

Deacidification

Deacidification with alkali (alkali refining) is widely practiced using batch or continuous operation, the latter is based largely on centrifugal separators for separating oil and soap stock, whereas gravity speculation of the phases is used in batch operation. Its ability to deal effectively with a wide range of oil qualities gives alkali refining 4 clear advantage over other processes, but oils of poorer quality suffer serious mustard oil losses, and the process generates considerable quantities of effluent. Neutral oil losses and effluent formation can be reduced by miscella refining an option best suited to a refinery closely integrated with a seed extraction plant.

Physical refining, or deacidification by steam stripping, constitutes the principal alternative to alkali refining and is always carried out in a semi continuous or continuous manner. This process, normally operated at 0.2 - 1.2 kpa (1.5-9 mm Itg) requires temperatures of 40-270°C for oils containing C16 or C18 fatty acids, but the lauric oils (C12) may be stripped at 200-20°C Neutral oil losses in stripping are significantly lower than those quoted for alkaline deacidification, although oil losses in pretreatment must be taken into account in making this comparison. Effluent formation is also lower in physical refining. The plants used are in many cases identical with the used for deodourisation, and upto 5 wt% of stripping steam may be used. The stripped fatty acids are recovered by means of a partial condenser or in a scrubber.

At the stripping temperature, carotenoids decompose rapidly, but chlorophyll is resistant to thermal decomposition and must be removed by absorption. The high temperature also leads to some loss of to copherol from the oil. Despite the process advantages, physical refining is not suitable for all oils, particularly those containing high levels of oxidized triglycerides or pigments likely to discolor at high temperature.

Bleaching

Bleaching of mustard oils has traditionally been carried out with natural or activated bleaching clay using temperatures of 90-110°C and preferably operating under vacuum. The amount of bleaching clay required depends on the history and prior processing of oil, but it is normally 0.5-2.0 wt% where deacidification has been carried out with alkali, the earth removes residual soap as well as pigments and various minor components. Reduction in pigment content as a function of contact time for rapeseed oil was used to characterize the kinetics of adsorptive bleaching because of its high cost carbon is little used in bleaching, but its ability to adsorbs certain hydrocarbons is valuable in some cases. The reduction of bleaching clay levels is an important objective for the refiner, since higher levels mean higher clay costs, greater losses of oil in spent day, and lower filter-press capacity. However, the reduction of the labour content of the process has also been important, and thus the industry in Europe has increasingly used one or other of the automatic centrifugal discharge filters, which are available sizes upto 100 m^2 filtration.

Deodorization

The volatile components present the deacidified, bleached oil are removed by deodorization, conventionally carried out at 0.2-1.2 kpa (1.5-9 mm Hg) and 175-270°C. The actual conditions used depends on the oil to be processed and the utilities available. Aldehydes and ketones formed by oxidative and thermal breakdown of unsaturated fatty acids predominated in thevolatile fraction, but many other compounds have also been found. Removal of pesticides from the oil requires a deodorization temperature of at least 240°C, but in some cases, e.g. in processing coca butter, it is essential to use a low temperature preferable C 180°C. A small amount of concentrated citric acid solution is normally added during deodorization to seavenge any metal present in the oil. Deeodorization is carried out batchwise by spanging steam into the oil through a distributor in the lower part of an upright cylindrical unressel. This distributor has many 2-3 mm openings to give a seem worthy at the point of entry into the oil phase sufficient to form bubbles of 3-5 mm dics. A head of Ca 2 m of oil is commonly provided above the distributor, which leads to a rapid change of presence as the bubble passes through the oil. Bubble expansion and fragmentation produce a continuous thick oil forth at the liquid surface, and transfer of the volatile components to the steam is facilitated by the enterfacial area thus aerated.

The principle of steam dispersion in a continuous oil phase is also applied in the design of semi continuous deodorizers. These consist of series of stages with the oil being held for a fixed time in each in the first two stages, the oil is heated to the deodorizing temperature, in part by exchanging heat with deodorized oil. The oil then passed to one or more deodorizing trays. The final tray is used to cool the oil to a temperature at which it can be discharged from the deodourizer. The temperature used in semi continuous operation, 220-270°C, facilitates removal of the volatile fraction and thus makes reduction of the cycle time possible. The conditions employed and constructional consideration lead to the use of shallower oil layers in semi continuous deodorizers, and in some designs the steam injection device is modified to give importance steam dispersion and more vigorous oil circulation. These principles are equally applicable to the design and operation of continues deodorizers, but in this case, a steam continuous steam - oil contacting system may also be used, e.g. in the form of a packed column, thus gaining the advantage of low pressure drop.

Deodorization is the most energy intensive of the process in the refining sequence, and the reduction of the energy equipment has attracted much attention. Energy is said to heat the oil to the operating temperature, to provide the live steam used for stripping, and to provide the motive steam normally used to operate the vacuum system. Batch deodorizers offer limited scope for energy conservation, as the recoverable energy is of a low grade.

PLANT ECONOMICS OF MUSTARD OIL AND CAKE

Rated Plant Capacity	=	44 MT/Day
Land & Building (Land Area 3000 sq.mt.)	=	Rented

PLANT & MACHINERY

1. Feeding elevator
2. Seed cleaning machine
3. Oil expeller
4. Filter press
5. Raw oil storage tank
6. Oil pump suitable

7. Weight bridge
8. Oil receiving tank
9. Neutralizer
10. Soap stock receiver
11. Oil-water gravity separator
12. Lye and Brine preparation tanks
13. Lye Brine and fresh water tanks
14. Neutralized oil storage tank
15. Chemical pumps
16. Centrifugal pump
17. Refined oil storage tanks
18. Filling vessel
19. Steam condensate
20. Catchells, cylindrical vessel
21. Cooler
22. Booster
23. Bleached storage
24. Deodourizer
25. Bleacher
26. Catchell
27. Vacuum pump
28. Air compressor
29. Other laboratory equipments
30. Baby boiler
31. Pipe lines, fittings valves, pumps and other miscellaneous

FIXED CAPITAL

1. Plant & Machinery		Rs.	22,90,000.00
2. Other Fixed Assets		Rs.	4,80,000.00
	TOTAL	Rs.	27,70,000.00

Mustard Oil (Edible Oil)

RAW MATERIALS

1. Mustard Oil seeds
2. Containers
3. Gunny bags
4. Miscellaneous expenses for sealing and labelling
5. Chemicals and others

TOTAL WORKING CAPITAL/MONTH

1. Raw Material	Rs.	71,15,000.00
2. Salary & Wages	Rs.	1,54,500.00
3. Utilities & Overheads	Rs.	3,89,000.00
TOTAL	Rs.	76,58,500.00

TOTAL CAPITAL INVESTMENT

Total Fixed Capital	Rs.	27,70,000.00
Total Working Capital for 1 Month	Rs.	76,58,500.00
TOTAL	Rs.	1,04,28,500.00

TURN OVER/ANNUM

1. By sale 4500 tonnes of Mustard oil
2. By sale 8700 tonnes of cake

TOTAL Rs. 12,72,90,000.00

PROFIT SALES RATIO = Profit / Sales x 100 = 26.36 %
RATE OF RETURN = Operating profit / T.C.I x 100 = 321.75 %
BREAK EVEN POINT (B.E.P)= 11.69 %

Chapter - 36

Menthol Crystals

Menthol has got wide range of applications ranging from perfumery cigarettes, liquors, as a horning agent in chewing gums and a number of pharmaceutical formulations, it is marketed in the form of flakes fine crystals as well as bold crystals each has its own application outlets.

Although there are a good number of firms manufacturing menthol, menthol bold crystals have got an increased demands because of increased formulations and growth in the pharmaceutical industry. This is an export oriented unit.

MANUFACTURING PROCESS

Menthol crystals are manufactured from mint oil by refining crystallization and centrifuging.

Mint oil is obtained by steam distillation of mentha leaves in a distillation still the vapours. A mixture of water and mint oil is condensed oil separated to get crude mint oil.

Crude mint oil is refined by vacuum filtration and then chilled in refrigerated chambers to temperatures ranging from 15 to 30°C. Where menthol crystallizes out. The mint oil is kept in the refrigeration unit for 90-120 hr., The chilled pieces are taken out and chipped into smaller bits by knives and filled in a synthetic fibre bag and put into the centrifuge.

The liquid percolates the rembrance during centrifuging and is drained off the centrifuge and the crystals are taken out from the bag and are sent for packing.

The liquor from the centrifuge is recycled to the chilling unit and the same process is repeated three times. Average yields of 15-20% are obtained by the first chilling. The second and third chillings yield 10 to 14% and 5 to 10% respectively depending upon the quality of the mint oil initially used.

Since chilling takes time and the operation is required a number of times, the refrigeration unit must be big enough to provide space for an adequate amount of oil required for an uninterrupted operation of the plant. The average yield of 30-40% depending upon the quality of the mint is obtained by repeated chilling in varying temperatures and centrifuging. The agent oil commonly known as dementholised oil has approximately the following composition.

Free menthol	30-35%
Methyl auatate	30-32%
Menthones	15%
Terpenese	18-25%

The dementholised thus obtained is subjected to chemical treatment for extracting the menthol further. This is accomplished by saponification with sodium hydroxide and subsequent esterification by boric acid. The white crystalline borate esters are formed which are separated and decomposed by steam after washing. A mixture of various isoness of menthol separates out by decomposition with steam. The menthol is recovered by subsequent chilling and centrifuging.

The residual oil is subjected to fractional distillation under reduced pressure in a fractionating column packed with rasching rings. The menthol recovered by distillation is rouged to refrigeration unit for chilling and subsequent centrifuging .

The residual oil after fractionating contains some amount of menthol, but it is not economical to is late it further. However this oil has a food resolve value and is easily marketed.

An additional yield of 10-20% of menthol can be obtained by this additional processing. Thus the total yield of the process ranges between 40-55%. The final yield is basically dependent upon the quality of the peppermint oil used.

Bold crystals can either be made from small crystals or by doing minor changes in manufacturing process. For making bold crystal from ordinary crystals, the hopes are melted in a vessel and required amount of mint oil is added and stirred well. The liquid is cooled in a pan and crushed to desired size.

Bold crystals can also be manufactured by making minor adjustments in manufacturing process. The menthone contained in peppermint oil can be catalytically hydrogenated to menthol, there by enriching the oil with menthol. Regardly the process also out 30°C of oil were hydrogenated for five hours at water bath temperature with hydrogen with a velocity of 8 to 10 litres per hour and with 2-3% of nickel oxide as catalyst.

After hydrogenation, the oil is cooled under the same conditions as given before during freezing. It is very important to rate that gradual and slow cooling permits the formation of larger and more regular crystals. The freezing plant proper consists of three tanks cooled with bromine solution or of numerous cells, such as used for malcing of ice blocks commersed into three tanks and which cold bromine solution of different temp. circulates.

PLANT ECONOMICS OF MENTHOL CRYSTALS

Rated Plant Capacity = 70.00 Kgs/Day

Land & Building (Land area 14.8 X 30 METER) = RENTED

PLANT & MACHINERY

1. Mixing tank (SS)
2. Jacketted Vessel
3. Distillation (Fraction column)
4. S.S. tank
5. Motor
6. Brine solution tank (PVC)
7. Water chiller
8. Manual packaing machine

FIXED CAPITAL

1. Plant & Machinery		Rs.	3,00,000.00
2. Other Fixed Assets		Rs.	29,500.00
	TOTAL	Rs.	3,29,500.00

RAW MATERIALS

1. Men' oil
2. Che ..icals, Caustic soda, Boric acid salts and others
3. Polyethene packets

TOTAL WORKING CAPITAL/MONTH

1. Raw Material		Rs.	10,62,000.00
2. Salary & Wages		Rs.	9,375.00
3. Utilities & Overheads		Rs.	14,200.00
	TOTAL	Rs.	10,85,575.00

Menthol Crystals

TOTAL CAPITAL INVESTMENT

Total Fixed Capital	Rs.	3,29,500.00
Total Working Capital for 1 month	Rs.	10,85,575.00
TOTAL	Rs.	14,15,075.00

TURN OVER/ANNUM

1. By sale of Menthol Crystal 16800 kg
2. Dementholised oil 19,200 kg

TOTAL Rs. 1,48,80,000.00

PROFIT SALES RATIO = Profit / Sales x 100 = 10.79 %

RATE OF RETURN = Operating profit / T.C.I x 100 = 113.46 %

BREAK EVEN POINT (B.E.P) = 18.34 %

Chapter - 37

Mineral Water

Potable spring waters containing, sulphur iron, magnesium and other mineral salts occuring in certain regions are claimed to be beneficial to human metabolism. They occur in specific and widely scattered locations best known of which are white sulphur springs (Virginia) Hot springs (Arkansas), saragoge springs (New York) Vichy (France Baden (Germany) and (U.S.S.R.) The therapeutic value of such waters is questionable carbonate mineral waters also contain lithium salts.

WATER SUPPLIES AND OTHER IMPURITIES

Natural fresh water supplies are derived indirectly from the oceans; Clouds form by solar evaporation and the winds move the moisture overland to precipitate as rain, snow or hail. The water flows back to the oceans, completing the hydrological cycle. Water supplies are classified as surface supplies and underground waters. Surface waters are rivers, lakes, creeks, ponds, and reservoirs, wells & springs are the sources of underground water.

Water vapour in clouds is generally pure but gathers dust and gases when it reaches the earth suspended organic matter and soil turbidy are picked up. Minerals are leached from the soil and socks and organic matter is added from municipal and industrial wastes and decaying vegetation. Well waters usually are free of suspended materials and organic matter due to filtration through the earth. Surface waters are generally low in mineral content but relatively high in suspended and organic materials.

MAJOR IMPURITIES IN WATER

Most surface waters contain 50-250 pm. dissolved salts well waters contain 150-500 ppm. Water from the great lake contains about 150 pm total dissolved solids TDS.

FORMULATION OF MINERAL WATER

	mg/litre
Total solids at 180°C	304.0
Bicarbonate	78.0
Sulphate	40.0
Calcium	9.0
Potassium	3.0
Magnesium	30.0
Sodium	39.0
pH	8.4

MANUFACTURING PROCESS

The basis manufacturing process consists of the following steps.

1. Filteration
2. Dimineralisation
3. Blending with Salts & gases.
4. Quality control & Testing
5. Bottling
6. Packing.

SOURCES OF RAW WATER

The raw water to be used for the proposed mineral water production unit shall be taken from an underground source or a nearby river. The water shall be pumped from the river or underground source to a storage tank. It shall be analysed and depending upon the quality of the raw water to be processed various processes like water treatment and blending shall be done. On the same before it is finally tested & boiled as mineral water.

SEDIMENTATION AND FILTRATION

Since most surface waters contain varying amounts of suspended solids, including salt, clay, bacteria, viruses, etc. it is necessary to remove them prior further treatment. The principal treatment processes are sedimentation and filteration sedimentation alone is rarely adequate for the clarification of turbid waters and is of little or no value for the removal of such very fine particles as clay, bacteria etc.

DEMINERALISATION UNIT

The demineralisation unit is equipped with a series activated carbon column. This carbon column allows, apart from very fine filtration sensible reduction of the dissolved organic matters and dechlorination of water. Periodic back washing every two weeks contributes to much better utilisation of activated carbon capacity. Independently back washing should be made, when filter resistance has risen to 5 MWC pressure difference.

Exhausted activated carbon needs exchanging or reactivating. Exhausting characteristics are decreasing filteration and dechlorination. Exhausting moment depends on degree of admission of above matters. According the experience, the carbon should be exchanged every year. In operation water flow is from top to bottom, back washing in counter flow upwards.

The demineralisation unit is designed with two lines, each line consisting of one cation exchanger and one anion exchanger and one mixed bed. Normal operation will be one line in operation and one line in stand by.

The cation columns are filled with a strong acid resin, regenerated with diluted hydrochloric acid. The necessary regeneration equipment common to both cation columns and mixed beds, consists of measuring tank, an ejector for diluting of concentrated acid and all connecting pipelines.

BLENDING

In the blending and mixing unit, the demineralise water is mixed and blended with the filtered water upto the desired concentrations of mineral water. At the next stage pH control is done with addition of lime and chlorine and carbon dioxide injected upto the required level to maintain the desired quality.

ANALYSIS AND QUALITY CONTROL TESTING

After blending, samples, are regularly taken at intervals of every one hour and tested and corrective action taken in the blending unit

BOTTLE FILLING & SEALING UNIT

The bottle used for this unit are initially purchased from the market and later on a unit is installed for manufacture of the plastic bottles. To produce the PET Bottles from PET preform the machinery and proforms are fluently available all over India.

'Automa' has developed and fine tuned the extrusion stretch blow technology (the first in Italy) for producing bottle in PVC and PAN upto 2 litre Cap. This technique allows for various benefits with respect to the traditional method of extrusion blow moulding PVC such as reduced cost of resin due to absence of impact modifiers reduction of bottle. Weight upto 25% increase in impermeability, superior bottle clearness and brightness superior mechanical resistance to compression, fluage and bursting and the possibility to produce bottles with special bottoms in order for them to contain medium gassed soft drinks and mineral water. These benefits permit the use of this technology in various sectors such as mineral water, soft drinks syrup, vegetable oil, cosmetics etc.

BOTTLE FILLING AND PACKING

After filling the quality mineral water in bottles the same are packed in cardboard boxes each containing 10 bottles.

PLANT ECONOMICS OF MINERAL WATER IN POUCHES

Rated Plant Capacity = 10000.00 PCH/Day
LAND & BUILDING (Land 800 sq.mt) = RENTED

PLANT & MACHINERY

1. M.S. Sand filters
2. DIMENERALIZATION UNIT 1M3/H
   Anion Exchanger FRP PVC lined
3. Activated carbon Filter FRP PVC lined
4. Cation Exchanger FRP PVC lined
5. Mixed Bed Exchanger FRP PVC lined
6. Piping, Valves, Accessories
   Instrumentation, pumps, blowers
7. Chemical Tanks
8. Misc. Tools & Spares and Lab. Testing Equipments
9. S.S. Mixir.g Tanks
10. Chlorination
11. Carbon dioxide injection equipment
12. FRP PVC lined storage tanks
13. M.S. Tanks
14. Pouch filling and sealing unit
15. Plastic crates
16. Laboratory testing and a quality
    control equipments
17. Pumps
18. Valves, Piping & Instrumentation
19. Tools Jigs & Fixtures

FIXED CAPITAL

1. Plant & Machinery	Rs.	6,00,000.00
2. Other Fixed Assets	Rs.	82,000.00
TOTAL	Rs.	6,82,000.00

RAW MATERIALS

1. Magnesium Carbonate
2. Sodium Carbonate
3. Potassium sulphate
4. Sodium sulphate
5. Carbon dioxide
6. Chlorine
7. Hydrochloric acid
8. Caustic Soda
9. Pouch

TOTAL WORKING CAPITAL/ANNUM

1. Raw Material	Rs.	18,05,340.00
2. Salary & Wages	Rs.	5,41,200.00
3. Utilities & Overheads	Rs.	5,34,000.00
TOTAL	Rs.	28,80,540.00

TOTAL CAPITAL INVESTMENT

Total Fixed Capital	Rs.	6,82,000.00
Total Working Capital for 1 Month	Rs.	2,40,045.00
TOTAL	Rs.	9,22,045.00

TURN OVER/ANNUM

By sale of 30 Lakh pouches of mineral water	Rs.	60,00,000.00

PROFIT SALES RATIO = Profit / Sales x 100 = 47.57 %

RATE OF RETURN = Operating profit / T.C.I x 100 = 309.57 %

BREAK EVEN POINT (B.E.P) = 19.58 %

Chapter - 38

Mini Flour Mill (Atta)

Mini flour mill serves the purpose of processing wheat to convert it into Atta, maida, Suji. Wheat grains are the seeds of the wheat plant which is able to grow in kinds of soil and under widely differing climatic conditions. The principle wheats of commerce belong to the botanical groups Triticum vulgane, Triticum drum and triticum compactum.

The grains of wheat consists of three main parts, the enveloping skins, the embroyo and the endosperm. The relative proportions of these parts vary with the plumpness of the grain but average composition of wheat is 85% endosperm, 2.4% embroyo and 14.5% enveloping skins.

The enveloping skins are pericarp which consists of the epidorumis, epicarp and endocarp. The percarp represent about 6% of the grain. The seed cost consisting of the tests the byaline layer which comprises about 2% of the grain. The aleuorone layer representing about 6.5% of the grain wheat show a wide range of analytical data which is not unexpected in view of the many varieties which are grown and the very different conditions under which they are cultivated. The range of data normally encountered is as follows :

	Percentage
Moisture	10.0 - 17.0
Protein	8.5 - 14.0
Fat	2.0 - 2.50
Fibre	2.0 - 2.50
Mineral matter	1.5 - 2.0
Sugars	2.0 - 3.0
Starch	63.0 - 71.0

MANUFACTURING PROCESS

The milling process breaks open the wheat kernel and reduces the particles formed as to separate the outer and inner portions of the kernel. Bran and gram are almost completely separated from the white interior portions in the milling of refined flour.

When the entire kernel is ground and no separations are made, the product is whole white flour. The following steps are involved in milling wheat, Wheat selection blending sieving, purifying reducing classifying and some combination of maturing bleaching and diastric or enriching treatment of the flour. It is not necessary that all these operations be performed is every flour mill. But either these operations are performed as such as or combination of these operations to serve the some purpose are performed in the flour mills.

1. WHEAT SELECTION AND BLENDING

There are different qualities of wheat being grown in India varying in the composition of proteins, carbohydrates, vitamins etc. The wheat chosen for mills milling depends upon the final products.

2. CLEANING

Cleaning is done with machines that use sieves and air current to separate, dirt, chaff and foeing seeds from wheat other devices are available to remove metal or stone contamination and wash wheat before it is milled.

3. CONDITIONING OR TEMPERING

Water and often heat are added in the process called tempering or conditioning before the actual milling operation beings, to prevent to the bran from fragmenting unusually during milling and to maintain proper milling conditions.

4. MILLING

The milling operations consists of breaking, bolting sieving, purifying reducing, classifying and some combinations of naturing, bleaching and static or enriching.

AIR CLASSIFIERS AND GRINDERS

In this high velocity process, finished flour from the roller mill is further reduced in size in special grinders. In these grinders the flour particles spin in air varieties created behind rotating blades and become smaller by rubbing on the other. This method breaks the protein matrix without undue starch damage. Following this the product is separated in air classified using flow dynamic properties (size, shape and specific gravity) to separate protein particles, starch granules and endosperm chunks. In such separators, centrifugal force keeps the heavy particles, being conveyed in the air stream to the outside of the chamber enabling a cut point separation to be made by a value located at the proper position in the air stream.

CONVEYING SYSTEM

Pneumatic conveying is the term applied to air conveying in flour mills. The higher power costs of pneumatic conveying are offset by cheaper construction less mill clean up, less infestation, cooler flour sock and metal rather than wood spouting. Pneumatic conveying depends upon the fluidizing effect of air flowing through a bed of particulate matter.

PATENT FLOUR:

The purest flour, selected from the purest flour streams released in the mill, is often called patent flour. It has very low mineral (or ash) content is remarkably free from impurities. The bulk of the approximately 72% released is suited to most bread making purposes, by special varieties are needed for some confectionery purposes. These varieties may have to be esp. fine for production of specialized cakes called high ratio cakes, that are esp. light and have good keeping qualities.

THE STORAGE OF FLOUR

Bulk storage has a number of advantages paramount is the ability to blend flour after milling to achieve optimum quality. Another advantages is that adequate storage of flours allows greater milling flexibility. Different grades can be milled and held until needed.

Packed flour is put up in bags holding from 2-100 lb. The larger bags are for bakery use, the smaller for the consumer market.

PLANT ECONOMICS OF MINI FLOUR MILL

Rated Plant Capacity	=	22.40 MT./Day
LAND & BUILDING (Land area 350 sq.mts.)	=	Rented

PLANT & MACHINERY

1. Reel Machine for wheat cleaning.
2. Elevator Conveyor
3. Emery Rula
4. Worm Conveyor
5. Chakki
6. Pneumatic Conveyor
7. Centrifugal Machine
8. Fan Low Pressure.
9. Piple
10. Pulley/Belting/Shafts etc.

11. Motors
12. Water Dampner
13. Storage Bins
14. Platform weighing Balance
15. Tube-well with storage tank

FIXED CAPITAL

1. Plant & Machinery		Rs.	7,57,000.00
2. Other Fixed Assets		Rs.	1,85,000.00
	TOTAL	Rs.	9,42,000.00

RAW MATERIALS

1. Wheat
2. Gunny bags/HDPE/PP/Sacks

TOTAL WORKING CAPITAL/MONTH

1. Raw Material		Rs.	37,15,000.00
2. Salary & Wages		Rs.	1,05,420.00
3. Utilities & Overheads		Rs.	1,78,700.00
	TOTAL	Rs.	39,99,120.00

TOTAL CAPITAL INVESTMENT

Total Fixed Capital		Rs.	9,42,000.00
Total Working Capital for 1 Month		Rs.	39,99,120.00
	TOTAL	Rs.	49,41,120.00

TURN OVER/ANNUM

1. By selling of Atta 6586 MTs		
2. By selling of Chokar 146 MTs.	Rs.	5,32,86,600.00

PROFIT SALES RATIO = Profit / Sales x 100 = 8.45 %

RATE OF RETURN = Operating profit / T.C.I x 100 = 91.13 %

BREAK EVEN POINT (B.E.P) = 32.40 %

Chapter - 39

Note Book, Register & Files

Exercise books & register are used in large quantities in school, colleges, Research laboratories & other educational Institutions. Private & Goverment organisation use these products of necessity for accounting and record keeping purposes with increased population and overall development, demand for Exercise Books & Register is increasing continuously.

Two types of paper are used for making exercise books & register viz. ruled & plain. For rulling, the paper is passed through a double sided disc rulling machine and the desired size. The required number of sheets are then sticked with cover printed page or bound in paper or card board depending on the type of product being made.

Due to rapid Industrialisation taking place in the country, the demand for office stationery is increasing day by day.

They are used for keeping the day to day correspondance, office records, important papers, etc in order. They are used in huge quantity by governmental offices/establishments, schools, colleges etc.

Boards first cut to the record size of the file covers, it is printed as desired & then creased and binded on the binding machine.

MANUFACTURING PROCESS

Note Books are made in varying dimensions and pages and having card board bound paper bound covers etc.

The paper is available in rims. The process as follows.

1. Cutting
2. Rulling
3. Printing of covers.
4. Stapling
5. Binding
6. Finishing

1. Cutting :

The paper which comes in rims is of bigger size which is cut into the required size.

2. Rulling :

This paper is rulled in rulling machines because the note books are generally rulled.

3. Printing of Covers :

Covers as the name suggest covers the book. It has got the purposes of saving the book from deterioration form handling.

Covers are made of many materials like hard board papers oridanary paper.

In case of hard board bound books, an ordinary printed paper is always pasted at the board. In case of hard paper and oridinary bound books an extra paper pasting is required and printing is done on itself.

Besides safeguarding the book from deterioration the cover also serves as a purpose of its identity in that title and the name of owner and subject is also written on the cover.

The small scale units generally get their cover, printed from other printers. The cover should have the following.

1. No of pages.

2. Name of the manufacturers.

3. Identity Chart, giving name of the owner subject, name of school class and address etc.

4. Stapling.

After cutting and rulling, the papers are stapled in a stapling machine and each stapled book contain certain number of pages. Two or more such stapled books are combined in order to make a book of required number of pages.

5. Handling :

If the book is bound by ordinary paper for hard papers, usually such printed papers are stapled while doing stapling.

In case of hard cover, the stapling books are placed between the proper sized board and outer printed cover is pasted to it with same gummy materials the inside page of books are also pasted to the inside the board both sides. Pasted to the inside the board at both sides.

6. Finishing :

Finishing means to cut the edges of the book a little so that edges are smooth. If the book is bound by ordinary paper or hard paper this step is done after stapling.

In case of card board bound books, this type is done before the binding of the books.

FILES

Files are made in different sizes, but very common size is 30 cm x 24 cms. The process of file cover consists of following steps :-

i) Cutting

ii) Bending

iii) Rivets Fastening

iv) Printing

i) Cutting :

The thick paper is purchased from the market in ready made form and indifferent. However, most common colour is khaki and next to it, yellow files are also used. Required sizes are cut on power driven machine. A gauge is set for continuous cutting but it is wisdom to check the cut paper size time to time as gauge may move due to vibrations observed in the machine. After the required quantity of a particular size papers has been cut, gauge may be reset for next job.

ii) Binding :

Binding is done with a small size press and dies. The press may be either hand driven or electrically operated. Before placing the paper for cutting, it should be checked that the paper is properly placed on the bending die. Odd bending is never desirable and file is completely useless.

iii) Rivets fastening :

Either one hollow rivet is fastened on the left corner of file or two rivets at a c.c. distance of 3.25 are fastened in between on central layer of life. This size is the general sizes being extensively used as punching machines of the same c.c. are available in the market. However, this size may be increased or decreased if asked by the customer. If not so, 3.25 cms c.c is very general size and file is easily saleable. Clips are also sometimes used in place of tags.

iv) Printing :

Printing is not necessarily done on out side of left cover. However, if that is to be done, generally a manufacturers of files likes to go to a printing press professional for the purpose. Printing may also be done by manufacturer if he likes but generally he avoids and printing is got done on charges basis. File is then ready & is sent to market for sale.

PLANT ECONOMICS OF EXERCISE NOTE BOOK, REGISTER & PADS

Rated Plant Capacity	=	1833.00 Nos./Day
Land & Building (Land 400 sq. mts.)	=	Rented

PLANT & MACHINERY

1. Disc Ruling Machine
2. Perforating Machine
3. Rotary type paper cutting machine
4. Shifting attachment with 2 sets of cutter 32"
5. Extra set of blades for machines 32".
6. Wire stitching machine
7. Printing Machine
8. Printing types (English/Hindi)
9. Spacing Materials
10. Sundry Items
11. Hand Operating Gumming Machine
12. DAB Press
13. Cost of equipments (Stop rulling attachment, brassrulling, Disc single and doubling)
14. Plastic rulling spaces, rulling powder(Blue, Red and Green)
15. Electrification and Installation Charge
16. Miscellaneous items
17. Thread Book sewing machine

FIXED CAPITAL

1.	Plant & Machinery	Rs.	3,00,901.00
2.	Other Fixed Assets	Rs.	27,000.00
	TOTAL	Rs.	3,27,901.00

RAW MATERIALS

1. Paper white (Cream wove/Maplitho)
2. Paper white for Register
3. Grey board, Card board
4. Stiching wires
5. Ink, glue, thread, cloth
6. Packaging expenses
7. Miscellaneous Items

TOTAL WORKING CAPITAL/MONTH

1. Raw Material	Rs.	96,833.00
2. Salary & Wages	Rs.	23,625.00
3. Utilities & Overheads	Rs.	24,900.00
TOTAL	Rs.	1,45,358.00

TOTAL CAPITAL INVESTMENT

Total Fixed Capital	Rs.	3,27,901.00
Total Working Capital for 1 Month	Rs.	1,45,358.00
TOTAL	Rs.	4,73,259.00

TURN OVER/ANNUM

1. By selling of 150000 exercise book 200 pages.
2. Register 96 pages 100000 exercises book
3. Pad 3,00,000 Nos.

TOTAL Rs. 27,00,000.00

PROFIT SALES RATIO = Profit / Sales x 100 = 30.32 %

RATE OF RETURN = Operating profit / T.C.I x 100 = 172.99 %

BREAK EVEN POINT (B.E.P) = 31.12 %

Chapter - 40

Paper Carry Bags

Paper bags are the oldest types of packaging material and are very much prevalent in the modern days in various fields. Infect, paper bag is one of the most common and popular form of packaging. The hand made bags of paper have been a commodity of common use. However, for the manufacture of bags, the introduction of machines is of recent origin about the middle of 19th century. Since then the manufacture of paper bags has become an important industry in itself, paper bag is the cheapest form of packaging. Such paper bags have the speciality that they are light weight, free from any contaminants like dust, and are, as well, free from shifting or 'puffing' which results in loss of contents. As for the share occupying these paper bags for general use require minimum possible space for storage and shipment, both before and after filling. However, one disadvantage of the paper bags is that they are not durable. Though the strength of the paper bags can be increased by lamination of the base paper with jute, scrim or other reinforcing materials, this however, increases the cost of the bag by making it more expensive.

Paper Carry bags are made from a variety of papers both bleached and imbleached. However, for making of the paper bags for general use, kraft, paper and imitation kraft paper are the most common papers used. Papers most commonly used for commercial and office envelopes include manilla, brown wrapping paper or white papers. The type of paper used for bags depends upon the requirements of the product to be packed. Kraft paper used for bag making is usually of 20 to 40 lb. basis weight.

SIZE OF PAPER BAGS

Paper bags are made in wide variety of sizes. However, the most common sizes are 15 cm x 7 cm x 42 cm to 22 cm x 8 cm x 53 cm in case of gusseted bags and 12 cm x 18 cm, 22 cm x 38 cm, 26 cm x 38 cm and 36 cm x 50 cm (in case of flat or satchel bags. Most popular sizes of envelopes include 10 cm x 5 cm, 15 cm x 9 cm, 18 cm x 13 cm, 23 cm x 10 cm, 26 cm x 12 cm, 25 cm x 20 cm and 30 cm x 23 cm.

Bags and envelops are also custom made in varying sizes according to the customers requirements and satisfaction. Pouches are made in various sizes depending upon the quality or the product to be filled in them.

SIZES OF PAPER BAGS (USED IN THE PROJECT) (FINISHED)

PAPER BAGS CAPACITY	SIZE
1/2 Kg.	19 cm x 14 cm
1 Kg.	21 cm x 16 cm
2 Kgs.	22.5 cm x 21.5 cm
5 Kgs.	31.5 cm x 26.5 x cm

PROCESS OF MANUFACTURE

The printed laminated paper carry bags are prepared by following processing steps.

1. Selection and procurement of paper for hand carry bags.
2. Printing (6-Colour Flexo Printing) of Paper rolls.
3. Lamination of printed papers in the desired thick lamination.
4. Drying of Printed Lamination Paper-Rolls.
5. Feeding into the automatic carry bag making machine in which (cutting, folding, adhesive coating, sides sealing, eyeletting and Handle Fitting) is done in one single operation.

PLANT ECONOMICS OF PAPER CARRY BAGS

Rated Plant Capacity	=	200000.00 Nos./Day
Land & Building (Land Area 1000 Sq.Mt.)	=	Rented

PLANT & MACHINERY

1. One complete Plant & Machinery Set-up for automatic One-colour flexoprinting,
2. Paper cutting, sides sealing, folding, eyeletting and tagging unit for paper carry hand bags of various
3. Automatic plant
4. Tools, jigs, fixtures

FIXED CAPITAL

1. Plant and Machinery		Rs.	8,35,000.00
2. Other Fixed Assets		Rs.	10,000.00
	TOTAL	Rs.	8,45,000.00

RAW MATERIALS

1. Kraft paper
2. Printing Inks (Various desired Colours)
3. Packaging Materials
4. Tags, Eyelets

TOTAL WORKING CAPITAL/MONTH

1. Raw Material	Rs.	17,64,440.00
2. Salary & Wages	Rs.	1,04,625.00
3. Utilities & Overheads	Rs.	67,550.00
TOTAL	Rs.	19,36,615.00

TOTAL CAPITAL INVESTMENT

Total Fixed Capital	Rs.	8,45,000.00
Total Working Capital for 1 Month	Rs.	19,36,615.00
TOTAL	Rs.	27,81,615.00

TURN OVER/ANNUM

1. By sale of 1,80,00,000 Nos. Paper Carry Bags (1/2 Kg. size)
2. By sale of 1,80,00,000 Nos. Paper Carry Bags (1 Kg. Size)
3. By sale of 1,80,00,000 Nos. Paper Carry Bags (2 Kg. size)
4. By sale of 60,00,000 Nos. Paper Carry Bags (5 Kg Size)

TOTAL Rs. 3,12,00,000.00

PROFIT SALES RATIO = Profit / Sales x 100 = 23.77 %

RATE OF RETURN = Operating profit / T.C.I x 100 = 266.61 %

BREAK EVEN POINT (B.E.P) = 15.60 %

Chapter - 41

Pan Masala

Pan Masala are widely used to remove bad odour of mouth and for scenting the breath in order to impart it a pleasant feeling. Pan masalas are available in the market in many different types, forms, brand, standards. Now a days Pan Parag, Prince Gutka, Pan mayur, Darbar type, Rajni Gandha, Tambul, Maruti, Pan Bahar, types pan masalas are commonly used.

These are the best Pan Masalas and are made of kutch , Lime betal-nuts and other sophisticated item and perfumes.

The other types of Pan Masalas are available in the form of fine powder, pills, or tablets or paste but the various constituents remain nearly the same. Pan masala is also Known as Tembul Bilas. A wide range of spices enters into its composition and if is put into tin pots in the form of powder or paste. But now packing of pouches are very much common and used all over the places. It is used to distinguish the bad odour of mouth and for scenting the breath importing a pleasant feelings. It is taken at the end of a tooth-pick. The sale and marketing of Pan Masala is increasing day by day. It is very clear from the fact that wherever you go in the market, in the town , in a village you will find same in panwari shops around every where in every mohalla and in every street.

MANUFACTURING PROCESS WITH FORMULATIONS

GENERAL FORMULA FOR PAN MASALA

1. Sandal Wood	26.00%
2. Kapur Kachri	10.00%
3. Cloves	1.20%
4. Cinnamon	5.80%
5. Dried Rose petals	11.80%
6. Liquorice powder	25.60%

7. Cardamom minor	3.50%
8. Mace	2.40%
9. Sugar	11.73%
10. Saffron genuine	0.25%
11. Peppermint	0.50%
12. Attar Rose	0.50%
13. Attar Panri	0.58%
14. Attar Koda	0.50%
15. Saccharine	0.08%
16. Musk Perfumes	0.25%

SAADA (PLAIN) PAN MASALA

Formula : As per 100 parts

Kutha	50 parts by weight
Lime	12 parts by weight
Betal Nuts	25 parts by weight
Cardomom minor	2 part by weight
Cardamom major	3 parts by weight
Pippermint	1 part by weight
Sandalwood oil	5 parts by weight
Saffron genuine	0.25 part by weight
Attar Rose	0.25 part by weight
Atter Panri	0.25 part by weight
Atter Keoda	0.25 part by weight
Saccharine	0.50 part by weight
Musk perfumes	0.50 part by weight

Pan Masala (ZARDA)

FORMULA

It consist of three sections

1.	Tobacco Leaves	70 parts
	Catechu (black variety)	4 parts
	Lime	4 parts
	Black pepper	4 parts
	Taj	2 parts

2	Cloves	10 parts
	Cardamom (Major)	15 parts
	Cardamom (Minor)	10 parts
	Mace	10 parts
	Cinnamom	15 parts
	Nagar Motha	10 parts
	Tejpat	5 parts
	Sugandhbala	10 parts
	Charils	5 parts
	White sandal wood (Powdered)	10 parts

PROCESS - (PLAIN & SWEET PAN MASALA)

Pulverise the solid or dry ingredients to convert them into fine powder, then sieve through a fine mesh sieve.

Now, in a stone mortar put the liquid ingredients, add perfume and work withpestle to form a uniform liquid. Add this liquid mixture, to the powder of dry and solid ingredients and rub well until they have mixed well. Pan masala in powder form is now ready to pack into pouches.

ZARDA PAN MASALA

Zarda making process is completed in four different steps, which are.

i. Tobacco leaves are dried in the sun and chipped which are dyed with various harmless food colours & granuled as discussed later.

ii. A thick extract which is technically called "Kimam" is prepared of tobacco leaves

iii. Powdered spices and tobacco extract is coated on the granule. This process is called 'spice coating'.

iv. Incorporation of perfumes. The details of the above four steps is given below :-

a. Making granules and their drying. It is the first step to make zarda. For this purpose a good formula is given earlier.

Spread the tobacco leaves on a cemented or smooth & clean floor in the sun light and let them dry. These dried leaves broken up into small pieces by pressing them in hands. All the leaves are broken by hands. Then these broken leaves are shifted through 150 mesh sieve to separate fine dust.

Breaking the tobacco leaves and sieving is done continuously till the midribs and large veins of leaves are left. These are separated by sorting and used in making Kimam. By this method tobacco leaves are reduced to almost uniform sized small granules (chura).

Black pepper and 'Taj' are reduced to a fine powder. Catechu is dissolved in some water, boiled for a few minutes and strained through fine cloth. Lime is also dissolved in some water and some strained when cold. Now black pepper, 'Taj' catechu extract & lime water are dissolved in about 20 litre of water and again strained through fine cloth.

This blackish water is sprinkled over tobacco 'chura' and rubbed between hands till all the water is consumed and the 'chura' gets a blackish tint. Now whole of the chura is made into a heep and left undisturbed overnight. It should be kept covered with a thick cloth or gunny bag. The next morning, this cloured 'chura' is spread on the flour in the sunlight to dry.

b. Preparing Tobacco extract

Take tobacco dust, veins and mid-ribs, cigarette cuttings from cigarette factories and leaves and soak in water. Keep for 3-4 days, stirring occasionally within this time all the nicotine of tobacco will be dissolved in water, which will become of brownish colour. This water is now strained through a fine cloth and powdered gum acacia and sugar is mixed in it. This extract is now boiled over at a mild temperature till its consistency becomes as that of honey and of blackish brownish colour.

c. Coating colour and dried chura with spices

For coating the coloured and dried chura with spices, an extract of selected spices is used. The composition is given earlier. Pulverised all the above ingredient to a very fine powder and dissolve in water. Now add gum acacia and already prepared 'thick tobacco extract'. Mix thoroughly. Coating

SUPARI CUTTER (ROLLER TYPE)

solution is ready. It is sprinkled over the coloured and dried chura then rubbed within both hands till all the solution is consumed. Now cover it with a cloth for 4 to 5 hours. Then again dried in the sunlight and rubbed over sieve, so that granules are made. These granules should be of the size of mustard seeds.

d. Addition of perfume

The last step is to add the perfume. Above prepared Zarda granules are spread in the sunlight to warm them a bit. When these granules have become somewhat, sprinkle the perfume mixture over them & rub the granules in both hands so that perfume is thoroughly and evenly distributed. The whole preparation is immediately put into an airtight pouches and packed.

PLANT ECONOMICS OF PAN MASALA

Rated Plant Capacity	=	200.00 Kgs/Day
LAND & BUILDING (Land Area)	=	Rs 5,30,000.00

PLANT & MACHINERY

1. Feeding and self sealing machine
2. Coarse pulveriser
3. Betal nut cutter
4. Ribbon blend mixer
5. Automatic weigh balance
6. Weigh Balance
7. Tin filling & sealing machine

FIXED CAPITAL

1. Land & Building	Rs.	5,30,000.00
2. Plant & Machinery	Rs.	5,75,000.00
3. Other Fixed Assets	Rs.	1,21,000.00
TOTAL	Rs.	12,26,000.00

RAW MATERIALS

1. Katha
2. Lime
3. Betel nut
4. Cardamom minor
5. Sandal wood flour
6. Cardamom major

7. Cloves
8. Cinamom
9. Sugar
10. Saccarine
11. Peppermint
12. Perfumes
13. Pouches
14. Tin pack

TOTAL WORKING CAPITAL/MONTH

1. Raw Material	Rs.	5,96,730.00
2. Salary & Wages	Rs.	48,187.00
3. Utilities & Overheads	Rs.	1,48,000.00
TOTAL	Rs.	7,92,917.00

TOTAL CAPITAL INVESTMENT

Total Fixed Capital	Rs.	12,26,000.00
Total Working Capital for 3 Month	Rs.	23,78,752.00
TOTAL	Rs.	36,04,752.00

TURN OVER/ANNUM

By selling of 60000 kgs of Pan Masala.	Rs.	1,26,00,000.00

RATE OF RETURN = 58.17 %

BREAK EVEN POINT (B.E.P) = 47.93 %

Chapter - 42

Pappad Plant (Automatic)

The Word "PAPPAD" is quite familiar with Indians. Pappad is a common Indian food normally taken with meals. Some people take it along with tea also. It is a food which is liked by people of all states, people doing all type of occupations. It is well within the reach of common people. Pappad can be exported to other countries and can earn valuable foreign exchange as people in other countries have also taken interest in this food item.

Some time before pappads were made at home by the ladies and most of them know, the process of making them. At present also some of the housewives are making these, but their number has decreased considerably. However, they used to make them for their captive uses, only. Whereas modern ladies don't want to take trouble of making them at homes because of a number of reasons at follows:-

1. They are not free as ladies have also started working in offices like men.

2. They don't have ample space in their houses for making them.

3. Fresh pappads are available in the market (all types).

4. They have become sophisticated and don't want to make them in their homes.

Pappad's are of different types i.e. made from urad dal, moong dal, potatoes, rice etc. However, process of making all of them is very simple and absolutely identical except the formulations which may change according to one's taste. Pappad's may be made by using red or black peppers and their quantities may also be altered to make the product strong or light in chilly.

Normally, pappads are made round in shape and are thin like paper. All sizes and types of pappads are available in the market and can be manufactured also under one shed with almost the same plant and machineries.

PROCESS OF MANUFACTURE

Pappad may be manufactured by a single type of pulse flour or combination of various pulse flour. The rice flour is also added to reduce the cost of the pappad. However, following formulation is suggested for the pappad making.

Urad Pulse Flour	1000 Parts
Black Pepper	250 Parts
Sodium Bicarbonate	10 Parts
Zeera	15 Parts
Hing Water	10 Parts
Salt	25 Parts

All the ingredients are first taken according to their weighted quantities and then pre mixed. Now, the premixed mass is taken into a dough kneading machine. Required quantity of water is added and the whole content is kneaded at minimium speed to get homogenous lump of the dough. After 30 minutes resting it is divided into balls of about 6-8 kg mass. Now, this ball is placed on the conveyor belt of the automatic dough sheeting machine. The belt is moved to and thickness is gradually decreased using the lever handle till the final thickness of about 2.5 to 2 mm sheet is obtained. The conveyor belt takes the sheet to the sheet cutting machine.

The sheet is now cut into round shaped and tailing materials are then again mixed fed to the sheeting machine. After round cut of the pappad, the pappad is sent for sundrying or a drying chamber in which hot air at 27-30% of moisture content.

The pappad are then packed into the printed plastic packs. This plastic pack may contain about 100 pappads or as per market requirements.

PLANT ECONOMICS OF PAPPED PLANT (AUTOMATIC)

Rated Plant Capacity	=	0.60 MT/Day
Land & Building (Total area 500 Sq. Mt.)	=	Rented

PLANT & MACHINERY

1. Sifter
2. Dough Mixer
3. Automatic Dough sheeting machine
4. Automatic sheet cutting machine
5. Air Drying Chamber
6. Pack Sealing machine
7. Weighing balance
8. Miscellaneous equipments

FIXED CAPITAL

1. Plant & Machinery	Rs.	8,98,000.00
2. Other Fixed Assets	Rs.	1,75,000.00
TOTAL	Rs.	10,73,000.00

RAW MATERIALS

1. Black Urad Dal Flour/Moong Dal Flour
2. Black Pepper
3. Sodium Bicarbonate
4. Zeera
5. Hing Water
6. Salts
7. Packaging materials i.e. poly pack etc.

TOTAL WORKING CAPITAL/MONTH

1. Raw Material	Rs.	4,94,625.00
2. Salary & Wages	Rs.	63,000.00
3. Utilities & Overheads	Rs.	50,750.00
TOTAL	Rs.	6,08,375.00

TOTAL CAPITAL INVESTMENT

Total Fixed Capital	Rs.	10,73,000.00
Total Working Capital for 1 Month	Rs.	6,08,375.00
TOTAL	Rs.	16,81,375.00

TURNOVER/ANNUM

Receipts by sale of 180 ton of pappad	Rs.	99,00,000.00

PROFIT SALES RATIO = Profit / Sales x 100 = 21.85 %

RATE OF RETURN = Operating profit / T.C.I x 100 = 128.66 %

BREAK EVEN POINT (B.E.P) = 31.23 %

Chapter - 43

PET Bottles From Pre-Form (Capsules)

PET bottles and containers are being used to pack mineral water, edible oils, coolant, shampoos etc.

The packing Industry has undergone a revolutionary change. Conventional packing materials like tins plate, glass, paper etc. have been replaced by P.E.T.

Glass container are not suitable due to their fragile toy nature and are heavy. Metal containers are not suitable at all for certain chemicals.

P.E.T containers are light, tough, unbreakable, hygienic durable and appealing. They reduce transport cost and damages, and increase the sale appeal of the products, P.E.T. containers like glass container can be made transparent, beside they may be given different colours also. They are not affected by humidity and is chemically, Inert therefore preserve the goods as such for a long time. It is therefore, increasingly used for packing food, chemical, and other consumable items.

In recent years, P.E.T. containers have become a major material in packing in comparison with paper, metal and glass in many markets. P.E.T. have virtually over taken these transitional material and have dominated in a good number of fields of packaging.

MANUFACTURING PROCESS

The one line processing system of the machine (stretch blow molding machine) is fully automatic in the sense that a well proportioned PET or PVC or Pp materials fed through the hopper and it convert itself into a ready bottle complete in all respects. The machine is designed to heat up the material and under spiral screw and barrel plunger force feed it to the mold where a perform called parison is formed This parison is reheated to its below melting temperature and the action of compressed air it is biaxially stretched to a dimension air it is biaxially stretched to a dimension about ten times bigger than the parison dimensions. Thus, the container becomes too thin walled and very light weight. But, due to stretching it gets harder, stronger, stiffer, The wall sections are very uniform in thickness as the some are precisely controlled in the machine automatically. The more the material is stretched the stronger it becomes after solidification and cooling. When the articles get cooled, these are auto matically ejected from the machine and stored for inspection, sorting, packing or dispatch.

PLANT ECONOMICS OF PET BOTTLE & PET CONTAINERS

Rated Plant Capacity	=	1900.00 BTL/Day
Land & Building (Land Area 250 Sq. Mt.)	=	Rented

PLANT & MACHINERY

1. One stage bi-axial orientation stretch blow moulding machine bottles,chiller,dryer,compressor & accessories

FIXED CAPITAL

1. Plant & Machinery	Rs.	4,50,000.00
2. Other Fixed Assets	Rs.	30,000.00
TOTAL	Rs.	4,80,000.00

RAW MATERIALS

1. Pet preforms (capsules)
2. Packaging Materials

TOTAL WORKING CAPITAL/MONTH

1. Raw Material	Rs.	69,775.00
2. Salary & Wages	Rs.	28,860.00
3. Utilities & Overheads	Rs.	25,650.00
TOTAL	Rs.	1,24,285.00

TOTAL CAPITAL INVESTMENT

Total Fixed Capital	Rs.	4,80,000.00
Total Working Capital for 1 Month	Rs.	1,24,285.00
TOTAL	Rs.	6,04,285.00

TURN OVER/ANNUM

By sale of 570000 Nos of PET Bottle	Rs.	19,95,000.00

PROFIT SALES RATIO = Profit / Sales x 100 = 15.77 %

RATE OF RETURN = Operating profit / T.C.I x 100 = 52.06 %

BREAK EVEN POINT (B.E.P) = 58.89 %

Chapter - 44

Plastic Injection Moulding Products

Injection moulding is one of the most important processes used in plastic articles manufacture both in terms of volume thermo-plastics handled and the range of articles manufactured.

the original injection moulding machines were similar in design to metal die casting machines, when this process was developed in 1934 for the rapid moulding of thermoplastics. During the subsequent years, especially as experience and increase in understanding of processing chracteristics of plastics led to the improvements in the design of such machines, this technique has proved highly successful and to the bulk of thermoplastics are manufactured by this technique. The injection moulding machine is now a sophisticated integrated piece of equipment and includes all the mechanisms and centralls required to carry out successfully each step of the injection moulding process completely in a single unit. During the past two decades, the demand has grown for larger capacity machines and today it is possible to inject as much as 5 Kg of material at one 'shot'. Injection moulding process has inherent advantages of high degree of repititive accuracy and adaptability for the production of a wide range of components. The process of injection moulding can be applied with modifications to thermosetting materials also and differs from transfer moulding in that the plasticizing chamber contains enough material to fill the mould several times.

The thermoplastics material in general used for injection moulding include polyethylene PVC polystyrene, polypropylene polymethyl methacrylate PTFFZ polyamides, cellulose, derivatives polyurethanes, CAB and polycarbonates.

USES AND APPLICATION

Injection moulded articles mostly are made by thermoplastics materials with some exception of thermosetting materials. The main thermoplastic material which are processed to make the finished articles are:-

1. Cellulose nitrate
2. Cellulose acetate
3. Cellulose Acetate Butyrate

4. Ethyl cellulose
5. Cellulose propionate
6. Polymethyl Methacrylate
7. Polystyrene
8. Polyvinyl chloride-Acetate copolymer
9. The polyamides
10. Polyethylene.
11. Polypropylene
12. Acetate
13. Rigid P.V.C.
14. Acrylonitrile Butadiene
15. Styrene Acrylonitrile (SAN)
16. Polypropylene (PPO)
17. Ionomer
18. Poly Sulphone
19. Poly Carbonates

The main thermosetting plastic which are now injection moulded are:-

1. Phenolic resins
2. Urea-formaldehyde compounds (Bakelite)
3. Melamines.

The above mentioned thermoplastics finds numerous application as injection moulded goods. Few of them are illustrated as here under:-

1. Buckets
2. Bottles
3. Goggles
4. Toys
5. Trays
6. Cycle seat.
7. Cabinets for radio transisters tape recorder T.V. and other electronic appliances
8. Rods.
9. Electrical switches, sockets and plugs
10. Electrical panel & Board.
11. Bottle closures
12. Ignition coil housings etc.
13. Salad bowls
14. Toggles.

PROCESS OF MANUFACTURE

For the manufacture of injection moulded articles mostly, screw guided injection moulding machine is used. The advantage of this machine is that thermoplastics as well thermosets can be processed with the same machine using different dies for defferent product. The injection moulding process comprises four stages, each of which must be closely controlled and regulated to obtain good quality mouldings.

These stage are :-

1. Plasticizing
2. Injection
3. After filling and
4. Cooling and mould release.

Plasticizing:

The resin is fed from the hopper of the moulding machine and heated and softned to make its plastics in a heated cylinder. To achieve a suitable state by plasticization which will ensure a good quality product requires close control of temperature of the cylinder and residence time of the resin in the cylinder. In addition, on preplasticizing machines (screw type), the speed of rotation of screw and the applied pressure also influences the state of plasticizations. During this operation, the resin compound is conveyed from one end to the other end of the cyclinder is heated, melted and plasticized during the operation.

INJECTION :

In the injection stage a correct a mount of plastized melt is injected from the plasticizing cylinder into the relatively cold mould, while closed under controlled pressure. The amount of material injected into a mould is controlled by the machine feed mechanism. On piston or plunger type moulding machines this is achieved by a volumetric measurement of unmelted granules or resin it self.

On a one a screw preplasticizing machine however, the central is by valumetric measurement of molten material the latter method being more accurate.

After-filling :-

The solidification of the plasticized melt begins in the cold mould soon after its injection in the mould from the walls of the mould. Then injected material is kept under pressure for some time to ensure adequate filling of the mold and prevent the backflow of the polymer, and to compensate for the decrease in volume due to solidification.

The quality of the article very much depends upon the temperature and pressure of material in the mold cavity at the moment it starts solidifying in the gate. When the mould is being filled, the temperature of the plasticized melt starts falling and there are two opposing tendencies taking place-the thermal contraction tries to reduce the volume of the molding and residual pressure in the melt tries to expend it. The above two tendencies exist simultaneously and in an ideal case they must counter-balance each other.

Cooling and Mold Release

Some further time is allowed to elapse for cooling of the molded article in the mold until it is sufficiently rigid to be ejected without any risk of deformation taking place subsequently. Control of mold temperature is also important if the quality of the article is to be maintained uniform and consistant throughout the entire range. The mold temperature control systems allow the mold temperature to be raised to its optimum value before start up, so that during the initial period of production, the manufacture of highly strained parts from a cold mold and wastage of material due to short is avoided.

The mold is then opened eject the molding and is closed again to receive the plasticized melt for the next cycle of operation.

TIME CYCLE :

The basic steps and operation of injection molding process are common in all injection molding machines, i.e, taking a quantity of plastics material softening it in a cylinder by heating forcing it under pressure by means of a plunger of screw into a mold, cooling the plasticized melt in the mold, and ejecting it out by opening the mold. The time cycle of the operation may be considered in terms of a clock in which the hand is rotating in a clockwise direction.

When the mold is closed, the cylinder is ready in position to enable the plasticized melt to be injected into the mold. The period during which the plunger or screw moves forward displacing the plasticized melt from the cylinder into the mold is called 'injection time'.

PLANT ECONOMICS OF PLASTIC INJECTION MOULDING

Rated Plant Capacity	=	923.00 Nos/Day
Land & Building (Land Area 200 sq.Yard (approx)	=	Rented

PLANT & MACHINERY

1. Injection Moulding machine with all fittings
2. Scrap Grinder
3. Extruder, Mixer, Take off etc.
4. Acrylic cutter, Grinder, Heater

FIXED CAPITAL

1. Plant & Machinery	Rs.	4,10,000.00
2. Other Fixed Assets	Rs.	1,40,000.00
TOTAL	Rs.	5,50,000.00

RAW MATERIALS

1. Plastic moulding powder PP
2. Plastic scrap
3. Acrylic Plastic Sheet
4. Packaging Materials

TOTAL WORKING CAPITAL/MONTH

1. Raw Material	Rs.	1,71,250.00
2. Salary & Wages	Rs.	18,590.00
3. Utilities & Overheads	Rs.	48,225.00
TOTAL	Rs.	2,38,065.00

TOTAL CAPITAL INVESTMENT

Total Fixed Capital	Rs.	5,50,000.00
Total Working Capital for 1 Month	Rs.	2,38,065.00
TOTAL	Rs.	7,88,065.00

TURN OVER/ANNUM

1. By sale of Patras 72000 Pc.
2. Ice Trays 50000 Pc.
3. Fridge Mats 25000 Pc
4. Small Plastic Misc. Parts 50000
5. Small Plastic Kits 50000
6. Plastic Waste Paper Baskets 30000
7. Misc. Items of Stationery

TOTAL Rs. 42,84,000.00

PROFIT SALES RATIO = Profit / Sales x 100 = 28.48 %

RATE OF RETURN = Operating profit / T.C.I x 100 = 154.83 %

BREAK EVEN POINT (B.E.P) = 30.19 %

Chapter - 45

Polythene Bags

Polythene bags are made of polythene sheets which is fast replacing cellulose acetate (cellophane film). Polythene sheet is transparent, tough non toxic, not affect by humidity and is chemically inert. Polythene bags are much suitable for packing purposes.

Polythene sheets has possibilities in the packing field where protection against moisture and monsoon condition are required. Polythene is available commercially in two specific types, a conventional branched low density polythene and a linear high density polythene has become familiar to common man due to its characteristics as exhibited in films sheeting plastic bottles, plastic piping and tube, dish, pans, baskets, television antena wire and tublers etc.

The properties of polythene vary as to type and molecular weight, Polythylenes are among the lights in all of the plastics. In appearance they are a translucent white the conventional polythylene being a little more transparent than the linear type.

In comparision with the well known plastic materials they are about midway between the extremely flexible vinyl plastics and the more rigid polystyrenes. The cut standing properties of polyethylene are listed below :-

1. Readily mouldable into various shapes and forms.
2. Food mechanical properties combining together, strength, flexibility and toughness.
3. Excellent electrical resistances.
4. Low moisture vapour transmission.
5. High resistance to most solvents and chemicals.
6. Wide range of moulds form highly flexible film to rigid moulded forms.
7. Tasteless and odourless.
8. Good water resistances.

PROPERTIES OF POLYTHENE

Tensile strength	2,000 to 3,000
Elongation	200 to 800
Tear Strength g/mill	100 to 300
Heat seal of	250 to 400
Water absorption %	24
hours	Very low.

MANUFACTURING PROCESS

The manufacturing process has been considered in the automation which is composed of an extruder using polythene pellets, printer, cutter and bottom sealer. Through this system production efficiency has been made effectively high, operation cost, reduced, operation and quality of product made constant. The following operations are described in details.

1. Extrusion of Polythene sheet

Polythene sheet is extruded in the extruder by charging polythene pellet into the hopper. For blowing the rubber film coming out of extruder, air is introduced at pressure through the die blowing the film to approximate two or three times. The air pressure should be carefully adjusted to obtain the desired sheet thickness. The thickness of sheet can also be adjusted through the control of the wind cut rate. Generally, the thickness are form 70 to 700 gauge. The sheet is wound on a pictrolle which permit maintenance of the air bundle. The cooling is effected by placing a special air ring at a suitable position after the die. The die should be generally operated & gives clearer film,. The die should generally be operated in vertical position and die operating temperature 375-450°F.

Extrusion consists of forcing the plastic to flow through a shaped orific called die. The shape and the dimensions of the orifice determine the shape and dimensions of the extruders the shape and dimensions of the extrudates or extruded products but orific and extrudate will usually differ at least slightly in dimension-s and in many cases in shape too. Nearly all extruder products are cylindrical in the broad sense of the word that is their cross sections in the directions, perpendicular to the direction of flow through the orific and are constant in shape and size.

An extruder principally is a tube or barrel fitted with a motor driven screw to homogenize and heat a compound, convey the melt through a die fitted to produce the desired shape. The heat is developed by friction of the particles and shearing of the size of viscous mass as well as through external heating of barrel.

3. Cutting & Making of Bags

Printed tubular film polythene is cut off from certain bag length and put pieces of film taken into the polythene bag making machine. Although heat sealing machines are also available by which the bags can be prepared but in this machine production capacity is little. In the heat scaling machine, the bottom part of the tubular film is sealed with a heat sealer.

The polythene bag making machine is available in the different size viz. 18 inch, 28 inch, 36 inch and 42 inches. The width of making bag's and sealing depends upon the sizes of the machine. For instances, if you have a machine of 18 inch. You can only bags of maximum upto 18 inch width the sealing.

Some cottage scale manufacturers purchases polythene films from the market and make by installing only heat sealing or bags making machine. These machines are available throughout India.

In this way, their investment is very little but at the same time profit ratio is less.

4. Inspection and Packing

The finished product is inspected thoroughly to see the thickness, uniformity. Some times due to improper air flow the thickness is not uniform. If it is so the attention should be paid immediately and trouble should be removed. The product should be removed. The product should be sorted and treated as waste.

In this way, their investment is very little but at the same time profit ratio is less.

PLANT ECONOMICS OF POLYTHENE BAGS

Rated Plant Capacity	=	150.00 KGS/Day
Land & Building Total Land 250 sq.mt.)	=	Rented

PLANT & MACHINERY

1. Automatic Bag making Plant (including Extruder, Die head, Control board, Air compressor, winder etc.)
2. Cutting & Sealing machine
4. Stereo Hydraulic Press
5. Grinder

FIXED CAPITAL

1. Plant & Machinery	Rs.	4,70,000.00
2. Other Fixed Assets	Rs.	65,000.00
TOTAL	Rs.	5,35,000.00

RAW MATERIALS

1. L.D.P.E. Granules
2. Miscellaneous as (Bag handles etc.)

TOTAL WORKING CAPITAL/MONTH

1. Raw Material	Rs.	1,52,800.00
2. Salary & Wages	Rs.	31,562.00
3. Utilities & Overhead	Rs.	40,750.00
TOTAL	Rs.	2,25,112.00

TOTAL CAPITAL INVESTMENT

Total fixed capital	Rs.	5,35,000.00
Total working capital for 1 month	Rs.	2,25,112.00
TOTAL	Rs.	7,60,112.00

TURN OVER/ANNUM

By sale of 45,000 kg. Polythene Bags.	Rs.	36,00,000.00

PROFIT SALES RATIO = Profit / Sales x 100 = 18.89 %

RATE OF RETURN = Operating profit / T.C.I x 100 = 89.45 %

BREAK EVEN POINT (B.E.P) = 45.42 %

Chapter - 46

Phenyl (Black and White)

Phenyl type disinfectants fall in the category of black oil disinfectants and are extensively used for sanitation purposes, for drains, floor, stables etc. and are prepared from coal tar distillates containing high boiling tar acids. These are, however, less, affected in contact with organic matter.

Phenyl is being used since very beginning for killing insects grown in nallahas, lavatory and kooradan. Most of the diseases causes due to insects.

The black coal tar disinfectants are intimate mixture of coaltar oils and phenols with water and a suitable soap in such a physical state that it is optically clear. Rosin and liquid rosin; fixed oils such as castor palm, kernel, coconut and fish oil or any of their fatty acid or naphthenic acid can be used, usually as mixture in the black fluids. These fluids dilute only with moderately hard water.

The white coal tar disinfectants are readily made concentrated emulsion in water and stabilized by some suitable protective colloid certain protective colloids such as gelatin and suitable casein well permit the dilution of the conc emulsion with any water hard or saline.

By varying the amount and type of the phenolic homologues and the tar oils (Carbolic acid or Crysylic Creosotes) these disinfectants can be produced to cover a wide range, both for phenol content and germicidal value.

Because the special dispersing agents (the protective colloids) are used in small quantities as compared to the soaps used in the manufacture of dark fluids, the white fluids are generally cheaper on the basis of expenses per germicidal unit of rideal walker value than the black fluid. White fluids seldom contain less than 45 percent water and often considerably more while the black fluids contain water only up to 10 percent although some of the cheaper household fluids mainly contains up to 20 percent water. However, the black fluids are more suitable than the white fluid and if properly stored the black variety well remain in good usable condition for years together while the white fluid deteriorates on prolonged storage. It is always better to use the white fluids within a few months of its preparation.

MANUFACTURING PROCESS

High Boiling Tar Acid Black Fluids (Phenyl):-

Formulation

H.B.T.A (Boiling range 90% between (220°C% - 310%C)	-	40
Creosote Oil (5- 7% Tar acids)	-	25
W.W. Rosin	-	12
Castor Oil (Commerial grade)	-	7
Linseed oil	-	3
Soyabean Oil	-	2
Caustic Soda	-	3.4
Soft Water	-	7.6

Process :-

The castor oil and linseed oil are mixed together in a saponification vessels and heated slowly to 90°C. A pre-prepared 33% caustic soda solution in water is then slowly added with stirring. After the complete addition the mixture is boiled for a few minutes for the complete saponification of the fats. The castor oil accelerates and assists the saponification or otherwise slowly reacting linseed oil and soyabean oil. After the complete saponification of the fats rosin's is added and again the mixture kept in boiling stage for the saponification of rosin.

During the saponification process whatever water is lost by it evaporation is compensated by adding water.

When the saponification is over, heated is stopped and sufficient quantities of water added to get a soap solution. To this soap solution, is added with stirring the high boiling tar acid and creosote oil followed by the remaining quantities of water. The disinfectant thus formed is stirred for a period of 15 minutes to get a stable emulsion in water which can be packed and put into the market.

Formulation

		(%)
H.B.T.A (Boiling range 90% between 220°C% - 310%C)	-	30
Creosote Oil (5- 7% Tar acids)	-	30
Chlorinated Xylenols (Holdol - D)	-	3
W.W. Rosin	-	12
Castor Oil (Commerial grade)	-	7
Linseed oil	-	3
Soyabean Oil	-	2
Caustic Soda	-	3.4
Soft Water	-	9.6

Process:-

The Castor oil, linseed oil and soyabean oil are mixed well in a saponification tank and slowly heated to 90°C. A solution of caustic soda of 33% cone water is prepared and is added to the fat mixture in the saponification tank with constant stirring and at slow rate. When the whole has been added, the mixture is boiled for some time to complete the saponification of the fats. Then rosin is added and the mixture boiled for some more time water lost by evaporation during the saponification is compensated.

When the saponification is completed, the heat source turned off and sufficient quantity of water is added to get a soap solution. To this soap solution, are added, the H.B.T.A Creosote and chlorinated xylenols with stirring then the remaining quantity of water is added and the mixture is stirred well for a period of 15 minute and stored in large tanks.

METHODS OF MANUFACTURING OF BLACK PHENYL

Coal tar disinfectant are generally manufactured in a steam jacketted kettle fitted with a stirring equipment commercially

Various methods are in practice. The rosin may be first heated and saponified with caustic soda solution after which the tar acid oil are stirred in. Heating is continued for several hours at about 90°C until the mixture is uniform.

During final mixing test should that the product in the kettle gives a definite emulsion when added to water. If the product gives more of a solution then an emulsion when added to water mixing & heating should contiune with occasional testing. If it is still facts to give an emulsion adjustments are needed. There may be in sufficient tar acids oils present or the alkalinity of the soap may be too high. Maximum water content of the finished product should be between 8 - 10%. The caustic soda should be governed by the saponification values of the rosin, tar oil or other material used while the total soap contained will depend on the character of the tar acid oil.

Tar acid distiller's have found it profitable to extract as much phenol as possible from tar acid oil. This producing a product better adopted to the manufacture of disinfectant.

The boiling range of the tar acid is another determining factor. Higher Coefficient may result with 25% tar acids of the higher boiling range than with 60% tar acids in the low boiling range. A correctly made coal tar disinfectant should form a milky emulsion when mixed in 220 parts of distilled water at 25°C. The emulsion should show no appreciate separation on standing for five hour at 25°C, other than possible traces of only float sendiment. The disinfectant should be made from chilled tar acid so that no napthlane precipitates when subjected to a temperature of 0°C for 12 hours. Germicidal strength should remain constant or nearly so without any appreciable variation.

Higher coefficient disinfectants are made commercially using "high boiling tar acid". In preparing such high coefficient disinfectant, one third or more of a castor oil or a castor oil fatty acid soap is preferable to a soap made wholly from-tall acid or from rosin because it gives a better emulsion and hence a higher coefficient.

About one third of the castor oil may be replaced by some other vegetable oil such as castor oil. The alkali may be potash or a combination of potash and 20% caustic soda. A mixture of 15% tar acids and higher boiling acid will yield a finished disinfectant having a coefficient somewhere between 3 and 20 depending upon how much of each is employed, although there is no definite relation.

FORMULATION (WHITE PHENYL)

Formulation - 1

H.B.T. A (Boiling range 220-310°C) (High boiling tar acid)	-	4%
Cresylic Creosote (20-30% phenol)	-	30%
Casein (fine powders)	-	4%
Borax	-	2%
Sodium dodecyl benzene sulphonate (SDBA)	-	0.1%
Water	-	59.9%

Process:-

Firstly, casein and borax are mixed in water at 30°C and stirred well for 1 hour to get a homogeneous fluid this is then filtered through a 100 mesh gauge. To the filtered solution a sodium dodecyl benzene sulphonate is added, and with vigorous stirring is then added the mixture of high boiling tar acid and cresylic creosate at a slow rate. The final solution is then homogenised in a shearing colloid mill.

In these preparation, care should be taken to use a freshly prepared solution of casein and it should not be allowed to stand for any length of time.

PLANT ECONOMICS OF BLACK AND WHITE PHENYL

Rated Plant capacity	=	1000.00 Kgs./Day
LAND & BUILDING (Land Area 600 sq.mt.)	=	Rented

PLANT & MACHINERY

1. Steam Jacketted kettle fitted with a stirring equipment motor & other accessories
2. M.S. tank for emulsification
3. Emulsifier, storage tanks
4. Liquid disinfectant (Phenyl) storage tank
5. Bottle filling & sealing machine
6. Pumps, valves, motors, starters & other ancillaries
7. Boiler
8. Caustic soda preparation tank
9. Lab testing equipments
10. Raw Material storage tank

FIXED CAPITAL

1. Plant & Machinery	Rs.	6,86,000.00
2. Other Fixed Assets	Rs.	2,00,000.00
TOTAL	Rs.	8,86,000.00

Phenyl (Black and White)

RAW MATERIALS

1. FOR BLACK PHENYL:- High boiling tar acid (H.B.T.A.)
2. Creosote oil
3. Rosin
4. Castor Oil
5. Linseed Oil
6. Soyabean Oil
7. Caustic Soda
8. FOR WHITE PHENYL:- High Boiling Tar Acid
9. Cresylic Creosote
10. Casein (fine powder)
11. Borax
12. Sodium Dodecyl Benzene Sulphonate,
13. Packaging material glass bottles, etc.

TOTAL WORKING CAPITAL/MONTH

1. Raw Material	Rs.	5,28,135.00
2. Salary & Wages	Rs.	71,500.00
3. Utilities & Overheads	Rs.	96,200.00
TOTAL	Rs.	8,86,000.00

TOTAL CAPITAL INVESTMENT

Total Fixed Capital	Rs.	8,86,000.00
Total working capital for 1 month	Rs.	6,95,835.00
TOTAL	Rs.	15,81,835.00

TURN OVER/ANNUM

1. BY sale of 1,50,000 Kgs of Black Phenyl.
2. By sale of 1,50,000 Kgs. of White Phenyl.

TOTAL Rs. 1,00,50,000.00

PROFIT SALES RATIO = Profit / Sales x 100 = 13.22 %

RATE OF RETURN = Operating profit / T.C.I x 100 = 83.99 %

BREAK EVEN POINT (B.E.P) = 46.96 %

Chapter - 47

P.V.C. Granules from P.V.C. Scraps

The waste plastic cannot be accepted quite at random. It seems that the feed should contain some 60 per cent polyolefins, but whilst the rest can well be other plastics, non-plastic waste, such as paper and glass, as commonly found in municipal waste, can be accommodated to some degree. No outside heat source is used, since this can degrade the material's phys properties. The waste mixture softens under pressure as it is forced through the extruder by a high shear mechanical screw, whilst the short residence time in the extruder ensures that no volatiles are release to pollute the atmosphere. The polyolefin fraction softens and becomes the carrier of the other materials in the mix, which then act as fillers, lending rigidity to the end product. Since there is no chemical change during processing, the final specification of the finished product is determined by the nature and mix of the input waste. Since this cannot be controlled with precision, given its provenance, the nature of the product-in particular its quality and colour- is determined by the skill of the plant operator in achieving some degree of uniformity. The batches and the rate of extrusion have to be adjusted in a manner determined by the experience of those running the plant. But there is no doubt that this is a very acceptable way to recyle plastic waste, and it should eventually make a substantial contribution towards minimizing this particular problem. Vehicle manufacturers are also looking to recycle the plastic materials incorporated into their products.

PROCESS OF MANUFACTURE OF PLASTIC GRANULES FROM SCRAP/WASTE

This versatile system to produce high quality plastic Industrial grade granules has got the following process of manufacturing.

1. Sorting
2. Smashing & washing
3. Concentrate and Blending
4. Section Extruding 1st stage
5. Filtration
6. Section Extruding 2nd stage

7. Drawing & Pelletizing
8. Cooling and Dehumidifying
9. Packaging & storage.

SORTING

The mentioned plastics are taken for plastic powder manufacture. It contains many impurities like dust, mud, wire and nails, first of all the matter is sorted out and the wire and nail etc. are removed.

SMASHING & WASHING

This versatile system capable to manufacture high grade industrial quality recycled plastic granules calls for plastic scrap of various types and grades. The first stage in production starts with the introduction of plastic scrap to the crusher where it is crushed to small pieces of desired sizes. Once this crushed pieces of plastic scrap is obtained it is fed to the washing unit where it is washed with the help of detergent and diluted hydrochloric acids, under this process, the scrap is cleaned and is ready for the next process.

CONCENTRATE & BLENDING

The clean scrap once of desired size is automatically fed to the concentrate/blending unit, where it is dried up and the required pigments (in case of coloured granules only) are added. Once the blending and drying of material is done automatically the semi-finished product is ready to be fed to a hopper.

SECTION EXTRUDING 1st STAGE

From the hopper the well blended and dried scrap is automatically fed to the 1st stage extruder. This extruder is a highly sophisticated piece of equipment where the scrap melted with proper temperature to keep the H factor intect. This melted scrap is pushed forward by the extruder to the filter chamber.

Moreover the basic extrusion process is designed to continuously convert a thermoplastics material into a particular form.

The basic sequence of extruders function are as follows:-

a) Plasticization of the granular raw material.
b) Metering of the plasticized product through a die which
c) Solidification into the desired shape and size.

FILTRATION

The melted scrap with proper H factor and melting index is sent to the filtration chamber and is filtered through six stage filtration process where the melted scrap is totally cleaned which the washing unit is not capable to do.

SECTION EXTRUDING 2nd STAGE

The cleaned melted scrap is now sent to second stage of extrusion where a facility exists to induce plastic hardness.

DRAWING & PELLETIZING

Once this process is completed, the melted scrap is transferred automatically to the drawing machine. Here, for certain grade of plastics die cutting takes place to form the pellets and in some types of plastics the drawn wires are passed through a cooling tank and sent to the cutting unit, where pelletization takes place.

COOLING & DEHUMIDIFYING

Once pelletization takes place at that point time, it is hot and is thus sent to the cooling unit and at the same time it is dehumidified from its moisture content.

PACKING & STORAGE

The dehumidified and cooled pellet is all set to be packed and stored for marketing.

MANUFACTURING PROCESS FLOW SHEET

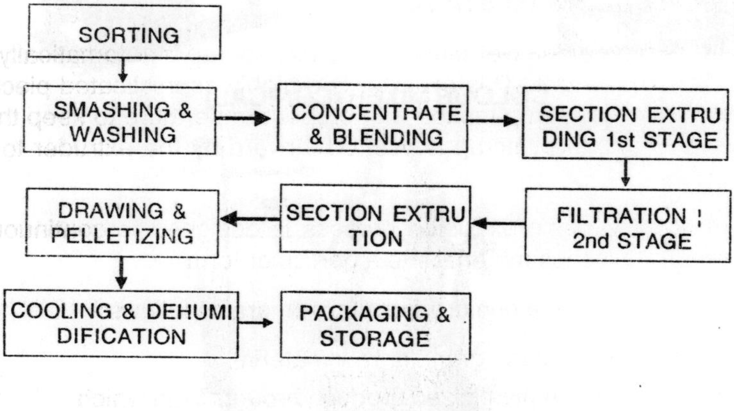

HOPPER AUTOLOADER

COLOUR MIXER (PARALLEL)

HOPPER DRYER

PLASTIC SCRAP GRANULATOT

COLOUR MIXER (CONICAL)

PLANT ECONOMICS OF PLASTIC GRANULES FROM SCRAPS/WASTE

Rated Plant Capacity	=	1.00 MT/Day
Land & Building (Land area 600 sq.mt)	=	Rented

PLANT & MACHINERY

1. Scrap Grinder
2. Magnetic separator
3. Washing Tank
4. Reaction vessel
5. Mixer
6. Activated carbon Treatment Tank
7. Filter
8. Distillation column
9. Vein-Screw
10. Solvent Recovery Unit
12. Dehumidifying
13. Granules formation
14. Solvent storage tanks
15. Weighing filling, sealing & packaging machine
16. Mini Boiler
17. Instruments & Process control & Lab Testing Equipment
18. Pipes, fitting, pump valves

FIXED CAPITAL

1. Plant & Machinery		Rs.	10,80,000.00
2. Other Fixed Assets		Rs.	3,81,760.00
	TOTAL	Rs.	14,61,760.00

RAW MATERIALS

1. Plastic Waste
2. Ethanol
3. Toluene
4. Xylene
5. Activated carbon
6. Dimethyl phthalate

7. Other miscellaneous Chemicals
8. Packing charges for packing

TOTAL WORKING CAPITAL/MONTH

1. Raw Material		Rs.	5,49,725.00
2. Salary & Wages		Rs.	1,39,150.00
3. Utilities & Overheads		Rs.	1,21,000.00
	TOTAL	Rs.	8,09,875.00

TOTAL CAPITAL INVESTMENT

Total Fixed Capital		Rs.	14,61,760.00
Total Working Capital for 1 Month		Rs.	8,09,875.00
	TOTAL	Rs.	22,71,635.00

TURN OVER/ANNUM

1. By selling 300 MT of plastic Granules (or all types)
2. Activated carbon for Regeneration

TOTAL Rs. 1,58,10,000.00

PROFIT SALES RATIO = Profit / Sales x 100 = 35.00 %

RATE OF RETURN = Operating profit / T.C.I x 100 = 243.61 %

BREAK EVEN POINT (B.E.P) = 24.61 %

Chapter - 48

P.V.C. Pipes and Fittings

Rigid (unplasticised) PVC pipes are strong but light in weight. As a result, these pipes are easily handled and are likely to be thrown about. Reasonable case, however should be taken in handling and storage of these pipes while loading and unloading. On to and for the vehicles and these should be lowered and not dropped to the ground, to prevent damage to the pipes. These pipes are supplied in six meter lengths and above.

Extreme cold and hot whether conditions pose limitations to the handling and storage of rigid PVC pipes, and these call for suitable precautions in handling and storage. Pipes should be given adequate support at all times, stacking in large pipes should be avoided, in particular during summer months in regions where the temperature goes upto 45°C and above, as the bottom of pipes may distort, thus giving rise to difficulty to pipe alignment and jointing. During summer months, pipes should preferably be stored in shade. For long term storage, pipe racks provided continuous support. For temporary storage in the field, where racks are not provided, care should be taken that the ground is level and free from loose stones. Pipes stored thus should not exceed three layers high and should be stacked to prevent movement. During summer months the pipes stored in the field should be under shade.

The impact strength of the rigid PVC pipes is reduced somewhat in cold weather, thus more care in handling is required to be exercised in these pipes in regions where the temperature goes below zero degree centigrade. At 10°C, the reduction has become marked and PVC pipes should not be laid in such conditions. While in transit, pipes should be well secured and supported over their entire length.

PROCESS OF MANUFACTURE

Rigid or unplasticized PVC pipes are made from polyvinyl chloride (PVC) which in resin form is hard and rigid material. This rigidity can be controlled by controlling the percentage of plasticizer at the time of compounding. The production of rigid PVC pipes consists of plasticizing and homogenizing PVC compound and metering through and extruder. This hot molten PVC compound is extruded by the extruder through a circular slit. This circular slit governs the size of the pipe to be extruded. Different dies are used for manufacturing different sizes of pipes.

The pipe thus extruded through the die is then passed through a vacuum sizing tank where the dimensions of the pipe can be accurately set. This also helps in the surface finish of the pipe. Vacuum sizing which is more sophisticated than other types of forming operations reduces the percentage of wastage considerably.

PVC PIPE FITTINGS:-

For manufacturing same procedure is applied as in the case of pipe manufacture. Fittings are manufactured by using different dies meant for different kinds of fittings. These dies are fitted on the moulding machine and molten PVC is charged in them. The dies are removed and the produced form is removed and the die is again set on the moulding machine. The same process is repeated.

Elbows and T-joints are manufactured using elbow moulding machine in which molten PVC is charged in the die and compressed air is injected in the die to get the desired product.

PROCESS FLOW SHEET FOR THE MANUFACTURE OF PVC PIPES

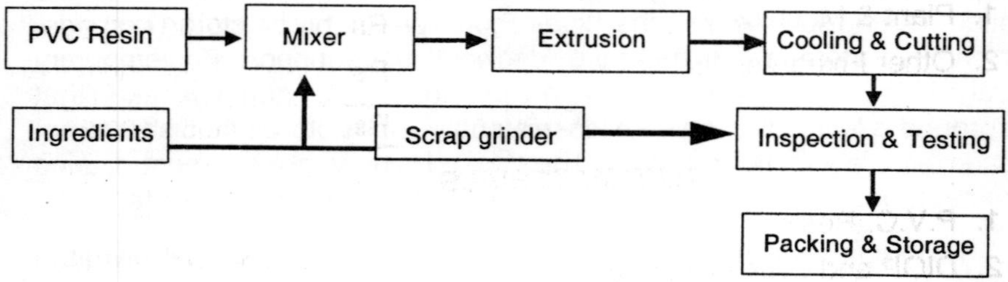

PROCESS FLOW SHEET FOR THE MANUFACTURE OF PVC FITTINGS

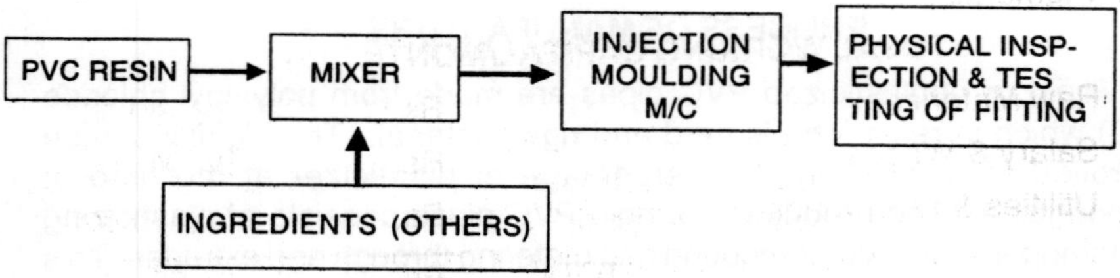

FORMULATION FOR PVC RIGID PIPES

Ingredients	Parts
1. PVC	100
2. DIOP & DAP	42-50
3. Basic Lead Carbonate	5-8
4. Calcium Stearate	1
5. Mineral Precipitated Calcium Carbonate	0.0.5

PLANT ECONOMICS OF RIGID P.V.C. PIPES AND FITTINGS

Rated Plant Capacity = 2.00 MT/Day

LAND & BUILDING (Land Area 1 Acre) = Rented

PLANT & MACHINERY

1. Total cost of Plant & Machinery	Rs.	35,00,000.00

FIXED CAPITAL

1. Plant & Machinery	Rs.	35,00,000.00
2. Other Fixed Assets	Rs.	5,50,000.00
TOTAL	Rs.	40,50,000.00

RAW MATERIALS

1. P.V.C. Resin
2. DIOP and DAP Plasticizer
3. Lead Stearate
4. Calcium Stearate
5. Precipitated Calcium Carbonate
6. Pigments/Dyes

TOTAL WORKING CAPITAL/MONTH

1. Raw Material	Rs.	25,52,960.00
2. Salary & Wages	Rs.	1,04,625.00
3. Utilities & Overheads	Rs.	3,58,000.00
TOTAL	Rs.	30,15,585.00

TOTAL CAPITAL INVESTMENT

Total Fixed Capital	Rs.	40,50,000.00
Total Working Capital for 1 Month	Rs.	30,15,585.00
TOTAL	Rs.	70,65,585.00

TURN OVER/ANNUM

1. By Sale of 450 MT P.V.C. Pipes of different Sizes 4" to 6"
2. By Sale of 150 MT Fittings (T,Elbow Joints Sockets etc.)

Rs. 4,80,00,000.00

PROFIT SALES RATIO = Profit / Sales x 100 = 21.00 %

RATE OF RETURN = Operating profit / T.C.I x 100 = 142.66 %

BREAK EVEN POINT (B.E.P) = 28.17 %

Chapter - 49

Paint Industry

The paints properties can be divided into two parts to ensure the exact requirements. In fact the paint is a chemical composition and mechanical mixtures which has physical fitness to ascertain the durability of the surface.

1. PHYSICAL PROPERTIES:-

The physical property in the paint has very importance to ensure its colour which should not fade and to be discoloured in any case which is a creditable property. It should be empowered to resist heat, water and the other atmospheric conditions. The paint should protect the surface from the above mentioned effects. Its main property should be of high hiding power ensuring the colour durability.

The paint which is applied on metals should be of corrosion resistant under all climatic effects in which the component has to live. In the same case the woodweares of every nature such as furniture, cots, etc. should also resist the normal climatic conditions when painted or polished.

2. CHEMICAL PROPERTIES:-

The painted surfaces should be of washable condition. The films which are produced by the painting, when dried well should be of cleaning condition in case of change, the colour and other things extra.

It should also consists the adequate the proper consistency for particular purpose for which the paint is applied.

The very important property in the paint in "GLOSS" which is the very must in paint manufacturing. There are no set methods for the prescribed formulations or recipe balanced for permanent in gloss. Only the trial and errors guide the paint manufacturers through their chemists who have really command to adjust the compound ingredients to obtain the proper gloss.

The properties under physical and chemical terms are mentioned in brief to enable manufacturers and to guide them to utilize the chemical and technical know-how in the paint manufacturing.

PRINCIPLES OF PAINT FORMULATIONS

The main constituents of paints are :

(a) Pigment

(b) Binder

(c) Thinner

In addition to these other additives like driers, plasticizers, fillers, extenders settling agents and dispersing agents, are also used in small quantities.

PAINT FORMULATION :

Formuiations of paint implies the proper selection of the pigments, binder and other ingredients suitable to impart the specific properties to the finished product, which is in turn depends on the function for which the paint is intended to the used.

For decorative paints in general use the emphasis is laid upon the factors such as colour, gloss and retention of these properties in service. In such cases character of the pigments and pigments volume concentration plays an important role along with the binder.

Thus it is very important to know the special purpose, the substance to which it is to be applied and environmental conditions prevailing before suggesting a paint formulation.

As a first step following general characteristics of ingredients should be known for a proper selection, suited to particular requirement.

DRY DISTEMPERS

Dry distemper is a powdered mixture of pigment and binder which when dispersed in water gives the required water paint.

Distempers have replaced white wash and calcimine, this is mainly due to the superior retention power, durability and light fastness on exposures to exterior conditions throughout the year. There is no possibility of cloths being spoiled when distempers and used whereas lime colours give their effect on clothes when they come in contact.

FORMULATIONS FOR DRY DISTEMPERS:-

1.	White distemper:	lbs
	Paris white	55
	Casein	10
	Barytes	25
	Lime	6
	Borax	4
		100

2. Yellow Distemper:

		Parts
Calcium carbonate	:	300
Titanium dioxide	:	4
Glue powder	:	20
Mid stone or ochere	:	900
Sulphonated castor oil	:	4
Hansa Yellow	:	5

3. General Dry Distemper:

		%
Pigment	:	74.4
Mica	:	10.0
Casein	:	12.0
Borax	:	1.1
Sodium fluoride	:	1.0
Potassium dichromate	:	1.5

For other color distempers different pigments are used in the same proportion. The pigments are the same as mentioned in lime color.

BALL MILL

MANUFACTURING PROCESS

LIME COLOURS:-

The process of making lime colours is very simple and involves only mixing of desired pigment into lime or gypsum according to formulation.

The pigment should be very finely ground. Lime or gypsum should also be ground separately. Then both ingredients are thoroughly mixed in a dry mixer or ribbon blender. Finally, it is suitably packed for selling.

DRY DISTEMPER:-

In the manufacture of dry distempers, the process involved is the same except that after grinding and mixing of all components, casein solution, which is nearly neutral is mixed slowly in the mass with vigorous agitation. After this, the product formed is dried, ground and packed for selling.

OIL BOUND DISTEMPER

Oil bound distempers are also known as washable distempers, and made by dispersing a mixture of lithopone and wetting it is a distemper emulsion, the pigment being dispersed in the aqueous phases. Distemper emulsion consists of a dispersion of drying oil or binder in an aqueous solution of glue or casein.

Formula for distemper emulsion based on glue and linseed oil is given below :

Solution A:-

Skin glue 7 lbs is soaked in 70 lbs of water over night and then warmed to 60°C to dissolve. Add this to carboxy methyl cellulose 1.5 ozs. and triethanolamine 8 ozs.

Solution B:-

Linseed oil 30 lbs, oleic acid 21 lbs, and 6% cobalt naphthenate 300 ozs. All these are mixed.

Solution C:-

Solution B is added to Solution A while stirring and then passed through an emulsifier. This gives a good quality emulsion containing about 25 - 28% of oil.

Glue or Casein Based Oil Bound Distemper :-

Oil bound distempers have greater washability and dustability. The binder generally consists of an emulsion of processed drying oil or of a varnish (oleoresinous or synthetic) in an aqueous solution of casein or glue. The emulsion is prepared in a high speed mixer or in a colloid mill. The pigment dispersion is accomplished in edge runners or pug mills.

Oil bound distempers are generally supplied in paste form to be thinned with water before application. Glue or casein may be added as protective colloids.

Oil bound distempers are used as interior wall coatings on both new and old surfaces. Conditions of storage of them are important and extremes of temperature should be avoided. Soyabean protein based oil bound distempers are most widely used in water paints.

Typical formula for soyabean protein based oil bound distemper :

Alpha Protein (Soyabean)	:	100 lbs
Water	:	400 lbs
Borax	:	15 lbs
Water	:	110 lbs
Phenol	:	6 lbs
Water	:	50 lbs
Diglycol laurate	:	5 lbs

Linseed Oil Containing (0.02%) :-

Cobalt	:	35 lbs
Pine oil	:	71 lbs
Phenol	:	20 ozs
Locust beagum	:	2.5 lbs
Water	:	50 lbs

It is soked for 10 minutes in water and heat it in a jacketed kettle with steam, with continuous stirring. Now add (3) and allow temperature to rise to 160°C and hold it at 165°C until the protein is thoroughly cut. Add others serially one by one, allowing about 5 min. between each addition and keeping temperature at about 150°C. Stir the Solution for about 20 minutes and pass through a colloid mill if possible. Add half of the total protein solution in a change can mixer and then add the following pigments.

Lithopone	:	825 lbs
Whiting	:	110 lbs

This will form a very heavy paste. Continue agitation until a thorough mix is obtained. Add remainder of the protein solution and continue agitation until the pigments are properly dispersed by grinding in a roller mill.

Formula for washable distempers and water paint which will brush out satisfactorily can readily be made with a mixture of casein and latex, but this is unsuitable owing to the tendency of the casein solution to harden up in the container on standing. To avoid this, part of the casein is replaced by glue.

Composition:-

Lithopone	:	100 parts
Latex	:	30 parts
Glue Solution	:	25 parts
Casein Solution	:	25 parts
	TOTAL	180 parts

The economics in this profile is based on the above formulation.

Plastic Wall Distemper Formula:-

Plaster	:	30 Kgs.
Asbestos	:	21.75 Kgs.
Glue	:	10.00 Kgs.
Casein	:	12.50 Kgs.
Lime	:	12.50 Kgs.
Lithopone	:	12.50 Kgs.

It is made a creamy paste with water directly before use.

ENAMEL PAINTS

Depending upon their use, the enamel paints are divided into two categories, namely enamels, for interior use and enamels for exterior use. The differnce is due to the quality of the vehicle used in each case. Enamels are painted on under costs applied first on the surface to be painted.

Formulations :-

Examples of a few types of enamels are given below :

1. Synthetic Enamel (Orange) :-

Components		% by weight
Middle chrome	:	5.0
Orange chrome	:	15.0
Zinc chrome	:	4.0
Linseed modified alkyd	:	15.0
Turpentine oil	:	5.0

All the above ingredients are mixed and made in paste form. To this paste the following components are added to get the final paint.

Alkyd resin varnish	:	40.0%
Cobalt naphthenate (10%Co)	:	0.17
Solution of elad naphthenate (20% ple)	:	0.85
Calcium naphthenate (6% Ca)	:	0.70

Manufacture of Enamels :-

In the manufacture of enamels the following steps are involved.

1. Mixing of pigments and sufficient vehicle binder to produce a paste with a good consistency for grinding.

2. Grinding the paste in a mill untill the aggregates are broken down to a certain grindness are as required.

3. Mixing and tinting of batch to the reqiured exact colour.

4. Filtering the enamel paint before transferring to storage tanks and packages.

For a small scale unit, all the operation involved are performed in a ball mill. In the manufacture all the pigments, about 20% of the resin and 50% of the mineral turpentine (or white spirit) are added, the mill is allowed to run for 1 or 2 days. If proper grinding has taken place, the remaining amounts of the resins and mineral turpentine along with the drier solutions are added. The mill is again allowed to run. The batch will be ready after one or two days. More the finished product is then filtered through 12-200 mesh sieve or through a filter cloth into the containers.

PLANT ECONOMICS OF PAINT INDUSTRY

Rated Plant Capacity	=	100.00 Kgs./Day
LAND & BUILDING (Land 300 sq.mt)	=	Rented

PLANT & MACHINERY

1 Grinder for grinding lime with porcelain balls,
2. Ribbon blender
3. Edge Runner for making dry distemper paste
4. Oil Distemper & Enamel Paints Sec :
   Edge Runner
5. Ball Mill
6. Mixer
7. Reactor
8. Steel Ball Mill
9. General Equipments :
   Weighing Balances platform type
10. Lab. Equipments
11. Alkyd Resin
    Heating eqpt with burner bhatties
    (Either gas or fired)
12. Stainless steel reaction vessel fitted
    with thermameter, stirrer, electric motor

FIXED CAPITAL

1. Plant & Machinery	Rs.	3,60,000.00
2. Other Fixed Assets	Rs.	50,000.00
TOTAL	Rs.	4,10,000.00

RAW MATERIALS

1. Phthalic-Anhydride
2. Glycerine
3. Linseed oil
4. Titanium dioxide
5. White antimony
6. Linseed oil
7. Alkyd Resin

TOTAL WORKING CAPITAL/MONTH

1. Raw Material		Rs.	1,40,970.00
2. Salary & Wages		Rs.	7,560.00
3. Utilities & Overheads		Rs.	16,000.00
	TOTAL	Rs.	1,64,530.00

TOTAL CAPITAL INVESTMENT

Total Fixed Capital		Rs.	4,10,000.00
Total Working Capital for 1 Month		Rs.	1,64,530.00
	TOTAL	Rs.	5,74,530.00

TURN OVER/ANNUM

1. BY sale of 30,000 kgs enamel paint
2. 24000 kg oil varnish

TOTAL Rs. 25,80,000.00

PROFIT SALES RATIO = Profit / Sales x 100 = 17.16 %

RATE OF RETURN = Operating profit / T.C.I x 100 = 77.05 %

BREAK EVEN POINT (B.E.P) = 38.41 %

Chapter - 50

Potato Chips/Waffers

Potato chips is a food item very popular for picnics, journeys, evening tea and may be served at any time as snack food.

In India, a large area is under cultivation of potato. Therefore potato is grown in large quantities, and is a short of food for the poor became when other grains are touching the soaring prices, the poor people depend upon the potatoes only. A number of preparation can be made from potato. Potato chips have a regular sale through out the year.

Snack food like potato chips in recent years have made impressive trends in food industry. The approximate composition of chips is as follows:-

Moisture	-	2%
Protein	-	6.7%
Fat	-	37.1%
Carbohydrate	-	51.1%
Minerals	-	3.00%

Potatoes from the basis of a very wide range of snack products ranging

POTATO CHIPS MACHINE

POTATO PEALER

from direct structured derivatives from whole potatoes. If potatoes are to be used for the production of chips, a great variety of constrains apply to the feed stock if eventually a final product is to be produced.

Different varieties of potatoes are usually used for chips. The penland series plus majestic are frequently used for chips. Only medium to large ware potatoes are necessarily suitable for chips over 45mm. A regular shape with shallow eyes is necessary for chips production. For chips, cream or while flesh with no blemishes is necessary. Freedom from rot, cracking, splitting and disease generally is demanded together with only a minimum of greening.

For chips manufacture, sugar contents of potatoes should be over S.G (Specific Gravity)1.080 i.e (minimum 20% solids content).

Sugar content must be low because if it is high it leads to excessive colour in the finished product and also to higher production losses by leaching . For chips a maximum of 0.25% is generally accepted. These level must be maintained during storage.

POTATO WAFER MACHINE

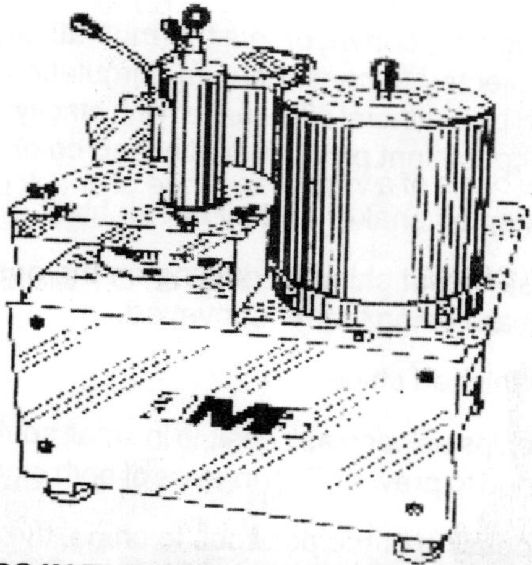

STEPS IN THE PROCESS OF MANUFACTURE

1. Inspection of feed stocks and manual removal of obviously trash on a conveyor belt.

2. Mechanical washing and stoning of potatoes using brushes with gravity separation of stones in a vertical fume.

3. Steam or water peeling of potatoes usually by steam jet surface loosing

of the skin followed by a dry abrasive skin removal treatment and then the use of brushes and water sprays thus minimize water usage and concentrating the skin residues.

4. Inspection and triming by hand in a conveyor belt.

5. To maintain continuity of production a buffer tank is usually provided at this point containing a weak solution of SO_2 or sodium meta bisulfate to avoid enzymic blackening during the holding period.

6. Slicing of potatoes to the desired thickness using multiple knives.

7. Washing slices free of starch and use chemical separation of slivers and nubbins concominatantly with dewating the slices.

8. Blanching of the slices in steam or hot water (160°– 200°F) (71–93°C) which amounts to a partial pre cooking. Blanching times will depend on slice thickness and the blanch temperature and can be from 3 or 4 times upwards.

9. Drying the slices by shaking and by air blast to avoid a water carry over and to start the dehydration continued in the next stage.

10. Frying or cooking on a conveyor in a thermostaticaly controlled bath of oil, the oil subjected to continuous re- circulation and filtration and indirectly heated by a mineral oil calorifier with strictly controlled cooking time to ensure consistent product quality and color.

11. Defaulting of crisp by shaker and by hot air blast.

12. Flavoring and salting of chips by dusting on the seasoning whilst the defaulted chips are being timber conveyed.

13. Cooling of the finished chips.

14. Packing of the chips as soon as possible in small sophisticated laminate package designed to prevent. The ingress of both oxygen and moisture.

During the processing or the potatoes to chips, the moisture contents of the potato has been reduced from 79% (Approx.) to 5% (Approx.) and of the 95% of dry malts in the chips 35-40% will be fat.

Taking into account peeling trimming and other small losses in the plant and the up take of fat the conversion ratio of potatoes, the chips is around 4:1.

PROCESS OF MANUFACTURE

Potatoes received from fields are first checked for quality on conveyor belt. The spoiled ones are removed from the lot. The hand picked potatoes are then washed well with jet of water to remove mud and other materials. Then, the clean potatoes are moved into the peeling section.

The peeled potatoes are sliced in a conscious slicing machine. The peeled potatoes are feed to the hopper of the slicing machine and are discharged out to dual potato slicing machine. The dual slicer are used to handle more potatoes continuously. Each slicer are separately powered by a variable speed gear head motor. The feed to the dual slicer are arranged in such a way that slice cutting rotor in either slice may be changed during operation. Rotary type slicer are used in most chips plants. Slice thickness varies from (1/15 to 1/30mm). Potato slices are washed in rotating reels in the additional jet of water under high pressure to remove starch from the potato slices.

The washed potato slices are dried in a dryer to remove moisture content.

The dried potato slices are treated chemically with sodium bisulfate alone or with phosporic acid, sodium citrate or citric acid to prevent the formation of dark chips during Trying. In this chemical treatment water or solution is heated up to 200°F and after rinsing slices are placed in the above hot solution fc' one or two minute and then sent into frying kettles.

For frying, two types of processes are in general use.

1. Batch frying
2. Continuous frying.

The simplest method for frying is batch frying provides for a slicer to be mounted on a batch directly above the frying vessel. This vessel may be either rectangular or flat bottom. Flat bottom tank with burner beneath or the tank may be of the immersion tube type.

After frying, the chips are salted and packed. A uniform application 1.5 to 2 lbs of salt is applied to 100 lbs of chips. Mono sodium glutonate is used for flavour. One part of mono sodium glutonate to 10 parts of salt provides a good mixture.

Then the chips are packed to protect the content against development of rancidily. Plant & Equipments are available in India to produce potato chips.

PROCESS FLOW SHEET

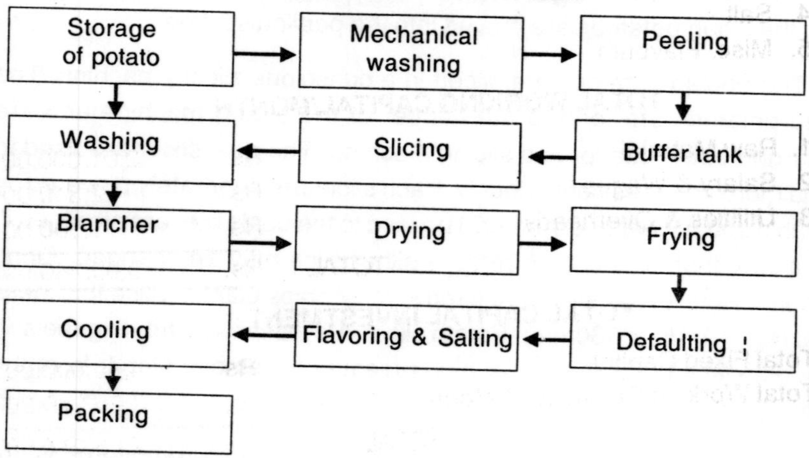

PLANT ECONOMICS OF POTATO CHIPS

Rated Plant Capacity	=	500.00 Kgs./Day
Land & Building (Land 400 Sq. Ft.)	=	Rented

PLANT & MACHINERY

1. Potato Peeler
2. Slicing Machine
3. Blender
4. Hydro extractor
5. Weighing Balance
6. Frier
7. Potato Chips Packing Machine

FIXED CAPITAL

1. Plant & Machinery		Rs.	3,55,000.00
2. Other Fixed Assets		Rs.	1,05,000.00
	TOTAL	Rs.	4,60,000.00

Potato Chips/Waffers

RAW MATERIALS

1. Hand Picked Potatoes
2. Edible oil
3. Chemicals
4. Salt
5. Misc. Flavours

TOTAL WORKING CAPITAL/MONTH

1. Raw Material	Rs.	2,01,000.00
2. Salary & Wages	Rs	32,340.00
3. Utilities & Overheads	Rs.	71,900.00
TOTAL	Rs.	3,05,240.00

TOTAL CAPITAL INVESTMENT

Total Fixed Capital	Rs.	4,60,000.00
Total Working Capital for 1 Month	Rs.	3,05,240.00
TOTAL	Rs.	7,65,240.00

TURN OVER/ANNUM

Receipt by Sale of 150 MT of Potato Chips per annum	Rs.	75,00,000.00

PROFIT SALES RATIO = Profit / Sales x 100 = 48.65 %

RATE OF RETURN = Operating profit / T.C.I x 100 = 476.78 %

BREAK EVEN POINT (B.E.P) = 15.88 %

Chapter - 51

Paper Envelopes (Including Self Sealing Type)

Paper envelopes is well known to all persons as it is a routine article of use, with the growth of education, industrialization and commercial activities, the demand for office stationery and allied items is increasing rapidly. Paper envelopes play an important role as a stationery material in any type of correspondence.

Now-a-days, the envelopes are used in the publicity-advertisement very frequently. There are various types and sizes of envelopes and also of various quality. The size and type of envelopes depend upon the quality of paper which is used in envelope making, demand of users and market. Various types and sizes of envelopes are now used quite extensively. Some envelopes are self adhesive type, due to already pasted gum on their brims. These self adhesive type envelopes are very convenient to use and have very important applications in post & telegraph department, offices and in many commercial departments.

Some other special type of envelopes are used in special fields as pocket envelopes. Some varieties of pocket envelopes are particularly suitable for substances such as seeds, powders, hairnets, postage stamps, wedges wireless parts, gramophone needles and their smail articles. Some important sizes of the envelopes are given here under:

1. 15. x 9 cm.
2. 18. x 13 cm.
3. 23 x 16 cm.
4. 26 x 12 cm.

The above sizes of envelopes are most important and well known sizes. These sizes are mostly used in offices and P & T Departments.

The basic raw material for envelopes manufacture is paper. Paper may be of any colour having good bursting. Strength, but mostly white or brown papers are utilized for this purpose.

Paper Envelopes (Including Self Sealing Type)

Plant & Machinery for envelopes manufacture are simple and indigenously available so there is no hurdle in setting up envelope manufacturing unit. The unit also comes under cottage-small scale.

MANUFACTURING PROCESS

The process of making paper envelopes is quite simple and involves the following steps :-

1. Envelope making
2. Flap Gumming
3. Packing.

The most common and popular machine for paper envelope is rotary sheet fed type envelope making machine. In this type of machine, blanks are put on the feeding table in high stack and the flap paint downwards.

While the envelope making machine is running, additional blanks can be put on the table. A sucking device takes the blanks from below and carried them to the receiving cylinder. The printing attachments are slewable and can be stopped individually. After this, the flap gumming follows. Now the blank is conveyed through turning cylinder and then brought rapidly to the format pit where it is aligned. The folding of the blanks is achieved by folding rules, thereafter the finished envelope falls into the drying chain.

When drying process is finished, the envelope is conveyed by means of sucking dies to the receiving table where the finished envelopes are stacked up and counted by 25 to 50 envelopes.

The brown, wrapper or white paper, white coloured or brown wrapper and also manila is usually employed for various types of envelopes. The gums (Gum arabic or local) are generally used as the common adhesives. The paste made from tapioca flour are also used to a lesser extent.

Now, the envelopes are allowed to affix the stamps and the different kinds of advertisement are stamped on the back of the envelopes. Now these envelopes are ready for use. They are bounded or packed in hundred or thousand bundle.

PROCESS FLOW CHART FOR PAPER ENVELOPE INCLUDING SELF ADHESIVE TYPE

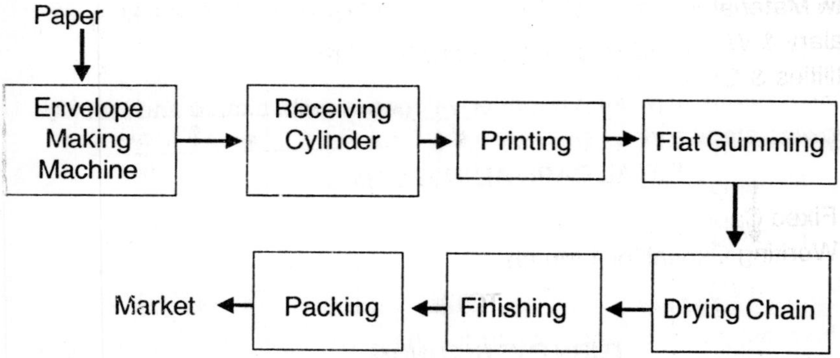

PLANT ECONOMICS OF PAPER ENVELOPES

Rated Plant Capacity	=	60000.00 Nos/Day
Land & Building (Land area 150 sq.mt.)	=	Rented

PLANT & MACHINERY

1. Paper cutting Machine
2. Envelope making machine
3. Flap Gumming Machine
4. Drying Chains
5. Receiving Tables
6. Sucking Desk
7. Other Miscellaneous equipments such as testing equipments etc.

FIXED CAPITAL

1. Plnt & Machinery	Rs.	1,06,000.00
2. Other Fixed Assets	Rs.	85,000.00
TOTAL	Rs.	1,91,000.00

RAW MATERIALS

1. Paper
2. Gums/Adhesives
3. Packing Boxes

Paper Envelopes (Including Self Sealing Type)

TOTAL WORKING CAPITAL/MONTH

1. Raw Material	Rs.	40,875.00
2. Salary & Wages	Rs.	44,125.00
3. Utilities & Overheads	Rs.	14,550.00
TOTAL	Rs.	99,550.00

TOTAL CAPITAL INVESTMENT

Total Fixed Capital	Rs.	1,91,000.00
Total Working Capital for 1 Month	Rs.	99,550.00
TOTAL	Rs.	2,90,550.00

TURN OVER/ANNUM

1. 1,35,00,000 Envelopes (Plain)
2. 4500000 Envelopes (Self Sealing Type)

TOTAL Rs. 16,65,000.00

PROFIT SALES RATIO = Profit / Sales x 100 = 23.97 %

RATE OF RETURN = Operating profit / T.C.I x 100 = 137.34 %

BREAK EVEN POINT (B.E.P) = 46.94 %

Chapter - 52

Readymade Garments

The readymade garments industry is a highly diversified one consisting of a large number of items based on various fabrics either woven or knitted, for ladies and girls, for men and for boys for sports and swimming. Under-garments, Outer garments, traditional institutional and also industrial garments.

The readymade garments Industries one of the few in country to have recorded a spectaculan export performance. Readymade garments are made in India both in the large scale as well as small scale sectors. At present there are nearly 2000000 large and small scale manufacturers producing readymade garments in the country. While the capacity position relating to readymade garments is not exactly known. The production figures for the same are available from the study made by Indian Institute of Foreign Trade.

OUTLINE OF PLANT

Here we take up the men's dress shift sewing plant which can be easily standardized with less diversification according to tastes assuming that the plant will be operated by persons with any experience of operating on industrial sewing plant.

SUPER HIGH-SPEED OVERLOCK SEWING MACHINE

However, it should be noted that shift sewing has complicated standards and sizes through it tends to seem to be otherwise.

For instance, there are more than ten kinds and sizes of collars and there are cloth of 100% cotton and that of polyester cotton blend as material cloth.

Further more, some markets have classification standards which must be taken into consideration in operating and industrial sewing plant.

In this plant, we have adopted the progressive bundle system so that products of uniform quality may be turned out reasonably and cheaply in large quantities.

TECHNICAL GUIDANCE

As for technical training in the sewing industry, since the technique of advance production control-system and of human engineering are indispensable factors for the industry, training system in which trainees receive training at an industrial sewing plant and a sewing plant and sewing machine manufacturing plant is preferable to technical coperation by experts dispatched from advanced countries.

In this way, the trainees will be able to acquire applied engineering by activity participating in the operation of the plant.

It is suggested that a prospective operation of the plant constructed whose duty will be guidance of operation of sewing machine operation of the plant constructed whose duty will be guidance of operation of sewing machines, should receive training together with other trainees.

The techniques of industrial shirt sewing which has acquired more laborate fields of sewing and be usually industrialised. In this sense we introduce the men's dress shirt sewing project here.

PROCESS DESCRIPTION

Here is the outline of the operation order which is the name as that for industrial sewing in general.

1. Pattern design and pattern making.

2. Cloth cutting by mechanical process.

3. Sewing by higher speed industrial sewing machine.

4. Trimming and inspection.

5. Ironing and pressing as finishing process.

For sewing process and operation analysis have been conducted on which is provided sewing group by group basis of a progressive bundles stemp help achieve the target of production. Furnished with one line each of sewing process for over type it is an economic small scale sewing plant.

DESIGN

Designers use five elements to create a design that will stimulate the potential consumer to buy (i) colour (ii) sil honette (iii) drape (iv) texture (v) ione balance on the products surface. Besides choosing textile and other raw materials with specifies properties and characteristics of colour, drape, hand and texture, the designer selects findings buttons, uppers, snaps, gromets, thread lace, tapes, braids, medallions, sequins and a variety of ornaments and closures a decorative devices to impart the desired design effect line balance is generally achieved by the sectional patterns of raw materials that the designer shapes to form the finished product.

The basis patterns that fit the form, last or block with minimum seams and skin tight precision form the foundation patters. In the drafting method of designing style patterns, the designer pulates the founds pattern to develop the style pattern. Which is used to cut the raw materials into the sections required for the garment. The drapery method is used by designers who prefers to drape the actual material for the garment on the form, block, or last, cutting patterns for cutting the raw materials are traced from the droped sections. Cutting pattern may be made rigid or semi rigid paper or plastics.

CUTTING PROCESS

Cutting involves three basic operations:-

Making the market, spreading the fabric and chopping then spread fabric into the marked sections. The marker or cutting lay, is the arrangement of patterns on the spread fabrics.

Six types of machines are available to chop or cut a lay into the component parts of the market rotary blade machines, vertical reciprocal blad machines, band knives, similar to band - raws, die clickers systems with straight blades and automated co%puterised laser beam cutting machines.

Round knife machines rotate a circular blade down into the lay where the straight kni&e machines oscillate a straight blade in out of the lay in jig raw fashion.

In hand knife cutting, block our from the lay with round or straight knife machines are trimmed precisely to pattern specifications as the blocks are manipulated against the band knife rotating in a fixed orbit. die clickers cut by pressing dies. Susperposed on the lay, through the depth of the lay. The cutting dies out line the pattern to be cut.

Two types of auxiliary equipment are used.

Cutting drills to drill holes through the super posed plies in a lay notches to notch the perimenter of the out section. These holes notches guides the sewing operations. Cut sections are techketed to insure proper siring and sheding during the assembly of the garment.

SERVING PRODUCTION

The prime characteristic of a serving machine is the stitch it makes. The manual paced serving machines have a separate dutch motor with stark speed breaking controlled by food treadle action to the motor's clutch. Which actuates or stops the belt drive while the motor runs continuously. The integrated sewing machine, eliminates the separated the belt drive. The integrated machine frame contains the motor module, which is actuated, controlled, stepped by a four speed switch operated by a device resembling foot treadle. The motor in this machine rotates only when the treadle is actuated so electricity is used only when treadle is actuated so electricity is used only when the machine is sewing.

Special purpose machines sew automatic cycles for operations such as button holing, button sewing contour seaming, profit stitching, seaming for patch pockets, doct stitching, tacking welt pocketing padding cycles such as blend stitching interlings to the outer shell.

The quality of manual packed serving depends on the integration of six variables: the needle, its size, shape and finish, the type of feed system, the co-ordination of needle and feed, thread tension adjustments. The tread, operator handling machine manufacturers make needles in variety of diameters points has per finishes as well as different types, shapes sizes of feds pressure feet to improve quality and output.

FUSING AND CEMENTING

Fusing and cementing are processes for stitching or decorative seaming. In fusing, the seam bond on decoration is formed by melting some fibre or finish content in the material in a manner that join the sections or decorates in the desired are. In comenting, the bond of decoration is made by an adhesive, such as cement, glue on plastic which is applied to the materials during or immediately preceding the cementing process. Fusing is either by direct heat, by hot head fusing presses, in which pressure surface are heated by electric heating grade or steam, cementing processes use mechanical pressure systems with in thout head application depending on the adhesive materials used. Fusing is replacing serving in some operations such as joining inter lining to collars, tuffs etc.

INDUSTRIAL SEWING MACHINE

PRESSING AND MOULDING PROCESSES :-

Moulding is any process that changes the surface character to photography of a garment of one of its stitch sections by application of heat, moisture or pressure. Pressing, ploating, blocking, mangling, steaming, creasing, curing and casting are trade terms for various molding processes.

Processing has two major divisions: buck press is a machine for pressing a garment or section between two contoured, heated pressure surface that may have steam vacuum systems in either or both surface.

PLANT ECONOMICS OF READYMADE GARMENTS

Rated Plant Capacity	=1,44,000 Shirts/Annum	
Land & Building (Land Area 450 Sq.Mt.)	=	Rented

PLANT & MACHINERY

1. Designing Section
2. Drawing Office Equipments
3. Cutting Machine
4. Electric adheshears
5. 60" cloth laying machine
6. Coller Printer
7. Checking Press

8. High speed lock stitch sewing machine
9. Two handle two thread machine
10. Automatic single thread chain stitch sewing machine
11. Automatic lock stitch button holes sewing machines
12. Finished Section Truneenised
13. Truneeinsed fusing press
14. Collar turning press
15. Contour trimming machine
16. Cuff turning press
17. Collar press
18. Body press
19. Double sleaves press
20. Shirts folding table
22. Embroidery & Design in single fixing machine
23. Electric irons
25. Miscellaneous & Equipments

FIXED CAPITAL

1. Plant & Machinery		2,20,000.00
2. Other Fixed Assets		20,000.00
	TOTAL	2,40,000.00

RAW MATERIALS

1. Cotton Cloth
2. Terecotton cloth
3. Threads, buttons, pins collards stiffners & other consumables etc.

TOTAL WORKING CAPITAL/MONTH

1. Raw Material		9,02,000.00
2. Salary & Wages		57,600.00
	TOTAL	9,59,600.00

TOTAL CAPITAL INVESTMENT

Total Fixed Capital		2,40,000.00
Total Working Capital for 1 Month		9,59,600.00
	TOTAL	11,99,600.00

TURN OVER/ANNUM

1. By sale of cotton shirts 60,000
2. By sale of Terecotton shirts 84,000

TOTAL 1,51,80,000.00

PROFIT SALES RATIO = Profit / Sales x 100 = 22.83 %

RATE OF RETURN = Operating profit / T.C.I x 100 = 288.92 %

BREAK EVEN POINT (B.E.P) = 12.06 %

Chapter - 53

Repacking of Medicines

The term repacking is purchasing the finished product in bulk from the market and pack the same in small packings and sell in the market with own name and trade mark. In some of the cases, the entrepreneur may improve the quality before repacking either by further processing or adding same additives or chemicals.

There are number of items which can be repacked and sold in the market but here we are only discussing about repacking of castor oil, Glucose D, Iodine, glycerine and petroleum jelly. Before we repack the material, it is quite necessary to discuss fundamental details of each materials.

The repacking business is being carried out in different trades particularly in chemicals, pharmaceuticals, fine chemicals and medicines. Such repacking units establish to a small unit and sell the sophisticated items with their names.

Such units have to register themselves with state government indicating their activities so that there may not be any possibility of adulteration.

The units for repacking of medicines have to be registered with the drug controller and they have to obtain a licence in this regards. The repacking units for medicines should be more neat and clean and the working persons have to use hand gloves. No any medicine is touched with hand.

FUNDAMENTAL DETAILS OF FEW ITEMS

1. Castor Oil :-

Castor oil is of vegetable origin which is extracted and refined to make it i.p. grade as well as edible oil. Extraction of castor oil and refining is a medium sized unit.

2. Glycerine :-

The term "Glycerine" refers to commercial produce of different grades and purity of a chemical compound known as "Glycerol" and having a chemical formula, $Ch_2OH\text{-}CHOH\text{-}CH_2OH$ which may also be designated as 1,2,3 propenetriol.

Refined "Glycerine" of commercial importance may be broadly classified as IP grade and industrial grade Ip grade required rigid specification as it has to be consumed by the drug, pharmaceutical and food industries. Hence it has requirements of extra purity. The industrial grade glycerine can be of various standards, such as Dynamite glycerine. Yellow distilled, industrial white and pale straw glycerine. Each of these industrial glycerines can be produced by different processing at the final stages depending upon the requirements of the consumer.

Glycerine is a clear colourless liquid having a sweet taste but no odour. It has a variety of industrial applications such as explosives, drugs and pharmaceuticals, dyes.

3. Petroleum Jelly :-

Petroleum jelly is also known as mineral jelly or petroleum. Petroleum jelly is a most important constituent for the manufacture of continents, emulsions, cosmetic products and other pharmaceuticals products.

Petroleum jelly is available in two forms one is commercial grade and the other is Ip grade. Commercial grade petroleum jelly is used as a lubricating agent for steel and iron products to protect from rust and corrosion . Generally, this grade is used while new steel products are packed so that rust may not be effected. Ip grade petroleum jelly is used in ointments, cosmetics, perfumes and other repellent lotions as a bases. Since it is a products for all these materials, the use in large quantity than other ingredients to be incorporated in formulations :-

4. GLUCOSE D:

Glucose is the main source of energy in living organisms. In plants, it is stored largely as starch. The starch must be converted into glucose by enzymes before it can be transported in solution to regions of cellular activity and growth. When the carbohydrates are consumed by animals, they are broken down into manoses, chiefly glycose and fructose, before passing into the blood, and the fructose is converted into glucose in the lever under normal circumstances.

The symptoms of hypoglycemica i.e. nervourness and perspiration developing into terms and conclusions coma, and finally death, when the blood sugar level falls below 0.05 per cent can be all-viated by the oral administration of glycose or sources or any other readily assimilated carbohydrate in the early stages or by the intravenous administration of glucose in the later stages.

Repacking of Medicines

The body is unable either to oxides glycose or to convert it into glycogen at the usual rate when ancrease secret insufficient insulin. Consequently, glucose, secrete accumulates in the blood. The resulting rise in the blood sugar level depends on the carbohydrate consumption and also on the degree of impairment of the pancrease. In severe diabetes, the oral administration of 1 g. of glucose per kg. of body weight may cause the book sugar level to rise with in an hour to as high as 0.4 to 0.5 per cent. In contrast to normal individuals the blood sugar level of diabetes may remain high for several hours and may exceed 0.2 per cent after passing over night.

Liquid glucose is a thick syrup containing 70 per cent of solids. It is used in the manufacture of pharmaceuticals e.g. the massing of pills of and the preparation of pillular extracts. Since it contain dextrains, maltose and some unhydrolyzed starch it is never used intravenously but it is a valuable form of carbohydrate used in many medical foods.

REPACKING PROCESS

1) Repacking of Castor Oil

The castor oil is obtained in the drums of 210 litres capacity. It is also available in 16 kg tin containers. The oil is purchased in bulk in drums packing. The colour of the castor oil is not appreciable, therefore it is decolourized before repacking. The treatment is done by activated carbon. In a canical tabk 2-4% activated carbon of the total weight of castor oil is incorporated and filtered well. It is then filtered and decolorized oil is packed.

2. Repacking of Glucose D:-

In repacking of glucose D, there are two methods :

1. Buying the prepared Glucose D from the reputed manufacturers in bulk and repack in 200 gm & 400 gms packs.

2. Buying dextrose monohydrate and mix with other ingredients.

Every minute of the day you use glucose for energy. When your body's glucose store gets reduced you feel tired and glucose D makes you energetic again.

Glucose D is a quick and convenient energy food for children teenagers, housewives, students, office goers, industrial workers, farmers, traders, professionals and sportmen.

Glucose D is recommended an excellent nutrients during travel sickness morning sickness during pregnancy, loss of appetite and run down conditions, it provides extra energy required by the body to beat the summer heat and to fight the winter cold.

3. Repacking of Iodine :-

Iodine itself is a chemical used for making number of iodided. It is purchased in bulk and small packings are done.

4. Repacking of Petroleum Jelly :-

The petroleum jelly is being manufactured on small scale. Repacking of petroleum jelly is not much economical is comparision to other items as it has a tough competition in the market .

Petroleum jelly manufacturing only involve mixing of paraffin wax and micro in the IP grade white oil and then packed.

5. Repacking of Glycerine (Process):-

The glycerine is purchased from the market, Glycerine is a compound of considerable interest in food industry besides, being nutritionally whole some. It posses a useful degree of surface activity and can be used either in its free from a source materials for the preparation of number of additives.

Glycerine is sold out in packs of 50 gm, 200 and 500 gm. 50 gm pack is the largest circulated pack. The very first step in its repacking is washing and cleaning bottles. Bottle washing machine is the machine which automatically do this mark and is available in different capacities. These washed bottles are sent to repacking machine where the bottle is filled by glycerine in required quantity. The smaller open packs are sealed with the help of sealing machines. Bottle sealing machine seals the cap of bottles and makes them ready for next step. The sealed samples are sent to lable pasting machine. The labelling of bottles is automatically performed by lable pasting machine.

These sealed and labelled samples are packed in card board boxes and these card board bottles are again packed in require any special treatment before repacking so it can be done with much difficult and sophistication.

PLANT ECONOMICS OF REPACKAGING OF MEDICINES

Rated Plant Capacity	=	9000.00 Pac./Day
Land & Building (Land 800 sq.mt)	=	Rented

PLANT & MACHINERY

1. Activated Carbon
2. Filter press
3. Bottle washing & filling machine
4. Bottle sealing machine
5. Powder packing machine for glucose D
6. Label pasting & glueing machine
7. Drying oven
8. Other Miscellaneous

FIXED CAPITAL

1. Pland & Machinery		Rs.	2,32,500.00
2. Other Fixed Assets		Rs.	1,08,000.00
	TOTAL	Rs.	3,40,500.00

RAW MATERIALS

1. Castor Oil
2. Glucose D
3. Glycerine I.P.
4. Petroleum Jelly
5. Activated carbon

TOTAL WORKING CAPITAL/ANNUM

1. Raq Material		Rs.	2,03,20,000.00
2. Salary & Wages		Rs.	5,55,128.00
3. Utilites & Overheads		Rs.	4,09,000.00
	TOTAL	Rs.	2,12,84,128.00

TOTAL CAPITAL INVESTMENT

Total Fixed Capital		Rs.	3,40,500.00
Total working Capital for 1 Month		Rs.	17,73,677.00
	TOTAL	Rs.	21,14,177.00

TURN OVER/ANNUM

1. By sale of 6,00,000 packs
   Castor oil.
2. 3,00,000 Glucose D packs
3. 1200000 Glycerine Packs
4. 600000 Petroleum Jelly Packs

TOTAL Rs. 3,81,00,000.00

PROFIT SALES RATIO = Profit / Sales x 100 = 43.32 %

RATE OF RETURN = Operating profit / T.C.I x 100 = 780.71 %

BREAK EVEN POINT (B.E.P) = 4.05 %

Chapter - 54

Rice Puff

Rice puff being one of the most nutritious food and is consumed as breakfast food not only in India but elsewhere in the world.

India is predominantly an agricultural country. Due to the progressive increase in farm produce a need has been felt to develop more agrobased food processing industries to make gainfull utilisation of the raw material resources and to provide remunerative prices to the growers.

Protein-calorie malnutrition (PCM) amongst children is prevalent in some parts of the country. Many efforts have been undertaken to ameliorate this socio-economic problem. One of these is the formulation of high protein foods. Rice puff is becoming increasingly popular in many states. Rice contains high amounts of fat and proteins, although there are some difference in varieties popularizing.

Children need extra food for their growth and metabolism. Therefore snacks for the children should be nourishing and contribute a fair share of needed nutrients. There are an almost unlimited number of wholesome snacks that can be easily prepared and stored. Puffed cereals (Rice) and legumes mixed with roasted oilseeds and desiccated coconut (salted and spiced) are a few popular snacks foods.

MANUFACTURING PROCESS

Usually Rice is used as the raw material for the puffed rice. It is cleaned before puffing to reduce the amount of bran present on the finished product.

PUFFED RICE:-

General Considerations:-

Puffing process may be conveniently divided into two types (i) atmospheric pressure procedures which rely upon the sudden application of heat to obtain the necessary rapid vaporization of water and (ii) pressure - drop processes which involve suddenly transferring super-heated, moist particles into a space at lower pressure. In the latter case the pressure drop may be achieved by releasing the seal on a vessel containing a product which has been equilibrated with high temperature steam or it may be secured by transferring the hot material from the atmosphere into an evacuated chamber.

The puffing phenomenon results from the sudden expansion of water vapor (steam) in the interstice of the granule. The particle is fixed in its expanded state by the dehydration resulting from the rapid diffusion of the water vapor out of it. Gun puffing may result in an increase of apparent volume (bulk density decrease) of sixfold to eightfold for rice.

Puffed products must be maintained at about three percent moisture (or less) in order to have the desired crispness. Even at five percent moisture a definite toughness becomes evident. These levels are more critical and harder to maintain in foods which have been gun puffed.

DETAILS OF PROCESS

Generally, Rice puff can be manufactured by following two process.

i. Oven-puffed process, and

ii. Gun-puffed process.

Oven - puffed process is most widely used for manufacturing of rice puff.

PLANT ECONOMICS OF RICE PUFF

Rated Plant Capacity	= 1.00 Tons/Day
LAND & BUILDING (Land Area 1000 sq.ft.)	= Rented

PLANT & MACHINERY

1. Automatic Puffed Rice making machine
2. Bag stiching machine
3. Hot pouch sealing machine
4. Weighing balance and Weight measurement

FIXED CAPITAL

1. Plant & Machinery	Rs.	1,26,200.00
2. Other Fixed Assets	Rs.	25,000.00
TOTAL	Rs.	1,51,200.00

Rice Puff

RAW MATERIALS

1. Rice
2. Salt
3. Jute bags
4. Polythene bags (Woven sacks)
5. Polypack

TOTAL WORKING CAPITAL/MONTH

1. Raw Material	Rs.	3,72,250.00
2. Salary & Wages	Rs.	25,935.00
3. Utilities & Overheads	Rs.	24,325.00
TOTAL	Rs.	4,22,510.00

TOTAL CAPITAL INVESTMENT

Total Fixed Capital	Rs.	1,51,200.00
Total Working Capital for 1 Month	Rs.	4,22,510.00
TOTAL	Rs.	5,73,710.00

TURN OVER/ANNUM

By sale of Puffed Rice 300 tons Rs. 55,50,000.00

PROFIT SALES RATIO = Profit / Sales x 100 = 7.16 %

RATE OF RETURN = Operating profit / T.C.I x 100 = 69.27 %

BREAK EVEN POINT (B.E.P) = 44.89 %

Chapter - 55

Shoe Polish

Shoes and boots are becoming more and more popular and due to this reason the production of footwear is steadily increasing in the country. With the increased use of footwear, boot polish consumption is also increasing. Different varieties of boot polishes are in use. This industry does not require costly machinery and can be profitably manufactured on small scale with a small investment. Variety of special surfaces are footwear furniture, automobile care, and floors.

The boot polish gives a free gloss to the shoes and actually makes them more durable by protecting these from friction, the grain finish of the upper leather and by rendening the surface somewhat water proof. It is profitable industry and can be started on a cottage scale/small scale sector.

GENERAL PROCESS FOR THE MANUFACTURE OF POLISHES

Any of the composition may be used for mixing waxes. Melt wax starting with the wax having the highest melting point and then add the other waxes in decenting other with continuous stirring of the mixture. When the mass has been started thoroughly then add a mixture of (tri-ethanolamine 1 part+ distilled water 2 parts). Add this mixture first at 85°C heating continued for half an hour. Then add a mixture of (mineral turpin 32 parts * turpentine oil 32 parts). It is mixed together and added gradually at a temperature of 30°C. while string. After this add dry stearate or a mixture of well mixed oil dye 0.75 + Turpentine 4 + Oil of mirbane 1) For better grains, the charge may be kept at a temperature of 50°C for pouring in containers. Care must be taken that the charge should not be allowed to cool rapidly. About 5% solent may be lost during the process. It is better that the pouring is done in an aconditined chamber as it would ensure an even and very gradual rate of setting and result in better quality polish with uniform grain of waxes in every layer and more uniform distribution of solvent then when pouring is done in open atmospheric conditions. The only equipments required are electric heater and water bath fitted with stainless steel vat and tunnel with level attachments.

MANUFACTURING PROCEDURES

For the manufacture of water-free black shoe cream, showing in the tins a wavy mirror surface with ring marking and giving a deep black polish with a very little brushing, the following procedure can be followed.

In a kettle, 4 parts of carnauba wax, broken into small pieces by hand or reduced in size by machine, are melted at 90-95°C. With constant stirring. As soon as the last piece is disappeared, 2-3 parts by weight of a 30-40% alobilized nigrosine base are added. After this has dissolved and has been mixed with the carnauba wax, 10 parts of crude montain wax, also broken into small pieces, are added and then 14 parts of paraffin wax, melting point 50-52°C. This is also metted with constant stirring, andthen 50 parts of turpentine are gradually run into at an initial temperature of about 80-85°C and the thinning completed by the addition of 20 parts of white spirit.

The quality retains between turpentine and white spirit depend on the market price of the day, and vary with season and the consistency desired. If overheating is to be avoided, the temperature of the finished cream-mass will now lie between 52° and 54°C, so that the contents of the kettle can be discharged suitable filling temperature lies between 32° and 48°C.

FORMULA

1. BLACK SHOE POLISHES (GROUP A)

INGREDIENTS	PARTS
1. Carnauba wax (green)	16
2. Crude montan wax	12
3. Ozokerite of melting-point Ca 58-60°	3.5
4. Paraffin of heating-point about 50°	30
5. With stearing prepared nigrosine base	6
6. Turpentine oil	185

The finished product showing formation on the surface, filling temperature 42-45°C.

2. Crude montain wax	30
Carnauba wax (grey)	5
Shellac wax	7
Paraffin or paraffin flakes melting point 50-52°C	50

With stearin prepared origrosine base	12
Turpentine	200
White spirit	50

The product shows a mirror smooth surface. Filling temperature 40-44°C.

MANUFACTURE OF GOOD QUALITY BOOT POLISH:

In a good quality boot polish there should be 35% waxes with a melting point of 70 to 75°C. Various ingredients of different waxes used for 100 parts of boot polish are as under:-

Hard paraffin wax	10 parts
Microcrystalline wax	17 parts
Bees wax	6 parts

PLANT ECONOMICS OF BOOT POLISH

Rated Plant Capacity	=	200.00 Kgs./Day
Land & Building (Land area 500 sq.mt.)	=	Rented

PLANT & MACHINERY

1. Mixer (Jacketed) and Temperature control system S.S.
2. Filling machine (automatic)
3. Heaters or miniboilers
4. Weighing machines
5. Other miscellaneous equipments, tools instruments

FIXED CAPITAL

1. Plant & Machinery	Rs.	1,45,000.00
2. Other Fixed Assets	Rs.	82,000.00
TOTAL	Rs.	2,27,000.00

RAW MATERIALS

1. Carnauba Wax (grey)
2. Crude montan wax
3. Crude Ozokerite
4. Stearin base migrosine base
5. White spirit
6. Paraffin flakes
7. Packing charges

Shoe Polish

TOTAL WORKING CAPITAL/MONTH

1. Raw Material	Rs.	1,40,650.00
2. Salary & Wages	Rs.	28,000.00
3. Utilities & Overheads	Rs.	18,250.00
TOTAL	Rs.	1,86,900.00

TOTAL CAPITAL INVESTMENT

Total Fixed Capital	Rs.	2,27,000.00
Total Working Capital for 1 Month	Rs.	1,86,900.00
TOTAL	Rs.	4,13,900.00

TURN OVER/ANNUM

Revenue by sales of 60,000 kgs. Boot polish Rs. 39,00,000.00

PROFIT SALES RATIO = Profit / Sales x 100 = 40.03 %

RATE OF RETURN = Operating profit / T.C.I x 100 = 377.21 %

BREAK EVEN POINT (B.E.P) = 16.92 %

Chapter - 56

Shampoo Industry

Shampoos are used to wash and clean hair. During old days, very rough soaps and other materials were used to wash hair. The rough type of soaps contained major proportion of caustic soda among their constituents. No doubt these soaps had good cleaning power due to caustic content in the shape of saponified materials yet they spoil the human skin by their drastic action. This actually produced irritation and in some it ended in the production of some skin diseases like irritation, skin itching and also in some cases gave rise to demodectic scabies.

With the introduction of shampoos all the above diseases and problems was removed as they replaced the soaps at a very high speed. These shampoos are available as solid, paste or liquid varieties.

The demand for shampoos especially the liquid type has never been greater than it is today. For several reasons these have superseded the ordinary shampoo powders owing to the abundance of soft lather produced and it is possible that the use of liquid shampoos does not entail so much trouble. Liquid shampoos are virtually solutions of soft soap in water with just sufficient spirit to aid through saponification. At one time more spirit was used to prevent a slight gelatnation. The popular demand in bulk shampoos being for those with a high viscosity, this can be obtained by leaving the shampoo exposed to air for a week, or a fortnight liquid variety but the demand for coconut preparation is probably not so great as it was. The reasons are the difficulty in covering the odour of the oil and the fact that some coconut shampoos have the hair in a slightly greasy condition.

The number of types of shampoos are available like coconut, which are described below:-

1. Liquid clear shampoo
2. Liquid cream shampoos or cream lotion shampoos.
3. Cream paste shampoos.
4. Egg shampoos.
5. Herbal shampoos.
6. Dry shampoos.
7. Liquid dry shampoos.

The formulation, process conditions etc. are different for different type of shampoos but all types of shampoos can be manufactured in the similar plant without change of set of machineries.

VARIOUS FORMULATION

1. **Liquid Shampoos :**

Formula No.1

Coconut oil	14%
Olive oil	3%
Castor oil	3%
Caustic Potash(8%Be)	4.7%
Glycerol	2%
Ethyl Alcohol	4%
Sodium hexametaphosphate	1%
Perfume	0.3%
Water	68%

Formulation No.2

Triethanolamine laural sulphate	35%
Sodium alginate	2.5%
Water	2.5%
Perfume	0.5%

2. **Vegetable oil Shampoo**

Formula oil Shampoo

1. Coconut	8%
2. Palm oil	4%
3. Potassium hydroxide(90%)	5%
4. Ethyl alcohol	8%
5. Glycerol	6%
6. Water	to make 100%
7. Perfume	0.5%
8. Olive oil	8%
9. Oleic acid	2.8%

Formula No.2

1.	Refined coconut oil	800 gms.
2.	Refined till oil	200 ,,
3.	Caustic Potash lye 44°be	500 ,,
4.	Glycerine	100 ,,
5.	Distilled water	2500 m.l.
6.	Iso propyl glycol	300 gms
7.	Perfume	50 cc.
8.	Saponax	4 gms
9.	Organize colour for cosmetic	2 ,,

3. Egg Shampoo :

1.	White of egg.	4 eggs.
2.	Water	10 oz.
3.	Ammonia water	6 oz.
4.	Cologne water	1/2 oz.
5.	Alcohol	8 oz.

Almond shampoo

23.8% Coconut oil	450 parts.
26.45 oleic acid	500 parts.
26.45% Trethanlance	500 parts.
23.28 Propyleneglycoal	440 parts.
.529 oil of almond	1 parts.
.026 perfumes	5 parts.

MANUFACTURING PROCESS FOR COCONUT OIL SHAMPOO

The shampoo based on coconut oil is prepared by two conventional methods viz.

1. Cold process.
2. Hot process.

1. Cold Process

In this process, caustic potash and soda is dissolved in 1/10 of total water requirement and the natural heat generated during the combination is sufficient.

Now, the coconut oil as per formula is melted. The exact calculated amount of lye and oil should be mixed together.

The melted coconut oil is poured in a thin stream in the lye with cntinuous stirring. In the last, when saponification is completed, the solution of spirit and perfume etc. is mixed. This solution is prepared separately. The stirring is continued until the liquid become a light amber colour.

The whole mass is now allowed to stand overnight and the remaining water is added. The shampoo is ready but before filteration and packing it is kept aside for a fortnight.

2. Hot Process

In this process, heating is required and the coconut oil is melted in a steam jacketed pan at a temperature of about 120°F. The alkali is dissolved in 1/5th of total water requirement separatejy and added in the hot coconut oil. The addition of lye should be done slowly and the temperature be maintained between 120 to 130°F. The stirring is done for a short time for emulsification of whole mass and then the spirit is added and the temperature is gradually raised to 180°F. This temperature is maintained till the saponification is Ompleted. The soap is allowed to cool and stand overnight.

Now the remaining water is heated to boiling and the soap as prepared, above is added and the stirring is continued till fully dissolved. A little quantity from 3 to 4 Oz. of potassium carbonate may be added in this shampoo if a much clear solution is desired. The prepared shampoo is now kept aside for 8-10 days and then filtered and packed in bottles.

In both the above processes, the cold process, although being much better and yield good quality. The investment on machineries is comparatively less than hot process.

In order to increase the lathering properties is the coconut oil shampoo, the mixture of following ingredients.

Glycerine	3 1bs.
Borax	1 1/2 1bs.
Potassium Carbonate	1/2 1bs
Oleic acid	1 1/2 1bs
Rectified spirit	1/2 gall.

The oleic acid is mixed with alcohol, then borax and potassium carbonate is dissolved separately in glycerine and added this solution in previous one.

After storing the final product in a tank, the shampoo is fed into the bottling machine where the shampoo is filled in bottles and packed.

PLANT ECONOMICS OF SHAMPOO

Rated Plant Capacity = 15,00,000 Bottles/Annum

Land & Building (Total area 250 sq.mt.) = Rented

PLANT & MACHINERY

1. Caustic lye tank
2. Coconut oil storage tank
3. Oil heating tank
4. Reaction Vessel
5. Storage tank
6. Botting machine
7. Plastic welding machine
8. Tube well and accessories
9. Extruder

FIXED CAPITAL

1. Plant & Machinery	3,10,000.00
2. Other Fixed Assets	80,000.00
TOTAL	3,90,000.00

RAW MATERIALS

1. Coconut oil refined
2. Triethanalamine
3. Propylene glycol
4. Oleic Acid
5. Oil Almond
6. Perfumes
7. Packaging materials i.e. bottles, pouches etc.

TOTAL WORKING CAPITAL/MONTH

1. Raw Material	15,14,520.00
2. Salary & Wages	50,875.00
3. Utilities & Overheads	90,000.00
TOTAL	16,55,395.00

TOTAL CAPITAL INVESTMENT

Total Fixed Capital	3,90,000.00
Total Working Capital for 1 Month	16,55,395.00
TOTAL	20,45,395.00

TURN OVER/ANNUM

1. Pay sale of 15,00,000 Bottles
2. Pay sale of 1,12,00,000 Pouches

TOTAL 2,81,00,000.00

PROFIT SALES RATIO = Profit / Sales x 100 = 28.16 %

RATE OF RETURN = Operating profit / T.C.I x 100 = 386.84 %

BREAK EVEN POINT (B.E.P) = 1.21 %

Chapter - 57

Socks Knitting

The production of hosiery goods in India dates back to 120 years. Hosiery industry can be traced to the beginning of 1830 when socks were knitted on a cottage scale by women folk with wooden and steel needles. Although the word hosiery originated from knitting of hoses/socks in India however use of socks in the past was confined to military personnel and the nobility. The first factory in Bengal for producing socks and stockings was set up in 1890 at kidder pare (Kolkata) with four hand driven machines. Gradual change over to power driven machines started from 1942 onwards. The hosiery machine manufacturing industry is located mostly in Ludhiana. Other centers for manufacturers are Saharanpur, Kolkata, Kanpur, Delhi and Ahmedabad. The following types of hosiery machines are now being manufactured.

a. Hand driven circular knitting machines for socks and stockings.
b. Hand driven outer wear machines e.g. plain rile machine, bala clava cap machine, half-jacquard machine, mattardana machine, checkputti machine, muffler machine, jack round machine and plain round machine.
c. Hand driven machine for underwear.
d. Circular power driven machines e.g. double jacquard machine, muffler making machine, plain rib machine and rib jacquard machine.
e. Warp knitting looms e.g. power driven rasehel looms (working width upto 96 inch)
f. Power driven circular machines e.g. non-sinker plain web machine, sinker body machine rib eyelet machine, plain eyelet machine and interlock machine.

PROCESS OF MANUFACTURE OF SOCKS ON AUTOMATIC SOCKS KNITTING MACHINE

The socks on automatic socks knitting machine are knitted by undergoing the following sequence of operations.

1. Procurement of raw material (Yarn)

It is advised to procure dyed or bleached and mercerized 2/2 is cotton yarn to avoid a lot of expenditures and botherations in the dyeing and bleaching process.

2. Conewinding

The dyed or bleached cotton yarn is to be wound on to paper cones as the package required on knitting machines is cone of a desired angle. If the elastic yarn is also received in hand form that is also to be wound on to the cones.

3. Socks Knitting

Usual socks knitting machines are equipped with feeding point on the creel. So the cones are placed in the creel and ends are drawn through the guide pins etc. and first row is knitted by hand often which all the settings are done and machines is handed over to the knitter who operates it properly and the socks are knitted automatically. The following two ways can be employed.

1: WARP KNITTING

Many yarns are set up, one to each knitting latch, and each yarn proceeds to form stitches in a wrap direction, i.e. lengthwise along the fabric, but, as it does so, the yarn also loops through the stitch on each side.

The machine may be flat with a row of needles at the base, producing a flat fabric with selvages, or it may be circular there by producing a tube of knitting. In both cases the fabrics are very wide.

Sharp knits can be identified by a characteristic wavy effect on the wrong side. The fabrics do not ladder when cut and firm to sew. There is a limited amount of 'give' in warp knit.

2: WEFT KNITS OR FILLING KNITS

One yarn traverses horizontally on either a flat or circular knitting machine. The produces a flat or tubular fabric that can be identified by lengthwise rows or wales of knitting on the right side, looking exactly like hand knitting. The stitch can be varied by the introduction of ribs, purl stitches, tucks for lacy effects, etc.

Weft knits 'give' considerably in both directions and they may ladder when cut, but they tend to be better quality fabrics that wrap knits. Cut edges tend to curl up in handling. Both wrap and weft knit fabrics may be plain or printed.

4. Washing and Drying

All the knitted socks are to be washed with the soap water and rinsed properly in clean water in the washing tank equipped with agitator and then dried in the hydraulic dryer.

5. Inspection and mending

Whole of the production is checked and inspected for damage etc. and the mandible faults are rectified.

6. Ironing & Pressing

This is one of the most important operations, pressing can be done by 3 modes such as heat, pressure and steam.

When using the iron directly on the fabric be guided by the setting indicated on the iron, but when pressing with a damp cloth, the cloth cools the base of the iron and so the iron should be used at a higher setting. If this is not done, the amount of heat actually reaching the fabric is incorrect, and the amount actually penetrating it is very little. The result is that the pressing is effective, as the heat is insufficient to put the fabric in position permanently. And worse than this is the possibility of harming some fabrics with too little heat combined with moisture. At best this makes the fabric warm and damp, at worst it leaves a permanent imprint of the iron.

Ironing after laundering is usually done by placing the iron directly on the fabric and sliding it. Pressing after sewing is done with the iron held in position until it has pressed the sewing process in position, and, as in nearly all cases the addition of steam is vital, the iron is used slightly hotter than when laundering.

PRESSURE

The process has literally to be pressed and to do it you use the weight of the iron. The amount of pressure needed varies with the type of fabric and is largely a matter for experiment. For example, too much pressure exerted on a pile fabric will flatten the pile, but too little on a twill weave polyester will have no effect at all. The iron, therefore, can be used lightly, even holding it just above the surface in some cases, or more heavily, while if you add the weight of your arm and body by leaning over and pressing hard, you extert the maximum pressure necessary for springly fibres and stubborn weaves.

Whatever you decide about the amount of pressure required. The iron should be used in short, sharp dabbing movements. Do not slide it when using a damp cloth. If using the iron directly on the fabric, make sure you press the process adequately with sharp movements then finish off by sliding the iron if necessary.

STEAM

With a few exceptions it is impossible forcibly to change the position of the fabric without applying steam. The best way to provide steam is by the use of a dampended cloth. It requires quite a lot of skill to use it properly, but it is well worth learning the techniques in order to produce good results. The cloth is squeezed out in water, leaving just enough moisture in the cloth for the fabric being pressed. The quantity is governed by the type of fibres involved as well as the absorbency of the weave, i.e. whether close or open. The cloth is placed over the process, the iron applied and the heat irnmediately converts the water to steam and it is the steam which is pressed into the fabric. The cloth must be removed immediately. Failure to have the iron hot enough to convert the water tc steam will result in soggy fabric, possibly stretched or out of shape, on marks. In addition, the process will not be adequately processed.

With fine fabrics the steam issuing from a steam iron will be sufficient, but with others it may not be. A steam iron is fine for use after laundering, but in that instance we are only removing creases, not including fibres to turn sharp corners. Because a steam iron makes laundering so easy, there is a tendency to use it for pressing when sewing, but with most fabrics the iron has to be held in position for too long, to allow sufficient steam to escape, and the result in an impression of the sole plate on the fabric, and possibly shine, too.

Good professional pressing while sewing is a combination of heat, pressure and moisture, all applied together but it varying amounts according to the fibres, weave, texture and finish of the fabric. Although, in the fabric section, recommendations are made as to the best method of pressing, it is still essential to try pressing a small scrap of the fabric first to be essential to try pressing a small scrap of the fabric first to be absolutely confident of good results. Our fabric may appear to conform in every respect to the one we have described, but it may have a particular surface finish which is invisible to us and which we do not know about.

One final point for emphasis. It is very important indeed to press each process before proceeding to the next stage in construction. This is something that is always mentioned in the inconvenient situation of the iron, or a lack of appreciation as to why it is necessary. We cannot emphasize too strongly that the persuation of the fibres to take on a new direction must be done immediately after the permanent stitching of that process has been completed. Poor and amateurish-looking sewing is always the result of trying to press only on completion.

7. Labeling and Packing

The socks are checked for proper size of the socks and labeled and packed for marketing.

The specifications of different type of knitting machine with vertical designing and elastic attachments, are given below:

Plain socks knitting machine :

Size	Needles
2.5"	72 x 35
3"	85 x 42
3 1/4"	90 x 45
3 1/2"	90 x 48
3 3/4"	100 x 54
4"	72 x 36
4 1/2"	90 x 40

Designs sock hand knitting machine :

Size	Needles
2 1/4"	96 x 108
3"	108 x 120
3 1/4"	120 x 132
3 1/2 "	132 x 144
3 3/4"	144

During knitting, attention should be paid, so that length of the foot is kept correct according to the desired sizes. Length of the leg is taken from the top and of sock to the joint at the heel and the distance between the joint of heel and joint at paws is called length of the feet.

In order to make the socks long last in, the heels in the socks should be doubled. After knitting of legs, heel etc. the whole sock is sewn in an ordinary hand operated machine. The various operations like winding on bobbins, sewing of sock paws and ironing etc. can be done by ladies who may be employed on contract or daily basis.

In case of socks knitting - problems are mostly observed in three different important places viz welt, heel and toe. To eliminate this except the English welt and French welt enturned welt is also introduced in single cylinder knitting machine. Different types of heels can also be produced on modern socks knitting machine to improve durability also to minimize slippage. Toe of the socks is mostly torn as it is not properly stitched on linked. Normally open toe is produced on socks knitting machine. Then it is stitched on loop forming machine or linking machine. In fact for this purpose modern linking or loop forming machines were introduced. Recently new machines are introduced to manufacture close toe socks. In socks knitting machine computer patterning device was also introduced to develop wide range of designs.

PLANT ECONOMICS OF SOCKS KNITTING

Rated Plant Capacity	=	1200.00 Pairs/Day
Land & Building (Land 250 sq.mt.)	=	Rented

PLANT & MACHINERY

1. Model CS Horizontal and vertical st rips, moeril, cordori motor driver
2. Model SP 3(MS) Three coloured Jacquered floating pattern, Mesh pattern and strips
3. Linking machine set complete with motor drive
4. Overlock machine complete
5. Electric Ironing
6. Miscellaneous other machinery

FIXED CAPITAL

1. Plant & Machinery		Rs.	5,19,300.00
2. Other Fixed Assets		Rs.	2,17,000.00
	TOTAL	Rs.	7,36,300.00

RAW MATERIALS

1. Synthetic yarn (like nylon)
2. Miscellaneous chemical
3. Packing material

TOTAL WORKING CAPITAL/MONTH

1. Raw Material		Rs.	3,66,000.00
2. Salary & Wages		Rs.	18,720.00
3. Utilities & Overheads		Rs.	13,000.00
	TOTAL	Rs.	3,97,720.00

TOTAL CAPITAL INVESTMENT

Total Fixed Capital	Rs.	7,36,300.00
Total Working Capital for 1 Month	Rs.	3,97,720.00
TOTAL	Rs.	11,34,020.00

TURN OVER/ANNUM

Return on sales of 360000 pairs socks	Rs.	61,20,000.00

PROFIT SALES RATIO = Profit / Sales x 100 = 16.93 %

RATE OF RETURN = Operating profit / T.C.I x 100 = 91.37 %

BREAK EVEN POINT (B.E.P) = 30.90 %

Chapter - 58

Shaving Cream

Shaving creams are emulsified forms of shaving soap, and are usually in flexible tubes. The main requirements of a wet shaving preparation are to soften the beard, to lubricate the passage of the razor over the face and to support the beard hair. To minimize the trauma of shaving, a wide range of preparations is now available that prepare the beard and face for shaving, increase speed and comfort during the shave and confer a feeling of well-being after shaving. The choice of shaving cream is highly individualistic, however, it is generally recognized that different forms of beard preparation are required for 'wet' and 'dry' shaving.

Lather type shaving cream is the most important shaving cream item. Although in recent years, the lather cream lost its importance due to the introductions of electric dry shaving, and aerosol products, the popularity of this type of cream is still great compared to the other shaving products all over the world.

Formulations based on stearic acid alone do not produce a sufficiently voluminous lather and it is usual to add some coconut oil, fatty acids.

Soaps for shaving are generally formulated by saponifying a mixture of coconut oil and stearic acid with mixed caustic potash and soda. Stearic acid (4-8%) may be left unneutralized to supply a pearly luster and 5-10% glycerol may be added for body.

Shaving preparation contribute a great deal to the comfort, safety and speed of shave.

MANUFACTURING PROCESS

The manufacturing is done by melting and filtering the free fats and saponifying them with the soda lye and part of the potash lye in the presence of the glycerin. The remainder of the potash lye together with some water is now run in, the heat being maintained all the time. The melted stearic acid is then added in a continuous stream. The whole being stirred throughout (slow stirring is preferable). Samples are tested, and the necessary additions of acid or alkali made. The cream is now super habbed by means of boric acid, additional stearic acid, lanolin or occasionally fixed oils and boiling is continued until a perfectly even cream is obtained with all formulae further examination is necessary so that the total fatty acid in the cream can be adjusted to the standard percentage. The steam is then turned off and qenole agitation continued while the cream cools. The perfume is then addeo and after manufacture, the cream is allowed to stand for a period of 3-4 weeks before packaging. During this time, which is sometimes referred to as the curing process, changes occur in the crystal formation of the cream. The cream is finally turned out by machine filling.

PASTE GRINDER

To obtain the good quality the raw materials be the best and purest form.

The oil should be used are coconut oil, olive oil, peanut oil, sesame oil or even best white neutral tallow, and replacing part of the potash lye with soda lye.

Purified stearic acid is now used as the fatty acid. Triple pressed has the highest melting point, is the purest, and yirld the whitest product. It is comparatively easy to calculate by analytical method the exact amount of alkali required to produce an absolutely neutral cream. Stearic acid alone, however does in fact posses the disadvantage of producing a cream which does not have the necessary lathering properties. This drawback is overcome by adding some coconut oil, or if desired, some tallow as well. In general, four to eight times as much fatty acid is employed as free fat. When coconut oil is added alone to the stearic acid the ratio of about 1 to 7 should meet all requirements as to creaniners of lather. Exceptional foaming properties may be obtained by replacing part of the stearic acid with mysteristic acid.

Shaving Cream

A mixture of potash and soda is also preferable but the latter is kept low proportions and seldom exceeds 15% of the total alkali. The total fatty acid in a cream varies between 35 and 50%, softeners being enhanced by the addition of about 5% of glycerin. The latter also have the advantages of improving the wetting properties, preventing too rapid drying of the lather, making the skin more elastic, softening the beard and facilitating the transit of the razor over the face. Other wetting agents of interest are alkyl sulfate and triethanolamine stearic which also enhance creaminess of the lather.

A few percent of free fatty acid is added after the completion of the saponification. Alternatively this may be necessary quantity of boric acid to the nearly finished cream.

The manufacturing process is commenced by melting and filling t... free tab and saponifying the potash lye together with some water is now run in, the heating being maintained below 80°C all the time. The melted stearic acid is then added in a continuous steam the whole being stirred throughout (slow stirring is preferable). Samples are tested, and the necessary additions of acid or alkali made. The cream is now superfatted by means of boric acid, additional stearic acid. Lanolin or occasionally fixed oils, and boiling is continued until a perfectly even cream is obtained. With the all formulae further examination is necessary so that the total fatty acid in the cream can be adjusted to the standard percentage. The steam is then turned off and gentle agitation continued while the cream cools. The perfume is then added. It may be stayed for 3-4 weeks before packing due to form crystal formation of the cream. The cream is finally turned out by machine filling.

TYPICAL FORMULATIONS

Formulation : 1

Stearic Acid	280
Coconut Oil	10
Tallow	30
Potash lye at 20° Baume (approx.)	300
Soda lye at 20° Baume (approx.)	50
Glycerine	50
Boric Acid	20
Sodium Alkyl Sulphate	20
Water (Softened or distilled)	210
	1000

Perfume 0.3 - 0.5 per cent

Proceed as given in manufacturing process making adjustments necessary after saponification.

Formulation : 2

Stearic Acid	300
Myristic Acid	100
Coconut Oil	50
Glycerine	60
Sodium Hydroxide (approx.)	2
Potassium Hydroxide (approx.)	18
Triethanolamine Stearate	10
Water (Softened or distilled approx.)	460
	1000

Perfume 0.3 - 0.5 per cent

Proceed as above adjusting the cream to 3 per cent free fatty acid.

Chapter - 59

Softeners (Cationic, An-ionic and Non-Ionic)

Softening of textile materials was probably carried out in prehistoric times and has continued till today. Most of the Softening agents are derived from straight chain fatty radicals containing 12 to 18 carbon atoms.

Softening agents may be divided into three main classes i.e.-

1. Anionic Softeners such as oil emulsions, sulphonated oils, soaps, sulphated fatty alcohols & tellows.
2. Cationic softeners - such as substituted quarternary ammonium compounds and
3. Nonionic Softeners such as polyoxyethylene derivatives, polyethylene emulsions & silicons.

Recently reactive softeners are available in the market which react directly with hydroxyl groups of cellulose macromolecule by means of functional groups.

In textile finishing articles, the past decade can be considered "the age of the acrylics" and the era of the multipurpose finish.

Numerous polymers farmed from acrylic monomers have been specially 'Tailored' to meet the finisher exacting requirements. Multipurpose finished have been big property-wise and economy wise. Multipurpose finishes such as combined water repellency, flame retardancy and rotproofness have contributed to continued use of cotton in outdoor application.

These finishes include softeners, bodying agent water repellents, flame retardants etc. Softeners are basically of three types

1. Anionic
2. Cationic
3. Nonionic.

MANUFACTURING PROCESS

The amine is preheated to 60°C and 35% hydrogen peroxide is added over one hour per period with good agitation. The reaction mixture is kept at 60-65°C during peroxide addition, as above this temperature the solution become yellow and at lower temperature a longer reaction time is required. During the one hour period of hydrogen peroxide addition the mixture is gel unless water is also added. The water required for dilution is added in portion. Just sufficient to keep the reaction mixture fluid. After all the peroxide has been added. The remaining water to give the desired final strength is added and the temperature of the reaction mixture is raised to 75°C.

The solution is cooled and the unreacted hydrogen peroxide is destroyed by adding stoichiometric amount of sodium sulphite. While with pure amine the conversion is 100% with commercial amine it is 80% using a 10% molar excess of hydrogen peroxide.

NON-IONIC SOFTENERS

Formulation - 1.

Tallow Polyglycerol ester	-	21.2
Alkyl phenol condensate (with 20 mol of Ethylene oxide)	-	3.75
Water	-	74.75

Formulation -2.

It is an emulsion of medialan A. tallow polyglycerol ester, alkyl phenol condensate, 20 molecules ethylene oxide and water.

		%
Medialan - A	-	25
Tallow polyglycerol	-	21.5
Alkyl Phenol Condensate	-	3.75
Water	-	49.75

PROCESS :

The tallow polyglycerol is made by heating 66.7 Kgs of tallow with 27.23 Kgs polyglycerol at 200°C and finally raising the temperature to 260°C for 30 minute to complete the reaction. Completion of the reaction is indicated by the solubility of the mixture in alcohol. Six grams sodium hydrosulphite is generally used as a catalyst along with tallow and polyglycerol.

ANIONIC SOFTENERS

The anionic softeners do not possess substantivity to the fabric under not wash fast as most of the textile materials are anionic in nature hence they repel the softeners. Thus anionic softener are mechanically deposited on the fabric by padding.

Softeners (Cationic, An-ionic and NGN-Ionic)

Formulation :-

		Kgs.
Castor oil	-	30
Mineral oil	-	23
Paraffin wax	-	15
Stearic acid	-	10
Olcic acid	-	10
Sodium dodecyl benzene sulphonate	-	2
Water	-	10

The various appropriate indegenously e.g. castor oil, Mineral oil, paraffin wax, stearic acid, olecic acid and surface acture agent are indigenously blended in a mixer fitted with agitator and motar into the finished product to fulfill the specific and requisite properties.

FORMULATION OF NON-IONIC SOFTENER

FORMULATION NO. 1

1.	Stearic acid polyglycerol sster	21.50
2.	Alkyl Phenol condensate (nonyel phenol condensate) (with 20 mols of ethylene oxide) or stearic acid ethylene oxide condensate	3.75
3.	Water	74.75

PROCESS:-

The stearic acid polyglycerol ester is made by heating 66.7 Kgs of stearic acid with 27.23 Kgs polyglycerol at 200°C and finally raising the temperature to 260° C for 30 minutes to complete the reaction completion of this reaction is indicated by the solubility of the mixture in alcohol. 6 gms of sodium hydrosulphite is generally used as a catalyst alongwith stearic acid polyglycerol.

PLANT ECONOMICS OF SOFTENER

Rated Plant Capacity = 300.00 Kgs./Day

Land & Building (Land area 400 sq. mts.) = Rs. 12,20,000.00

PLANT & MACHINERY

1. Reaction vessel made of S. S.
2. Storage tank.
3. Baby boiler
4. Distillation equipment for water
5. Laboratory equipment
6. Miscellaneous pipe fitting pump

FIXED CAPITAL

1. Land & Building		Rs.	12,20,000.00
2. Plant & Machinery		Rs.	3,28,000.00
3. Other Fixed Assets		Rs	1,64,000.00
	TOTAL	Rs.	17,12,000.00

RAW MATERIALS

1. Tallow poly glycerol ester
2. Alkyl phenol condensate
3. Dimethyldodecyl amine
4. Hydrogen peroxide
5. Castor oil
6. Mineral oil
7. Paraffin wax.
8. Stearic acid
9. Oleic acid
10. Sodium dodecyl benzene sulphonate
11. Packaging material
12. Miscellaneous

TOTAL WORKING CAPITAL/MONTH

1. Raw Material		Rs.	2,41,527.00
2. Salary & Wages		Rs.	40,768.00
3. Utilities & Overheads		Rs.	93,000.00
	TOTAL	Rs.	3,75,295.00

TOTAL CAPITAL INVESTMENT

Total Fixed Capital		Rs.	17,12,000.00
Total Working Capital for 3 Month		Rs.	11,25,886.00
	TOTAL	Rs.	28,37,886.00

Softeners (Cationic, An-ionic and NGN-Ionic)

TURN OVER/ANNUM

Receipt by sale of Softener
(Cationic, Anionic, Non Ionic). 90,000 Kgs. Rs 58,50,000.00

PROFIT SALES RATIO = Profit / Sales x 100 = 14.30 %

RATE OF RETURN = Operating profit / T.C.I x 100 = 29.47 %

BREAK EVEN POINT (B.E.P) = 57.94 %

Chapter - 60

Silver Extraction from Waste Hypo Solution X-Ray Film, Colour Paper Bleach and Cinema Film by Chemical Process

Hypo solution contains a good percentage of silver which can be extracted either by chemical or electrolytic method. The extraction of silver from hypo solution, X-Ray and cinema film is quite economical and can be started with a small investment. A plant of 2 to 10 kgs silver per day of extracted silver is quite feasible on small scale.

Silver is widely distributed in nature, but the total amount present is quite small as compared to other metals. It occurs both native and in combination with many other elements in a large No. of naturally occurring minerals. Main forms of ores of silver are:-

1. Native silver (100% silver)
2. Argenite (Ag2s, 87.1% silver)
3. Cerargyrite (Agcl,75.3% silver)
4. Polybasite (Ag16 sb,59.9% silver)

Some of the other ores of silver which are less important are Tellurides, Argentiferrous Tetrahyrdrite, Strom-eyerite, Steepharite and Pearcite.

In India, the silver are deposits which are primarily mined for silver and of any commercial importance have not been reported. Silver occurs in association with lead and zinc ores in the form of argentiferrous. The argentiferrous lead Zinc ores found in Rajasthan are the principal sources of silver in the country. The lead ores of Andhra Pradesh, Bihar, Gujarat, Jammu & Kashmir and Uttar Pradesh are also reported to contain a fair amount of silver.

Films and the Silver:-

Photographic or X-ray films are made of transparent bare material generally a cellulosic plastic coated with a highly light sensitive emulsion.

These emusions are composed mainly of microscopic crystals of silver bromide suspended in gelatine; silver chloride and silver iodide are also present but in much smaller quantities.

These silver compounds are called silver halides. The gelatine is transparent and tough hard, it permits the penetraion of developer during processing and at the same time protects the silver halide crystals with in it in such a way that only those crystals which have been effected by light can be acted upon the developer to produce silver deposits of varing density in the negative. The gelatine a substance extracted from the bones and skin clipping of cows and pigs contains certain organic compounds which include sulphur in their composition and their help to make the halides more sensitive to light.

The next step in the photography after exposure to light is the development of the negative and standard developers are used for this purposes.

The main ingredients in developer is the reducing agent. This reduces the silver salts in the gelatine of the fims emulsion which have been affected by the light the latest image, to black metallic silver.

The stronger the light has been an a part of negative, the heavier and the deeper will be the silver deposit. The agent will not seriously affect those silver salts which have not been exposed to light and these will be washed away by the acid fixer. Metal hydro quanane, glycerine etc having its own characteristics. Now the film contains the reduced metallic silver and the silver halides which have not been effect by the light.

In the next step is the fixing which consists of removing by chemical means the substances in the emulsion which have not previously been affected by the light and by the developer, thus rendering the negative or print fixed, that is unalterable by any subsequent action of light. Sodium sulphate called hypo is the main chemicals fixing agent which dissolved all the silver halides unaffected by light from the film. This the film is deplected of all silver content except the light affected metallic silver which forms the base of the photographic image.

Silver in pure form is recoverable from the made film and other photographic film as well as wastes such as Hypo - Solutions.

Available Silver from Photographic Material

Photographic films contain silver in the form of silver halides.

The next step to photography after exposure to light is the development of the negative. Standard developers are used for this purpose. The main ingredients in developer is the reducing agent. This reduces the silver salts in the gelatin of the film emulsion which have been affected by the light the latent image to black metallic silver. The stronger the light has been on a part of the negative, the heavier and the deeper will be the silver deposit. The agent will not seriously affect those silver salts which have not been exposed to light and these will be washed away by the acid fixer. metal hydro quanane, glycine etc. are the best known of these reducing agents each having its own characteristics. Now the film contains and reduced metallic silver and the silver halides which have not been affected by the light.

The next step is the fixing which consists of removing by chemical means the substances in the emulsion which have not previously been affected by the light and by the developer thus, rendering the negative the as print fixed i.e. unalternate by any subsequent action of light sodium thio sulphate, commonly called 'Hypo solution' is the main chemical fixing agent which dissolves all the silver haldies unaffected by light from the film. Thus the film is deplected of all the silver content except the light affected metallic silver which forms the base of the photographic image.

Recovery of silver from photographic materials have been achieved by chemical means as well as electrolytic process.

PROCESS OF MANUFACTURE

The whole process can be divided into 2 parts.

1. Recovery of silve from waste used hypo solution.
2. Refining the silver recovered.

Recovery of Silver from used hypo solution :

Chemical Process

The first step is the recovery is the dissolution of metallic silver or silver salts in nitric acid. For this dilute nitric acid can be prepared by mixing one volume of con. Nitric acid (Sp. gravity 1.2) with 1.6 volume of water. Depending as the concentration of silver in the solution, the required quantity of nitric acid is added. About 1 ml. of the diluted nitric acid containing 0.67 gm of silver. The addition of acid is done in the lead lined or glass lined tanks containing required amount of acid as mentioned above. The contents may be gently warmed till whole of silver gets dissolved.

Silver Extraction from Waste Hypo Solution X-Ray Film

The silver halide which the major part of used hypo solution is also the major sources of silver recovey in this case, the baest way of dissolution is by fusion with about six times the weight of salt present in the solution of the sodium carbonate. This converts the silver into carbonate and the halide radical combines with solution to form sodium haide which is soluble in water and is therefore dissolved out in the water. The silver carbonate is washed to free it of halide and dissolved in dilute nitric acid. The fusion is carried out in a fusion tank by heating the solution with sodium carbonate.

The silver nitrate is then precipatated as silve chloride from the above solution by treating it with a 0.2 N hydrochloric acid. This strength of the acid can be prepared by adding 1 part of concentrated hydrochloric acid to 60 parts of water.

The treatment is carried out in lined vessel equipped with jacket. The silver nitrate solution is first heated to 70°C. 9.2N hydrochloric acid is then added to precipitate the silver present. The acid is added in 10 to 20% in excess. The addition of acid is done slowly and with continous stirring. The heating and stirring is continuous until the precipitated of silver chloride coagulated and show a tendency to settle.

The solution is cooled to room temperature and a sample is withdrawn to test it for completeness of the precipitation using a litte more 0.2 N hydrochloric acid. The precipitate is ten allowed to stand for several hours or over night, if possible in the dark.

The precipitate is then removed by decanting liquor and is washed with fresh water. It is then filtered. The precipitated is separated by means of a contrifuge. After washing it several time, the precipitate is dried which not contains about 70 to 75% by weight of silver.

The drying should be done at a round 130-150°C to remove all moisture as well to reduce any organic matter. When silver chloride is precipitated as above, it form a spongy mass which does not conclude much supernatent liquid and is easily washed and transferred.

In the next step, silver is separated from chloride. The precipitate is dissolved in ammonium hydroxide solution. This solution is added in little excess. To this solution is added sodium hypo sulphite ($Na_2S_2O_4$) to form metallic silver.

This is again separated by filteration. The precipitated silver is dried and mixed with about 1% o sodium carbonate, is packed in a claycrucible, the inside of which has been glazed with borax-glas and covered with a layer of crushed charcoal. The silver melted in the tightly covered crucible is pured into as iron mould which have been chalked or blade leaded.

If the cove of charcoal is ommitted or burned away during fusing, the metallic silver is capable of absorbing oxygen from the atmosphere to the extent of about 0.25 per cent of its weightage. This gas is expleed out during the passage of the metal into the solid state and produce a casting which can not be rolled into smooth sheets.

As a great number of operations are involved in this process, it is advisable to start the project either on laboratory scale (around 2 kg per day) or on very large scale. This profile deals with the project of 2 kg per day capacity.

PLANT ECONOMICS OF SILVER EXTRACTION

Rated Plant Capacity	=	2.00 Kg/Day
Land & Building (Land 300 sq.mts.)	=	Rented

PLANT & MACHINERY

1. Fibre glass lined vessel with heating arrangement and stirrer
2. Centrifuge
3. Fusing Tank
4. Filter press
5. Storage tank
6. Laboratory equipments
7. Installation
8. Electric Fittings and Accessories
9. Miscellaneous

FIXED CAPITAL

1. Plant & Machinery	Rs.	3,09,000.00
2. Other Fixed Assets	Rs.	25,000.00
TOTAL	Rs.	3,34,000.00

RAW MATERIALS

1. Hypo solution
2. Waste X-Ray & Cinema Film
3. Other chemicals including nitric hydrochloric acid and ammonium hydroxide, sodium carbonate etc.

Silver Extraction from Waste Hypo Solution X-Ray Film

TOTAL WORKING CAPITAL/ANNUM

1. Raw Material	Rs.	19,20,000.00
2. Salary & Wages	Rs.	2,89,080.00
3. Utilities & Overheads	Rs.	1,94,000.00
TOTAL	Rs.	24,03,080.00

TOTAL CAPITAL INVESTMENT

Total Fixed Capital	Rs.	3,34,000.00
Total Working Capital For 1 Month	Rs.	2,00,256.00
TOTAL	Rs.	5,34,256.00

TURN OVER/ANNUM

Receipt through sale of 600 kg of silver	Rs.	36,60,000.00

PROFIT SALES RATIO = Profit / Sales x 100 = 30.34 %

RATE OF RETURN = Operating profit / T.C.I x 100 = 207.87 %

BREAK EVEN POINT (B.E.P) = 23.42 %

Chapter - 61

Tooth Brush

Tooth brush occupies a prominent and very important place among the dentifice available today.

Due to the increasing awareness and importance of dental hygiene in the upkeeping of human health, the use of tooth paste was confined to the upper and upper middle classes ot urban society, but with increasing awareness the use of tooth brush has become well established in even rural house hold. Tooth brush being consumer product and its market being quite competitive and also acceptable.

For keeping good health, care of teeth is one of the essential step. The particle of food that sticks to our teeth give birth to fouling smell and many dreadful diseases, which destroy the gums and results in tooth decay. A man, who do not have teeth in his mouth, only knows as how important are these. A man having fouling smell coming out from his mouth can not even get the close company of his companion, and if some one has got a dental diseases, one can blame only one's carelessness in the past.

Fortunately people have become conscious of tooth brushing. In rural areas mostly natural cleaning material like Neem, charcoal are used. But in urban areas either the tooth powders or tooth paste are used. The latter is preferred because it is easier and hygeinic and gives more freshness.

MANUFACTURING PROCESS

Various kinds of brushes are available in the market depending upon their quality, size and material used in its manufacture. In respect of size they can be divided into following class.

1. Big size
2. Medium size
3. Children size

In respect of the material used for the fibre.

1. Bristlle brushes : black and grey hair bristles white brushes
2. Synthetic fibre brushes -Nylon fibre.
3. Vegetable fibre brushes.

Different materials are also used for the manufacture of the handle parts of the brushes.

1. Wood.
2. Plastic

A common tooth brush is made up of nylon fibre filled in plastic handle. Therefore this profile will give the manufacture of plastic-nylon fibre brushes in various sizes. In brief, the plastic handles are drilled and then filled with cut and dressed fibre bundles in an automatic machine, and brush is sent for trimming in a trimming machine. In a blocking press the trade marks etc. are embossed on the brush, the process may be described in the following steps:-

1. Handle making
2. Fibre dressing
3. Filling
4. Trimming.
5. Embossing the marks etc.
6. Packing.

PLANT ECONOMICS OF TOOTH BRUSH

Rated Plant Capacity	=	10000.00 Nos./Day
Land & Building (Land area 600 sq.mts.)	=	Rented

PLANT & MACHINERY

1. Injection moulding machine
2. Scrap grinder
3. Tuffine machine.
4. Packing machine.
5. Printing machine.
6. Dies hand tools, weighing scale & other misc. machinery etc.

FIXED CAPITAL

1. Plant & Machinery		Rs.	13,45,000.00
2. Other Fixed Assets		Rs.	2,55,000.00
	TOTAL	Rs.	16,00,000.00

RAW MATERIALS

1. Polypropylene Granules
2. Nylon bristle (tynex bristle)
3. Miscellaneous, wire, packaging materials, colour etc.

TOTAL WORKING CAPITAL/MONTH

1. Raw Material		Rs.	4,14,000.00
2. Salary & Wages		Rs.	53,500.00
3. Utilities & Overheads		Rs.	1,36,000.00
	TOTAL	Rs.	6,03,500.00

TOTAL CAPITAL INVESTMENT

Total Fixed Capital		Rs.	16,00,000.00
Total Working Capital for 1 Month		Rs.	6,03,500.00
	TOTAL	Rs.	22,03,500.00

TURN OVER/ANNUM

Receipt by sale of tooth brush of different size & colour, 3000000 Nos.	Rs.	1,05,00,000.00

PROFIT SALES RATIO = Profit / Sales x 100 = 25.23 %

RATE OF RETURN = Operating profit / T.C.I x 100 = 120.23 %

BREAK EVEN POINT (B.E.P) = 36.43 %

Chapter - 62

Suppliers of Plant and Machinery

ADHESIVE MIXERS

Jay Shree Industries
Mr. Kirtisinh Chavada
(Proprietor)
44, Kamdar Estate, Near Shastri Stadium, Murga Farm, Virat Nagar Road
Ahmedabad - 380050, Gujarat, India
Mobile:
+(91)-9925280242
+(91)-9428118351
Email:
jayshree2007@yahoo.com

Shiv Shakti Engineering
Mr. Ramesh Bhai Patel
Mr. Govindbhai
Mr. Shankar Patel
(Proprietor)
D/13/B, Diamond Park, Near Railway Line, Opp. Hitendranagar, N. H. No. 8, Naroda
Ahmedabad - 382330, Gujarat, India
Mobile:
+(91)-9328056649
+(91)-9376102293
+(91)-9586391861
Telephone:
+(91)-(79)-22820268
Fax:
+(91)-(79)-22820268

Karnavati Engineering
Mr. Vitthalbhai M. Patel
Mr. Prakash D. Patel
(Partner)
64, New Shiv-Vijay Saw Mill Compound, Opp Unipol Plastics, Near Sardar Patel Ring Road Circle, Odhav
Ahmedabad - 382 415, Gujarat, India
Mobile:
+(91)-9427041755
+(91)-9427698758
+(91)-9824095805
Telephone:
+(91)-(79)-22901488

Pledge International
Mr. Pragnesh Patel
(Proprietor)
AF-4, Soham Complex, Soni Ni Chawl
Ahmedabad - 382415, Gujarat, India
Mobile:
+(91)-9909538022
+(91)-9662047327
Telephone:
+(91)-(79)-22970077
Fax:
+(91)-(79)-22970077
Email:
info@pledgeinternational.com
pledgeinternational@gmail.com

BAKERY MACHINE

SAS Bakery Equipments
Mr. V. V. Shaji
(Chairman & Managing Director)
No. 763, R. C. Road, Rajevgandhi Nagar, Bommanahalli
Bengaluru - 560068, Karnataka, India
Mobile:
+(91)-7204549036
+(91)-8123619283
Telephone:
+(91)-(431)-2740482

Rite Equipments Private Limited
Mr. Ramesh Babu V. C.
(Manager-Operations)
No. 31, 1st Floor, 1st Main, Domlur Layout
Bengaluru - 560071, Karnataka, India
Mobile:
+(91)-9739992022
+(91)-9886052126
Telephone:
+(91)-(80)-43406000
Fax:
+(91)-(80)-43406060

Sun Kitchen Equipments
Mr. K. S. Siva Murugan
(Partner)
8/2, Nayudu Layout, Yarandahalli,

Henagara Post, Near Bommasandra Industrial Area
Bengaluru - 560105, Karnataka, India
Mobile:
+(91)-9940174272
+(91)-9043007001
+(91)-9611237811
+(91)-8095933853

C. S. Aerotherm Private Limited (Customer/Presales)
Mr. Prashanth Jairam (Manager)
No. 143 H, Bommasandra Industrial Area, Hosur Road
Bengaluru - 560 099, Karnataka, India
Mobile :
+(91)-9632221860 (Between 9 AM to 8 PM)
Phone :
+(91)-(80)-40895000.

C. S. Aerotherm Private Limited (After Sales)
Mr. Deshpande
No. 143 H, Bommasandra Industrial Area, Hosur Road
Bengaluru - 560 099, Karnataka, India
Mobile :
+(91)-9243720034, 9611195407
Phone :
+(91)-(80)-40875000

C. S. Aerotherm Private Limited
(Purchase Manager)
Mr. Senthil Kumar
No. 143 H, Bommasandra Industrial Area, Hosur Road
Bengaluru - 560 099, Karnataka, India
Mobile :
+(91)-9611195412
Phone :
+(91)-(80)-40895000

BLOW MOULDING MACHINE

Mittal Plast & Tech Industries
Mr. Kirit Vaisnani (Proprietor)
No. 313/11, Behind Lions School, Near Intex Boil, Near Asopalav Apartment, Phase-I, G.I.D.C, Naroda
Ahmedabad - 382330, Gujarat, India
Mobile:
+(91)-8141810049
+(91)-9714845004

U. V. Tech Systems
Mr. Salil S. Nair (Proprietor)
No. 24, 1st Floor, Dr. Ambedkar Road, Kodambakkam
Chennai - 600 024, Tamil Nadu, India
Mobile:
+(91)-9444033699
+(91)-9445195788
Telephone:
+(91)-(44)-23726691
+(91)-(44)-23726693
Fax:
+(91)-(44)-23726699

Windsor Machines Limited
Mr. Vikas Deo
Mr. Hitesh Chauhan
No. 5403, Phase- 4, G. I. D. C, Vatva, Industrial Estate
Ahmedabad - 382445, Gujarat, India
Mobile:
+(91)-9825084691
+(91)-9925011215
Telephone:
+(91)-(79)-30262131
+(91)-(79)-30262154
+(91)-(2764)-233646
+(91)-(79)-25841111
Fax:
+(91)-(79)-25842145
Email:
sales.emd@windsormachines.com
vikas.deo@windsormachines.com

Kartar Hydraulic Industries
Mr. Ranjit Singh (Owner)
Plot No. B-244/4, Street No. 1, Maan Nagar, Amar Puri, Daba Road
Ludhiana - 141003, Punjab, India
Mobile:
+(91)-9216517293
+(91)-9914117293
Telephone:
+(91)-(161)-2533032

BOILERS

Ashoka Machine Tools Corporation
Mr. Gautam Khanna
D-62-67, EPIP,
Site- V, Kasna,
Greater
Noida - 201301,
India
Mobile :
+(91)-9810296963
Factory Tel :
+(91)-(120)-2340031
+(91)-(120)-2340032
Factory Fax :
+(91)-(120)-2340033
Office Tel :
+(91)-(11)-46420000
Office Fax :
+(91)-(11)-46420011
E-Mail :
gkhanna@ashokamachines.com
mdhawan@ashokamachines.com

Ashoka USA
Mr. Harish Saluja
P.O. Box 1335
McMurray,
PA 15317, USA
Tel :
724 969-2565
Fax :
724 942-2558
E-Mail :
ashokausa@gmail.com

Akshaya Enterprises
Mr. V Balan
(Managing Director)
No. 4-1, Navy Nagar,
5th Cross West,
Meena Estate
Coimbatore - 641 028,
Tamil Nadu, India
Mobile:
+(91)-9629968102
Telephone:
+(91)-(422)-2313612
+(91)-(422)-2410272
Fax:
+(91)-(422)-2313612
Email:
balanakshaya@yahoo.com
info@akshayaboilers.com

Joyan Engineering Corporation
Mr. Arvind Solanki
5, First Floor, Gupta Chamber, Opposite
Vijay Co- Operative
Bank, Odhav,
G.I.D.C., Odhav
Ahmedabad - 382415,
Gujarat, India
Mobile:
+(91)-9825090993
+(91)-9427028315
Telephone:
+(91)-(79)-22970993
Fax:
+(91)-(79)-22970993

The Excell Corporation
Mr. Bipin Kumar Mishra
(Owner)
House No - 3124,
Sector - 32A,
Behind Mohini Resort,
Chandigarh Road
Ludhiana - 141010,
Punjab, India
Mobile:
+(91)-9216541624
+(91)-9971541624
+(91)-9023241624

COATING MACHINERY

Happy Mechanical Works
Mr. Kuldeep Singh
(Proprietor)
N. W. - 114,
Vishnu Garden
New Delhi - 110018,
Delhi, India
Mobile:
+(91)-9990600779
+(91)-9891378531
+(91)-9971569534
+(91)-9968388085
Telephone:
+(91)-(11)-25985925

Shiv Pharma Engineers
Mr. Mayank Joshi
(Sales Manager)
34-36,
Tejandra Industrial Estate,
Opposite C. M. C.,
Odhav Road
Ahmedabad - 382 415,
Gujarat, India
Mobile:
+(91)-9974999064
+(91)-9377535927
+(91)-9824169934
Telephone:
+(91)-(79)-22871399
Fax:
+(91)-(79)-22871399

Samarika Pharma Equipments
Mr. Vipul Panchal
(Owner)
Behind Mahadev Vas
No. 2, Near Shak
Market, Nava Vadaj

Ahmedabad - 382729, Gujarat, India
Mobile:
+(91)-9879084027
+(91)-9327779171
+(91)-9925024027
Telephone:
+(91)-(79)-65426647
+(91)-(79)-27640221
Fax:
+(91)-(79)-27640221

Dev Engineering
Mr. Arvind Prajapati
No. 156/B/9/A, Kailashnagar Estate, Opp. New Telephone Exchange, Phase-I, GIDC, Vatva Ahmedabad - 382445, Gujarat, India
Mobile:
+(91)-9825902848
Telephone:
+(91)-(79)-25894674
Website:
http://www.devextrusion.com

CONFECTIONERY MACHINE

Pack Care Enterprises
Mr. Rathan Chnadavath
No. 81/1 C, Maheswari Nagar, Thanneer Pandal, Vilankurichi, Road, Peelamedu Coimbatore - 641 004, Tamil Nadu, India
Mobile:
+(91)-9842873822
Telephone:
+(91)-(422)-2512812
Website:
http://www.packcare.in

Sehgal Industrial Works
Mr. Vikas Sehgal (Manager)
T-1698, Malka Ganj Road, Subzi Mandi New Delhi - 110007, Delhi, India
Mobile:
+(91)-9811706010
+(91)-9711706010
+(91)-9810136096
Telephone:
+(91)-(11)-23857381
+(91)-(11)-23850636
+(91)-(11)-32988722
Fax:
+(91)-(11)-23857381

Miranda Automation Private Limited
Mr. Albert Miranda (Managing Director)
Plot No. R-632, M.I.D.C., T.T.C. Industrial Area, Rabale, Thane-Belapur Road Navi Mumbai - 400701, Maharashtra, India
Mobile:
+(91)-9820059903
+(91)-9820062237
Telephone:
+(91)-(22)-27642533
+(91)-(22)-65135938
Fax:
+(91)-(22)-27690128

Eletech Engineering
Mr. S. P. Yadav
No. 15, Polo Ground, Industrial Estate Indore - 452015, Madhya Pradesh, India
Mobile:
+(91)-9425313140
Telephone:
+(91)-(731)-2424052
+(91)-(731)-2411118
Website:
http://www.etengineeringco.com

CORRUGATED PAPER BOX MACHINERY

Essar & Co.
Mr. Rajiv Venugopal (Managing Partner)
No. 207/D2-B, M. P. G. Nagar, Bharathiar Road, Ganapathy Coimbatore - 641006, Tamil Nadu, India
Mobile:
+(91)-9944494980
+(91)-9047794980
Telephone:
+(91)-(422)-6542012
Fax:
+(91)-(422)-2494663

Preet Machinery Corporation
Mr. Gaganpreet Singh
Plot No. 523, Ravi Dass Marg East, Mohan Nagar Amritsar - 143 006, Punjab, India
Mobile:
+(91)-9815861616
+(91)-9814888844
Telephone:
+(91)-(183)-2580358

Friends Engineering Overseas Exports, Delhi
Mr. Manjit Singh (Proprietor)
J - 126 - B,
Vishnu Garden
New Delhi - 110018,
Delhi, India
Mobile:
+(91)-9810626661
+(91)-9810626665
Telephone:
+(91)-(11)-25984953
+(91)-(11)-64686666

Friends Engineering Overseas Exports, Delhi
Mr. Manjit Singh (Proprietor)
J - 126 - B,
Vishnu Garden
New Delhi - 110018,
Delhi, India
Mobile:
+(91)-9810626661
+(91)-9810626665
Telephone:
+(91)-(11)-25984953
+(91)-(11)-64686666

COSMETICS PRODUCTS MACHINERY

Yash Pharma Machineries
Mr. Bhupendra Panchal (CEO)
No. 16, Abhinadan Industrial Estate,
Girnar Scooter Compound,
Behind Bank of India,
Odhav-Kathwada Ring Road, Odhav
Ahmedabad - 382415,
Gujarat, India
Mobile:
+(91)-9376148872
+(91)-9426040661

Global Project Consultants
Mr. Afzal Khan
No. 176/ 21,
Zakir Nagar
New Delhi - 110025,
Delhi, India
Mobile:
+(91)-9313165720
+(91)-8307590890
Telephone:
+(91)-(11)-64711921
Fax:
+(91)-(11)-26984272
Email:
globalproject99@yahoo.com

Sehgal Industrial Works
Mr. Vikas Sehgal (Manager)
T-1698, Malka Ganj Road, Subzi Mandi
New Delhi - 110007,
Delhi, India
Mobile:
+(91)-9811706010,
+(91)-9711706010,
+(91)-9810136096
Telephone:
+(91)-(11)-23857381
+(91)-(11)-23850636
+(91)-(11)-32988722
Fax:
+(91)-(11)-23857381

Emkay Engineering Works
Mr. M. Hasan (Partner)
B-33, DDA Shed,
Okhla Industrial Area, Phase - II
New Delhi - 110020,
Delhi, India
Mobile:
+(91)-9811301650
+(91)-9873231650
+(91)-9873241650
Telephone:
+(91)-(11)-41610110
+(91)-(11)-26388489
+(91)-(11)-26830350
Fax:
+(91)-(11)-26388489
+(91)-(11)-41610110

Parth Enterprise
Mr. Roopesh Dave (Proprietor)
3, Jivan Vihar Society,
Opp. Bank Of Bikaner & Jaipur,
Maninagar (East),
Ahmedabad - 380008,
Gujarat, India
Mobile:
+(91)-9909018406
Email:
roopesh_dave2000@yahoo.com,
parthenter@gmail.com

Apex Industries Thane
Mr. Salil Pradhan
No. 27,
Gupta Despande Industrial Estate,
Pokran Road No. 1,
Upavan
Thane - 400 606,
Maharashtra , India

Mobile:
+(91)-9892522986
Telephone:
+(91)-(22)-25856039

SHAMPOO MAKING AND FILLING MACHINE

Sakun Engineers
Mr. Hiten Bhavsar
Mr. Bharat Bhavsar
(Proprietor)
33/a New Arbuda Estate,
Near G.s.t Crossing Road, Ranip,
Ahmedabad - 382 470,
Gujarat, India
Mobile:
+(91)-9825339820
Telephone:
+(91)-(79)-27523886

Neelam Industries
Mr. Nilesh Patel
Plot No. 3735,
Behind New Nirma,
Phase - 4, G. I. D. C.,
Vatva,
Ahmedabad, Gujarat - 382 445, (India)
Email:
neelam@neelampharmamech.com
Mobile
+(91)-9925170468
(91)-9824314469
Phone:
+(91)-(79)-25840049 / 25842653 / 55237536
Fax:
+(91)-(79)-25842894

Unitek Packaging Systems Private Limited
Mr. Diwakar Sharma
(Director)
S - 23, G. F. Okhla Industrial Area,
Phase - 2
New Delhi - 110020,
Delhi, India
Mobile:
+(91)-9560992709,
+(91)-9810014265
Telephone:
+(91)-(11)-41045551
+(91)-(11)-41045552
Fax:
+(91)-(11)-40503166
Email:
info@unitek.in
ds@unitek.in

The Bombay Engineering Works
Mr. Mayur Joshi
1 Unit Nos. 12, Navyug Industrial Estate,
Tokersey Jivraj Road,
Sewree West
Mumbai - 400 015,
Maharashtra (India)
Phone:
+(91)-(22)-24137094
+(91)-(22)-24135959
Fax:
+(91)-(22)-24135828
Mobile:
+(91)-9821042408
+(91)-9820026383
E-Mail:
bomeng@vsnl.com
bombayengg@yahoo.co.in

BLENDERS

Prism Pharma Machinery
Plot No. 3713,
Phase 4, G. I. D. C.,
Vatva,
Ahmedabad - 382445,
Gujarat, India
Phone: 08376805843

Shiv Shakti Process Equipment Private Limited
Shiv Shakti, No. 407,
Shivam Chambers,
S. V. Road, Goregoan West,
Mumbai - 400104,
Maharashtra, India
Website:
www.shivshaktiequip.in

Hexamide Agro Tech LLP
Plot No.-11,
Aditya Industrial Estate,
At Post Kumbiwali,
Taluka Khalapur,
District- Raigad, Navi Mumbai - 410210,
Maharashtra, India
Phone: 08447556832

Namdhari Industrial Works
D - 26, Focal Point,
Khanna - 141 401,
Punjab, India
Phone: 08377804783

Sanskruti Engineers
Gate No. 7,
Chimbali,
Tal- Khed,
Pune - 410501,

Maharashtra, India
Phone:
09953363082

Surya Techno Chem
Opp. Radha Swami Satsang,
Village Morta,
Meerut Road,
Ghaziabad - 201003,
Uttar Pradesh, India
Phone:
09953354911

DRYERS AND DRYING OVENS

Metal Press Industries
A- 17, Pushpak Estate,
Gujarat Bottaling,
Char Rasta,
Rakhial,
Ahmedabad - 380023,
Gujarat, India
Phone: 08377806497

Shiv Pharma Engineers
34-36, Tejandra Industrial Estate,
Opp. C. M. C., Odhav Road,
Ahmedabad - 382 415,
Gujarat, India
Phone: 08373904427
Website:
www.gmpmachines.com

Richard Engineering Bom Private Limited
First Floor,
Brij Complex,
K. B. Road,
Railway Flyover Junction,
Ambarnath (W),
Thane - 421 501,
Maharashtra, India
Phone: 08447558651
Website:
www.chemicalpharmaequipment.com

Krishna Scientific Works
D - 23, Site - C,
Surajpur Industrial Area,
Dadri Road, Greater Noida - 201306,
Uttar Pradesh, India
Phone:
08377805857

Ahlada Industries Private Limited
Sy. No. 66-68,
Bahadurpally,
Qutbullapur Mandal,
Ranga Reddy District,
Hyderabad - 500043,
Andhra Pradesh, India
Phone: 08376808108
Website:
www.ahladaindustries.net

MIXERS

Kwality Process Equipments Private Limited
Plot No. 198,
Sector - 1,
Vasai Taluka,
I. E. Gauraipada,
Thane - 401208,
Maharashtra, India
Phone: 08447520194
Website:
www.kwalityengineeringcorporation.com

Maharashtra Enterprises
Rani Residency, Shop No. 7, Ground Floor,
Chirag Nagar,
Ghatkopar West,
Mumbai - 400086,
Maharashtra, India
Phone:
09953360621

Vinayak Industries
D-3, Sheetal Industrial Estate,
Behind Tirupti Gas Godown,
Meera Bhayandar Phatak Road,
Bhayandar East,
Thane - 401105,
Maharashtra, India
Phone: 08447525218
Website:
www.resinplants.com

Gangaa Machines
No. 13/ 62 - C, Trichy Main Road,
Chinthamani Pudur Post,
Coimbatore - 641103,
Tamil Nadu, India
Phone: 08447501162
Website:
www.gangaamachines.com

Haifa Engineering
5, BR Nath Pai Marg,
Pine Building,
Opp. Hajee Cassum Compound,
Mazgaon,
Mumbai - 400010,
Maharashtra, India
Phone:
09953358657

DRY CLEANING UNIT

S. V. Garment Machineries
Mr. Vijaya Kumar K. R. (CEO)
A 1/5, First Floor, Above Bluedart Courier Office, SVCIE,
Opp. IDPL, Balanagar
Hyderabad - 500037, Andhra Pradesh, India
Mobile:
+(91)-9848749582
+(91)-9246874018
+(91)-9246824011
Telephone:
+(91)-(40)-23871414
Fax:
+(91)-(40)-23871414

Vidhi Creations
Mr. Jagjit Sharma (Proprietor)
WH -34, Mayapuri Industrial Area, No. 1, Phase- 1
Delhi - 110064, India
Mobile:
+(91)-8750295060
+(91)-9013781120
Telephone:
+(91)-(11)-41833586
+(91)-(11)-41833596
+(91)-(11)-28113495

Lucky Engineering Works
Mr. Rajeev Sharma (Proprietor)
No. 779- A, Faridpuri, West Patel Nagar
New Delhi - 110008, Delhi, India
Mobile:
+(91)-9868156501
+(91)-9818867187
Telephone:
+(91)-(11)-25880514
Fax:
+(91)-(11)-25880514
Email:
luckyworks.rajeev@gmail.com
deepanshusharma0007@gmail.com

Sunrise Technical Services
Mr. P. Prem Kumar (Executive Director)
1065, Tughlaqabad
New Delhi - 110 044, Delhi, India
Mobile:
+(91)-9810133919
+(91)-9312959559
Telephone:
+(91)-(11)-65631999
Fax:
+(91)-(11)-65631999
Plastic Extruding Machinery

Amrut Plastic Engineers
Mr. Gunvant Mistry
Mr. Dhaval Mistry
Mr. Nikhil Mistry
No. 34, Hari Om Shivshankar, Opposite Jay Ambe Farsan Dairy, Behind Ambica Hotel, C. T. M., Amraiwadi
Ahmedabad - 380026, Gujarat, India
Mobile:
+(91)-9376098267
+(91)-9725426450
+(91)-9510030007

Hillson Mechanical Workshop
Mr. Amlesh Mistry (Proprietor)
222, Puskar Estate, Nr. Ferometic Milacron, Opp. Mecons, GIDC, Phase 1, Vatva
Ahmedabad - 380026, Gujarat, India
Mobile:
+(91)-9924206316
+(91)-8141563767
Telephone:
+(91)-(79)-65530134
+(91)-(79)-40308856
Email:
hillson_machinery@yahoo.in
amleshmistry@yahoo.com
amleshmistry228@gmail.com
hillsonmachine@gmail.com

Swaraj Engineering
Mr. Gulab Parmar (Proprietor)
1-Honest Complex, Decora Cement Street, Shapar Main Road, Shapar Veraval
Rajkot - 360006, Gujarat, India
Mobile:
+(91)-9327601200
Telephone:
+(91)-(28)-27253412
Email:
swaraj7eng@gmail.com

Rama Engineers
Mr. P. R. Yadav (Proprietor)
Plot No. 159/ B, Sector- 1, Lane 3, IDA, Phase-2, Cherlapally
Hyderabad - 500051, Andhra Pradesh, India

Mobile:
+(91)-9391159045
+(91)-9393159045
+(91)-9493390877

FLOUR MILL MACHINE

Universal Sales Agency
Mr. Shabbir Siyawala
Mr. Hussain Patel
No. 71/ B,
Netaji Subhas Road,
Gupta Mansion,
Ground Floor, Room No. A-57
Kolkata - 700001, West Bengal, India
Mobile:
+(91)-9831211470
+(91)-9163786287
Telephone:
+(91)-(33)-22434868
+(91)-(33)-28611074
+(91)-(33)-39855551

Hind Engineering Works
Mr. S. P. Shrivastwa (Proprietor)
36/4/2, Madhusudan Paul Choudhary Lane, Bantra
Howrah - 711101, West Bengal, India
Mobile:
+(91)-9432325298
+(91)-9830093502
Telephone:
+(91)-(33)-26544895

Dahela Engineers, India
Mr. Harpal Singh (CEO)
H. No. B - 21- 3368, Opposite Arora Palace, Gill Road
Ludhiana - 141003, Punjab, India
Mobile:
+(91)-9855101405
+(91)-9814226707
Telephone:
+(91)-(161)-2490315
+(91)-(161)-5047315
Fax:
+(91)-(161)-5047315

Technocraft, Kolkata
Mr. B. N. Majumder (Proprietor)
No. 5- B, Kundu Lane, Belgachia
Kolkata - 700037, West Bengal, India
Mobile:
+(91)-9830214207
Email:
technocraft2013@gmail.com
bnmtechnocraft@gmail.com

FOOD PROCESSING MACHINE

Ludhiana Engineering Works
Mr. Bhupinder Singh
Mr. Amrinder Singh
Tehsil Chopala Garh, Delhi Road, Near Suri Sweet
Hapur - 245101, Uttar Pradesh, India

Mobile:
+(91)-8439050307
+(91)-9837119909
+(91)-9837390950
Telephone:
+(91)-(122)-2303129

Sun Kitchen Equipments
Mr. K. S. Siva Murugan (Partner)
No. 8/2, Nayudu Layout, Yarandahalli, Henagara Post,
Near Bommasandra Industrial Area
Bengaluru - 560105, Karnataka, India
Mobile:
+(91)-9940174272
+(91)-9043007001
+(91)-9611237811
+(91)-8095933853

Parishram Industries
Mr. Arvind Khristi (Marketing Consultant)
B-90, Maruti Estate, Near Kiran Industries, Phase-1, G. I. D. C, Vatva
Ahmedabad - 382445, Gujarat, India
Mobile:
+(91)-7929094171
+(91)-9825362549

E & S Food Technologies Pvt. Ltd.
Mr. Sarang Dongare (Director)
No. 401, Barkha Bahar CHS, MG Road, Naupada, Thane West
Mumbai - 400602, Maharashtra, India

Mobile:
+(91)-9892157154
+(91)-8097910495
Telephone:
+(91)-(22)-25414803
Fax:
+(91)-(22)-25414803
Garment Machine

Geekay Group Of Companies
Mr. G. Krishnamoorthy (Managing Director)
No. 8/2, 2nd Main, Near Bata Show Room, Chamrajpet
Bengaluru - 560018, Karnataka, India
Mobile:
+(91)-9845333777
+(91)-9448333777
Telephone:
+(91)-(80)-26622777
+(91)-(421)-4333777
Fax:
+(91)-(80)-26500777

Bengal Sewing Mart Private Limited
Mr. Manoj Sikdar
Corp.O:69MIE,Part A Bahadurgarh Industrial Area, haryana, H.O.K-62 Udyog Nagar Industrial Area ,Nangloi ,Delhi-41
Delhi - 110 035, Delhi, India
Mobile:
+(91)-9310623242
Telephone:
+(91)-(1267)-321967
+(91)-(1267)-267069
+(91)-(1267)/25484297
Website:
http://www.bengal sewing.com

Millenium Garment Machine
Mr. Santosh Rajput
Shop No. 9,
Mahavir Estate,
Opposite Munjalshowa,
Sector No. 18
Gurgaon - 122001, Haryana, India
Mobile:
+(91)-9818073551
Telephone:
+(91)-(124)-4039049
Website:
http://www.milleniumgarmentmachine.com

Jalal Sewing Machine Company
297/A, Dasna Gate Road, Jatwara,
Opp. Ambedkar Bhawan
Ghaziabad - 201001, Uttar Pradesh, India
Telephone:
+(91)-(120)-2793649
+(91)-(120)-2792916
Website:
http://www.jsmc.biz/

ICE CREAM MAKING MACHINERY

VCS India Pvt. Ltd.
Mr. Hasmukh Gajjar
No. 96/7,
Behind Shiv Estate,
Opp. Ravirandal Society,
Near Jasodanagar Cross Road,
N. H. No. 8, C. T. M.
Ahmedabad - 380026, Gujarat, India
Mobile:
+(91)-9825023410
+(91)-9375523410
Telephone:
+(91)-(79)-25893038
+(91)-(79)-25890128
Fax:
+(91)-(79)-25893038

New National Refrigeration Engineering Company
Mr. Zuber Hawa
Mr. Azhar
Mr. Irshad (Owner)
No. 1256/3-4, Opposite Amdupura Petrol Pump, Naroda Road
Ahmedabad - 380025, Gujarat, India
Mobile:
+(91)-9825693796
+(91)-9909820546
+(91)-9979204673
Telephone:
+(91)-(79)-22203773

Mitora Machinex Pvt. Ltd
Mr. Mihir Patel (Owner)
Plot No. 2903, Phase-4, GIDC, Vatva
Ahmedabad - 382 445, Gujarat, India
Mobile:
+(91)-9825050144
Telephone:
+(91)-(79)-25840204
+(91)-(79)-25842636
+(91)-(79)-40083559
Fax:
+(91)-(79)-25842636

Sakthi Engineering
Mr. M Shanmugam
Ms. Sakthi Maheshwari (Partner)
No. 20, 2nd Floor, Bharathi Nagar, Ganapathy
Coimbatore - 641006, Tamil Nadu, India
Mobile:
+(91)-9150136807
+(91)-8643096918
Telephone:
+(91)-(422)-2136807
Email:
diamondshanmugam2015@gmail.com
diamondshanmugam2015@yahoo.com

SAS Bakery Equipments
Mr. V. V. Shaji
(Chairman & Managing Director)
No. 763, R. C. Road, Rajevgandhi Nagar, Bommanahalli
Bengaluru - 560068, Karnataka, India
Mobile:
+(91)-7204549036
+(91)-8123619283
Telephone:
+(91)-(431)-2740482

Matrix Kitchen Makers
Mr. Mir Mohd. Faheemuddin
(Managing Director & CEO)
No. 945, 1st Main Road, 6th Cross Road, Near Shreya Hospital, Kengeri Satellite Town
Bengaluru - 560060, Karnataka, India
Mobile:
+(91)-9880229452
+(91)-9632112221

PLASTIC INJECTION MOULDING MACHINE

Ghanshyam Engineering Co.
Mr. Vinod Patel
(Director)
No. 12,
Samrat Industrial Area, Behind S.T. Workshop, Gokuldham Road
Rajkot - 360004, Gujarat, India
Mobile:
+(91)-9825293732
+(91)-9825020210
Telephone:
+(91)-(281)-2360283

Natraj Industries
Mr. Naranbhai / Dinesh Mistri / Gopal Mistri/ Mahesh Mistri
(Managing Partner)
Plot No. 564, Kathwada G I.D.C., Opposite Road No. 10, Near Tribhuvan Estate Gate, Phase- 2, Kathwada, Tal- Daskroi
Ahmedabad - 382430, Gujarat, India
Mobile:
+(91)-9909421763
+(91)-9376105240
Email:
info@natrajind.com
mahesh@natrajind.com
sales@natrajind.com

Charmi Machinery Industries Private Limited
Mr. Rakesh Bhimani
(Director)
B-95, 96,
Bileshwar Estate, Kathwada, GIDC
Ahmedabad - 382415, Gujarat, India
Mobile:
+(91)-9898000188
+(91)-9898991310
Telephone:
+(91)-(79)-22900086
Fax:
+(91)-(79)-22900086

Tex Shine Plastic Hydralic
Mr. Vincent Xavier
Mr. Muthusamy
125, Kannimar Nagar, Sathy Road, Ganapathy
Coimbatore - 641006, Tamil Nadu, India
Mobile:
+(91)-9566615551
+(91)-9566615552
* +(91)-9443059638
+(91)-9843134874
Telephone:
+(91)-(422)-2539055

MINERAL WATER PLANTS

Nishu Enterprise
Mr. Bhavesh Jhaveri
(Proprietor)
Shop No. 4, Building No. 2, Aditi Apartment, Iraniwadi Cross Road 2, Near Vasant Aishwarya, Kandivali West

Mumbai - 400067, Maharashtra, India
Mobile:
+(91)-9820142424
+(91)-9820632212
Telephone:
+(91)-(22)-28614422
Fax:
+(91)-(22)-28614422

Cristal Aqua Systems
Mr. U. A. Sakthivel (Managing Director)
DP-112/G, 2nd Main Road, Ambattur Estate, Near Wavin Bus Stop
Chennai - 600058, Tamil Nadu, India
Mobile:
+(91)-9840042565
+(91)-9381038136
Telephone:
+(91)-(44)-42060135
+(91)-(44)-42060136
Fax:
+(91)-(44)-42060135

EXERCISE NOTEBOOK MANUFACTURING MACHINERY

Mecintell Technologies Private Limited
Mr. Sandip Poriya (Marketing Director)
5, Narayan Krupa Complex,
Opposite Satyam Flats, Near Chandan Farm Party Plot,
Jodhpur, Satellite
Ahmedabad - 380015, Gujarat, India
Mobile:
+(91)-9979787971
+(91)-8128829339

Acme Machinery (India) Pvt. Ltd., Mumbai
Mr. Ketan Shah
G 16,
Shalimar Industrial Estate, Near Tata Power House,
Matunga West
Mumbai - 400019, Maharashtra, India
Mobile:
+(91)-9820147274
Telephone:
+(91)-(22)-24037398
+(91)-(22)-24038823
Website:
http://www.acmeindia.com

NAMKEEN MAKING MACHINE

Odtin Food Solution Pvt. Ltd.
Mr. Shekhar Odak (Director- Business Development)
Mahak Market, Talawali Chanda, Opposite Miraj, Near Panchawati Colony, A. B. Road
Indore - 452010, Madhya Pradesh, India
Mobile:
+(91)-9993020331
+(91)-7879560415

Aim Engineering
Mr. Jitendra Singh / Mr. Satendra Singh (Owner)
A - 37, Adarsh Estate - 2, Opposite Guru Dwara, Odhav
Ahmedabad - 382415, Gujarat, India
Mobile:
+(91)-9904512503
+(91)-8690880382
+(91)-9723670176
Telephone:
+(91)-(79)-22890689
Email:
info@aimsteamboiler.com
aimboiler@gmail.com
satya_rajput2000@yahoo.com

Multipurpose Engineering Works
Mr. Naresh Agrawal (Proprietor)
No. 244, Hukumchand Colony, Gali No. 3, Panchkuian Road, 420, Papad Wala
Indore - 452002, Madhya Pradesh, India
Mobile:
+(91)-9826096420
+(91)-9826021420
Telephone:
+(91)-(731)-2417420
Fax:
+(91)-(731)-2418420
Email:
machine420papad@gmail.com
info@machine420papad.com

PAN MASALA MAKING MACHINE

Vishwakarma Engineering Works
Mr. Manger
Plot-56/B/3 /10,Gayatri Estate, Bharat Cement Compoud, Opp.

Shaswat Gam,Nr. Bank of India,
Phase -1,
G.I.D.C.,Vatva
Ahmedabad - 382 440,
Gujarat, India
Mobile:
+(91)-9558826415
Telephone:
+(91)-(79)-25895935
+(91)-(79)-25895935
Website:
http://www.vishwakarmaeng.com

PAPPAD MAKING MACHINE

Sara Commercial Kitchen Equipments
Mr. R. Hariraj
(Proprietor)
51, Bajanai Kovil Street, Choolaimedu
Chennai - 600094,
Tamil Nadu, India
Mobile:
+(91)-9566234547
+(91)-9566234542

EDIBLE OIL MILL MACHINERY

Tinytech Udyog
Mr. Siddharth Jivani
(Director)
Plot No. 2648, Road-H, Kranti Gate,
G.I.D.C., Metoda
Rajkot - 360021,
Gujarat, India
Mobile:
+(91)-9904225493
Telephone:
+(91)-(2827)-293366
+(91)-(281)-2574853
Fax: -
+(91)-(2827)-287869
+(91)-(2827)-293366
Email:
tinytech@oil-refinery.com
tinytechudyog@gmail.com

Gopal Expeller Co.
Mr. Kuljit Singh
(Manager)
Plot No. 4146, Guru Nanak Street No. 7, Shimla Puri, Maya Shop Street
Ludhiana - 141003,
Punjab, India
Mobile:
+(91)-9888333997
+(91)-9815033997
Telephone:
+(91)-(161)-2500093
Fax:
+(91)-(161)-5017916
Email:
info@gopalexpellercompany.com
gopalexpeller@gmail.com

Forsberg Agritech (India) Pvt. Ltd.
Mrs. Nivedita Thakore
(Executive Director)
123, G.I.D.C. Estate,
Makarpura
Vadodara - 390010,
Gujarat, India
Mobile:
+(91)-9377287246
+(91)-9377287245
Telephone:
+(91)-(265)-2636752
+(91)-(265)-6590584
Fax:
+(91)-(265)-2638583

PAPER CONVERTING MACHINERY

Sky Engineering Company
Mr. Altamash
F-292, 25FT Road, Opposite Bhajanpura Petrol Pump, Chand Bagh
Delhi - 110094, India
Mobile:
+(91)-9810707028
+(91)-9711877752

Sandip Machinery Mfrs. Co.
Mr. Pragnesh Mistry
(Chairman And Ceo)
L-92, GIDC Estate, Near Telephone Exchange, Near Bhikshukgruh, Odhav
Ahmedabad - 382 415,
Gujarat, India
Mobile:
+(91)-9426050933
+(91)-8866115588
Telephone:
+(91)-(79)-29093464
+(91)-(79)-22970933

Potato Chips Machine

Renuca Enterprises
Mr. B. Prabhakar
(Proprietor)
S. No. 44/1, Shanti Heights, NDA Road, Ganpati Matha, Warje, Malwadi
Pune - 411058,
Maharashtra, India
Mobile:
+(91)-9822658092
+(91)-9730033572

Super Metal & Co.
Mr. Mukesh Sablok
(Proprietor)
No. 3/33, L.I.G. Colony, L.I.G. Chouraha, Behind Maya Medical Store, A. B. Road
Indore - 452008, Madhya Pradesh, India
Mobile:
+(91)-9827212950
+(91)-9406630066
Telephone:
+(91)-(731)-2554272
+(91)-(731)-2557517
Fax:
+(91)-(731)-2557517
Email:
india@supermetalcompany.com
info@omshrisaiseva.org
info@supermetalindia.com

PVC PIPE MACHINE

Maruti Nandan Plastic Machinery
Mr. Riken Patel
(Managing Director)
No. 19, Shri Hari Estate, Opposite Surti Society, Near Ramol Police Station, Ramol C.T.M Ramol, Amraiwadi
Ahmedabad - 380001, Gujarat, India
Mobile:
+(91)-9724420196
+(91)-9601591999

Sant Engineering Industries
Mr. Charanjeev Malhotra
(CEO)
No. 580, Main Faiz Road, Street No.17, Karol Bagh,
New Delhi - 110005, Delhi, India
Mobile:
+(91)-9868107361
+(91)-9717263888
Telephone:
+(91)-(11)-23521090
+(91)-(11)-23679498
Email:
charanjeevmalhotra@gmail.com

SOAP & DETERGENT MACHINE

Rising Industries
Mr. Asim Kuila
Teghoria Loknath Mandir, Jhowtala, Ghosh Dutta Para, Tanushree Apartment
Kolkata - 700157, West Bengal, India
Mobile:
+(91)-9804212381
+(91)-9830260440
+(91)-9733037425
Telephone:
+(91)-(33)-25700181

Golden Heavy Engineering Company
Mr. Ramanjeet Singh
(Owner)
Village Majri Kishne Wali, Khanna Road, Amloh
Khanna - 141402, Punjab, India
Mobile:
+(91)-8872166000
+(91)-9876063162
Telephone:
+(91)-(1765)-232789

CANDLE MAKING MACHINE

Gayathri Match Industries & Veni Match Industries
Mr. P. N. Senthil Kumar
(Proprietor)
S. F. No. 28/1, Pattanamputhur, Pattanam
Coimbatore - 641016, Tamil Nadu, India
Mobile:
+(91)-9843027204
+(91)-9486217385
+(91)-9486129144
Telephone:
+(91)-(422)-2272047
+(91)-(422)-2270770
+(91) 9486476660
+(91)-9443116770

Rlumen Exim Private Limited
Mr. Rahul Singh
(Director)
Office No. 202, 2nd Floor, Jaina Tower-2, Janak Puri
New Delhi - 110058, Delhi, India
Mobile:
+(91)-9211701777
Telephone:
+(91)-(11)-65411227
+(91)-(11)-65023077

AGARBATTI MAKING MACHINE

Shreeji Incense Stick
Mr. Sanjay Patel
Mr. Arvind Patel
(Partner)
Patel Industries Area,

Near Natraj Plastic, Dhebar Road, Atika South
Rajkot - 360002, Gujarat, India
Mobile:
+(91)-9974323158
+(91)-9898022612
+(91)-7698535453

Soham Industrial Machinery Ltd.
Mr. Jagpal Gajera (Sales Manager)
Plot No. A-13/22-23, Opposite Calcutta Bearing, Near Puspa Restaurant, Central Road No. 7, Udhna, Udyognagar
Surat - 394210, Gujarat, India
Mobile:
+(91)-9978987748
+(91)-9825527848
+(91)-9879697091
Telephone:
+(91)-(261)-6507848
Email:
sohamtexaac@gmail.com

Bread Plant

Autobake Productions
Mr. Yusuf (Owner)
No. 191, Mutton Street, Nal Bazar
Mumbai - 400003, Maharashtra, India
Mobile:
+(91)-9892908633
+(91)-7208679975
+(91)-8082432436

Arun Rega Bakery Machineries (Pvt) Limited
Mr. Nand Kumar
F.S.No 213, Site No 4, Sitra Kalapatti Road, Kalapatti Post
Coimbatore - 641048, Tamil Nadu, India
Mobile:
+(91)-9600965636
Telephone:
+(91)-(422)-6544899
+(91)-(422)-6458111
+(91)-(422)-6458222
Fax:
+(91)-(422)-2665633

VSA Machines India
Mr. Sreekanth Yarlagadda (Proprietor)
Plot No. 117, Sy. No. 172, S. V. C. I. E., IDA, Bollaram
Hyderabad - 502325, Andhra Pradesh, India
Mobile:
+(91)-8686031434
+(91)-9246354744
+(91)-8332892495
+(91)-8330934825
Fax:
+(91)-(8458)-279789

SPICE MAKING MACHINE

Arihant Engineering Corporation
Mr. Ankit Verma (Owner)
No. 37, Guru Nanak Timber Market, Near Dev Krishan Baug; Dhar, Road
Indore - 452002, Madhya Pradesh, India
Mobile:
+(91)-9425082586
+(91)-9425062437
Telephone:
+(91)-(731)-2380535
+(91)-(731)-2380537
Fax:
+(91)-(731)-2380537
+(91)-(731)-2385355

PAPER CARRY BAGS MACHINE

Happy Mechanical Works
Mr. Kuldeep Singh (Proprietor)
N.W. 114, Vishnu Garden
New Delhi - 110018,
Mobile:
+(91)-9990600779
+(91)-9891378531
+(91)-9971569534
+(91)-9968388085
Telephone:
+(91)-(11)-25985925

Satgur Paper Machines
Mr. Gurnam Singh (prop)
N -26, Street No. 10, Anand Parbat Industrial Area, New Rohtak Road
New Delhi - 110005,
Mobile:
+(91)-8010854248
+(91)-9891641341
+(91)-9891313350
Telephone:
+(91)-(11)-25986697
Email:
satgur_paper_machines@yahoo.com
satgur.paper.machines1975@gmail.com

Chapter - 62

Suppliers of Raw Materials

COSMETIC

Shankar Dyes & Chemicals
No. 1209, Shankar Building,
Gali No. 11, Sadar Bazar,
New Delhi - 110 006,
Delhi, India
Phone: 08447498163
Website:
www.shankardyes.com

Cosmetics Of India
Plot No - 221,
Pocket-C, D sidc,
Sector-5, Bawana Industrial Area,
Delhi - 110039, India
Phone: 09811230720

Dev International
No. 301, 3rd Floor,
Solitaire Complex,
Opposite Bombay Garage, Shahibaug,
Ahmedabad - 380004,
Gujarat, India
Phone: 08377800758

Chemical Corporation
No. 2, Rajputpara No. 4, Amardeep Complex,
Nr Khodiyar Chamber,
Rajkot - 360 001,
Gujarat, India
Phone: 09427209556

Microtrol Sterilisation Services Private Ltd
No. 355-65-3, Sarjapur Road, Agara, Near Hsr Layout,
Bengaluru - 560 102,
Karnataka, India
Phone: 09902366779

HERBAL COSMETIC RAW MATERIALS

Vasavi India
No. 122, Varadhamuthiappan Street, Geroge Town,
Chennai - 600 001,
Tamil Nadu, India
Phone: 09840123444

Indian Commercial Company Pvt. Ltd.
Oriental House, 5th Floor, No. 7,
Jamshedji Tata Road,
Churchgate,
Mumbai - 400020,
Maharashtra, India
Phone: 08588802838

Kirpal Export Overseas
BP-130, Shalimar Bagh West,
New Delhi - 110 088,
Delhi, India
Phone: 08447557523
Website:
www.henna-manufacturers.com

Hennex India
Unit- II, No. 489, Link Road, Delhi Gate,
Old Faridabad,
Faridabad - 121002,
Haryana, India
Phone: 08376807668

Nathubhai Cooverji & Sons
No. 417, Vasant Nivas,
3rd Floor,
Bhaudaji Cross Road,
No. 10, Matunga,
Mumbai - 400019,
Maharashtra, India
Phone: 08447523788
Website:
www.ncsons.com

Aadi Enterprises
F-25, Bhram Tower,
Harimarg, Bajaj Nagar,
Jaipur - 302006,
Rajasthan, India
Phone: 09460587905

COSMETICS PACKAGING MATERIALS

Global Print & Pack
A-110, Okhla Industrial Area,
Phase-2,

New Delhi - 110020, Delhi, India
Phone: 08588873511

Akar Shrink Packs
C-40, MIDC, Sinnar, Nashik-Pune Highway, Nashik - 422113, Maharashtra, India
Phone: 08377801577

Sudham Packaging
Unit No. 101, Dewan & Shah Industrial Estate No. 1, Navghar Road, Vasai, Thane - 401210, Maharashtra, India
Phone: 09953354927

Excell Plastics
Shailesh Industrial Estate No. 3, Unit No 24/ 25/ 26, Vasai East, Thane - 400 601, Maharashtra, India
Phone: 08447526256
Website: www.excellplastics.com

Abhinav Enterprises
A - 67, D. D. A. Shed Okhla Industrial Area, Phase - 2, New Delhi - 110 020, Delhi, India

DETERGENT CHEMICALS

Vijay Sree Chemicals
Mr. Vijay Loya (Owner)
No. 8-2-55, Sri Nagar Colony Road, Panjagutta
Hyderabad - 500 082, Andhra Pradesh, India
Mobile:
+(91)-9246545121
+(91)-9848189693

Aman Enterprises
Mr. Aman Gupta (Owner)
No. 901, G. D. I. T. L. Tower- B- 08, Netaji Subhash Place, Pitampura
Delhi - 110034, India
Mobile:
+(91)-8588866951
+(91)-9811027816
Telephone:
+(91)-(11)-27357516
+(91)-(11)-27357515
+(91)-(11)-27357517
Fax:
+(91)-(11)-45629959
Candle Wax

Paragon Metachem
Mr. Maulik Shah (Proprietor)
Kabibai Trust Building, Ground Floor, No. 14/ 16, Bhandari Street, Cross Lane, Vadgadi
Mumbai - 400003, Maharashtra, India
Mobile:
+(91)-9820126082
+(91)-9323036261
Telephone:
+(91)-(22)-23426844
Fax:
+(91)-(22)-23454075

Mahendra Traders
Mr. Narendra Mehta (Proprietor)
No. 52, A. S. Char Street
Bengaluru - 560053, Karnataka, India
Mobile:
+(91)-9342853329
+(91)-9845026770
+(91)-8453229563
Telephone:
+(91)-(80)-22351428
+(91)-(80)-41223073
+(91)-(80)-41223854

AGARBATTI RAW MATERIALS

Shri Aromas
Mr. P. V. Sunil Kumar (Proprietor)
No. 50, Kathayani Niliya, 2nd Cross, Obaiah Lane, Akkipet Cross
Bengaluru - 560053, Karnataka, India
Mobile:
+(91)-9481028864
Telephone:
+(91)-(80)-41404843
+(91)-(80)-22871010

Soham Industrial Machinery Ltd.
Mr. Jagpal Gajera (Sales Manager)
Plot No. A-13/22-23, Opposite Calcutta Bearing, Near Puspa Restaurant, Central Road No. 7, Udhna, Udyognagar
Surat - 394210, Gujarat, India
Mobile:
+(91)-9978987748
+(91)-9825527848
+(91)-9879697091
Telephone:

+(91)-(261)-6507848
Email:
sohamtexaac@gmail.com

BAKERY RAW MATERIALS

Chemical Corporation
Mr. Jay Shah
No. 2, Rajputpara, No. 4, Amardeep Complex, Near Khodiyar Chamber
Rajkot - 360001, Gujarat, India
Mobile:
+(91)-9427209556
Telephone:
+(91)-(281)-6624546
+(91)-(281)-2226357
Website:
http://www.chemicalcorporation.in

Raj Dhanvantry
Mr. Rajen. J. B.
Bedi Port Road, Opposite Ashapura Gas Godown
Jamnagar - 361002, Gujarat, India
Mobile:
+(91)-9328811161
Telephone:
+(91)-(288)-2756366
+(91)-(288)-2753079
Website:
http://www.rajdhanvantry.com

CONFECTIONERY RAW MATERIALS

Raj Dhanvantry
Mr. Rajen. J. B.
Bedi Port Road, Opposite Ashapura Gas Godown
Jamnagar - 361002, Gujarat, India
Mobile:
+(91)-9328811161
Telephone:
+(91)-(288)-2756366
+(91)-(288)-2753079
Website:
http://www.rajdhanvantry.com

PLASTIC RAW MATERIALS

Vardhman Plastics
Mr. Sanil Jain / Mr. Anil Kumar Jain (Proprietor)
M-219, Sector-5, Bawana Industrial Area
New Delhi - 110 039, Delhi, India
Mobile:
+(91)-9811090568
+(91)-9899290568

Jain Plastics
Mr. Manoj Jain (Prop)
No. 487/29, National Market, Peera Garhi
Delhi - 110087, India
Mobile:
+(91)-9810078383
+(91)-9717078373
Telephone:
+(91)-(11)-25266531
+(91)-(11)-25258203
Fax:
+(91)-(11)-25258203

SEEDS FOR OILS MILL

Sakura Seed Corp.
Mr. Raj Kumar (President)
No. 1240, 14th Main, GKVK Post, Judicial Layout
Bengaluru - 560065, Karnataka, India
Mobile:
+(91)-9880090364
+(91)-9671396161
Telephone:
+(91)-(80)-28561923

Balaji Trading Co.
Mr. Anil Kumar (Dir.)
I. O. C. Link Road, Sojat Road Marg
Sojat - 306104, Rajasthan, India
Mobile:
+(91)-8769761111
Telephone:
+(91)-(2960)-221586
Email:
balaji.trading@sify.com
anilkumarnewara@sify.com

PET BOTTLE

Techni Plast
Mr. Pankaj Jain
C - 24, Ambey Garden, Samaypur Extension, Industrial Area, Libaspur
Delhi - 110042, India
Telephone:
+(91)-(11)-27831622

Heti Industries
Mr. Vijay Kumar Sharma (Proprietor)
No. 68, GIDC, Por
Vadodara - 390 020, Gujarat, India
Mobile:
+(91)-9904974434
Telephone:
+(91)-(265)-2830062
+(91)-(265)-2830063
Fax:

+(91)-(265)-2830063

PAINT RAW MATERIAL

Vardhman Plastics
Mr. Sanil Jain / Mr. Anil Kumar Jain (Proprietor)
M-219, Sector-5, Bawana Industrial Area
New Delhi - 110 039, Delhi, India
Mobile:
+(91)-9811090568
+(91)-9899290568

S. S. Conversions
Mr. K. Sheik Abdullah
Plot No. - 31, S. I. P. C. O. T Industrial Growth Centre, Gangaikondan
Tirunelveli - 627352, Tamil Nadu, India
Mobile:
+(91)-9443102924

GARMENTS MATERIALS

Pushkar Fashion Industry
Mr. Vinod Kumar Rohila (Proprietor)
Plot No. 17, Sanskar Vihar, Kankpura Malgodam, Near Railway Police Chowki, Sirsi Road
Jaipur - 302021, Rajasthan, India
Mobile:
+(91)-9214873512
Telephone:
+(91)-(141)-2470493

Dev Exports
Mr. Deven Purohit (CEO)
No. 204, 2nd Floor, Shilp 2, Near Sales India, Ashram Road
Ahmedabad - 380009, Gujarat, India
Mobile:
+(91)-9898171120
Telephone:
+(91)-(79)-65217844
Email:
inq.devexports@gmail.com

KR Enterprises, Jaipur
Mrs. Kavita Verma (Proprietor)
No. 137, 1st Floor, Sun & Moon Plaza, Near S.K. Soni Hospital, Vidhyadhar Nagar, Siker Road
Jaipur - 302013, Rajasthan, India
Mobile:
+(91)-9875100961
+(91)-8952993816
+(91)-9660216245
+(91)-8561800960
Telephone:
+(91)-(141)-5107961
Fax:
+(91)-(141)-5107961

ALL FOLLOWING PROJECT REPORTS ARE READILY AVAILABLE

AUTOMOBILES, MECHANICAL, STEEL & IRON & METALLURGICAL

- Agricultral Equipments
- Aac & Acsr Aluminium Conductors (All Aluminium Conductors)
- Agricultral Equipments Including Threshers
- Air Brake Helical Coil
- Air Cooler
- Air Filters (For Scooter Car & Excavators Etc.)
- Aluminium & Aluminium Alloys From Aluminium Scrap To Make Utensils (Induction Furnace Melted)
- Aluminium Alloy Wheels
- Aluminium Alloys From Aluminium Scrap To Make Utensils (Induction Furnace)
- Aluminium Hot & Cold Rolling Mill
- Aluminium Conductors
- Aluminium Bottle Manufacturing (Cold Extrusion Of Aluminium)
- Aluminium/Copper Cable Lugs
- Aluminium Cans For Beer Pkgs.
- Aluminium Cans For Capacitors
- Aluminium Caps For Injection Vials
- Aluminium Extrusion
- Aluminium Furniture & Hardware
- Aluminium Sheet Rolling Mill
- Alloy Steel Casting (Foundry)
- Aluminium Utensils
- Aluminium Utensils & School Boxes
- Aluminium Wire Drawing And Super Enamelling For Winding
- Anodised Aluminium Utensils
- Anodizing Of Aluminium
- Antimony Oxide From Lead Scrap
- Anti Scale Compound For Adding In Sugar Boilers
- Arc Welding Filter Glass
- Aluminium Foil Cutting & Roll Making
- Auto Flaps For Trucks & Buses
- Automobile Workshop (Garage & Service Centre)
- Auto Bulb
- Auto Electrical Parts (Armature)
- Auto Gears
- Auto Horns
- Auto Leaf Spring
- Auto Tubes
- Auto Piston Ring
- Auto Piston
- Auto Parts (Electricla And Electronic)
- Auto Rubber Parts And Turned Components Silent Block Bush And Ceiling Fan Shaft+
- Auto Wire Outer (Outer For Auto Wire)
- Bakery And Biscuits Equipments Fabrication
- Ball Point Pen Refills
- Ball Roller & Taper Bearing
- Band Saw Blades
- Barbed Wire
- Barrels (Oil)/(Metalliic Barrels)
- Bath Fittings, Turned Components (All Type) Sheet Metal (Job Work) And Hdpe/Pp Moulded Articles
- Battery For Car (Dry)
- Battery Operated Three Wheelers
- Benefication Of Chromite Ore Processing Charge Chrome
- Bicycle Spokes
- Bicycle Assembly
- Brake Lining Asbestoes/Resin Based & Asbestoes Free
- Brass Artware/Hollow Ware Casting (With Thehelp Of Phenolic Resin)
- Brass Casting
- Brass Pipes From Brass Sheet With Longitudinally Welding
- Brass Ware By Casting Method (Brass Articles Viz. Brass Pooja Lamps And Other Casted)
- Bright Bars
- Buffing And Polishing Industry (Job Work)
- Butt Hinge (Brass Sheet)
- Carbon Brush Holder & Slip Ring
- Co Welding Wire Electrodes (Copper/Copper Alloy Coated M.S.Wire)
- Carbon Film Resistors
- Car Dealership (Hyundai)
- Carburettors
- Cast Steel Body Valve
- Cast Steel Panes For Melting Furnace
- Ceramic Coated Steel Pipes
- Chemical Etching Of Stainless Steel
- Chemical Resistant Iron & Steel
- Concast Steel Bars
- Cold Form Section Mill
- Cold Rolled Forming Of Section And Other Sections
- Cold Rolling Of Ms Strip
- Cold Twisted De-Formed Ribbed Steel
- Cold Rolling Mill
- Compressor (Hermetic) For Air Conditioners
- Compressed Natural Gas (Cng Kit) For Autovehicle
- Continuously Cast Steel Wire Rods (5 Mm)
- Continuous Casting Copper Wire Rods
- Conveyor Beltings
- Conveyor Belt, Transmission Belt & V Belts
- Cooking Ranges
- Copper/Brass Sheets,Circle & Utensils
- Copper Foil
- Copper Ingots, Rods Making & Wire Drawing
- Copper Products From Copper Scrap
- Copper Smelting Plant
- Copper Wire Rods From Copper Scrap
- Corrugated Box Making Machinery And Other Their Parts
- Cylinder Liner For Automobiles
- Disposable Plastic Razors
- Door Locks/Pad Locks
- Drill Bits & Tool Bits
- Drum Closures
- Erw Steel Pipes And Tubes
- Erw Steel Conduit Pipe
- Earth Moving Eqpt.
- Engine Valves For Automobiles
- Fabrication Of Heat Exchanger
- Fabrication Of Storage Tanks And M.S. Drum
- Ferrous Alloy Ni-Hardy I.V Casting
- Ferrous Mn Alloy Casting By Alumina Thermic Process
- Ferro Alloys
- Ferro Silicon & Ferro Manganese From Dolomite (Sms Grade)
- Fire Extinguishers
- Fire Fighting Equipments And Appliances
- Flip-Tone Cans
- Forged Conecting Rod
- Forging Unit
- Fountain Pen Nibs
- Foundry Sand
- Free Wheels, Free Wheel Bushes And Free Wheel Plates For Autorickshaws
- Fuel Briquettes From Agro Waste
- Fuel Injection System
- Fused Magnesia
- Generator Canopy
- Galvanized M.S.Strips
- Galvanizing Plant
- Galvanized Iron Wire (G.I. Wire)
- G.I. Pipes
- Gas Welding Torches And Nozzles
- Gasket Sheet
- Gate Grills & Window Frames
- Generating Set (Diesel)
- Hard Anodised Aluminium
- High Pressure Cylinder

Market Survey Cum Detailed Techno Economic Feasibility Report on all Projects are available Contact.
"ENGINEERS INDIA RESEARCH INSTITUTE". 4449, Nai Sarak (D), Main Road, Delhi-110006 (India)
Ph. : 09811437895, 91-11-23918117, 23916431, 45120361, 64727385 Fax : 91-11-23916431
E-mail : eiriprojects@gmail.com, eiribooks@yahoo.com • website: www.eiri.in, www.eiriindia.org